"See you on the way back."

In the beginning were the words: lots of them.

On Monday, February 22, 1965,
Metro-Goldwyn-Mayer announced that it
would finance production of Stanley Kubrick's
next motion picture, *Journey Beyond the Stars*.

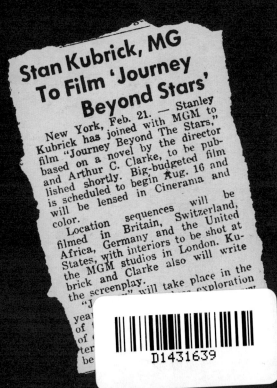

Stan Kubrick, MG To Film 'Journey Beyond Stars'

New York, Feb. 21. — Stanley
Kubrick has joined with MGM to
film "Journey Beyond The Stars,"
based on a novel by the director
and Arthur C. Clarke, to be published shortly. Big-budgeted film
is scheduled to begin Aug. 16 and
will be lensed in Cinerama and
color.

Location sequences will be
filmed in Britain, Switzerland,
Africa, Germany and the United
States, with interiors to be shot at
the MGM studios in London. Kubrick and Clarke also will write
the screenplay.

"J   " will take place in the
yea   exploration
of
of
ter
be

"Dave. Stop.

Stop. Will you.

Stop, Dave.

Will you stop, Dave.

Stop, Dave.

I'm afraid.

I'm afraid, Dave.

Dave.

My mind is going.

I can feel it.

I can feel it.

My mind is going.

There is no question

about it.

can feel it.

can feel it.

can feel it.

'm afraid."

The Making
of Kubrick's *2001*

Edited, with lots
of legwork, by

JEROME AGEL

SUN IN GEMINI
MOON IN ARIES
CANCER RISING

A SIGNET BOOK
NEW AMERICAN LIBRARY
TIMES MIRROR

SIGNET TRADEMARK REG. U.S. PAT. OFF. AND FOREIGN COUNTRIES
REGISTERED TRADEMARK——MARCA REGISTRADA
HECHO EN CHICAGO, U.S.A.

SIGNET, SIGNET CLASSICS, SIGNETTE, MENTOR AND PLUME BOOKS
are published by The New American Library, Inc.,
1301 Avenue of the Americas, New York, New York 10019

FIRST PRINTING, APRIL, 1970

    6 7 8 9 10 11 12 13 14

PRINTED IN THE UNITED STATES OF AMERICA

JEROME AGEL, the editor-producer of *The Making of Kubrick's 2001*, is the author and/ or co-author and/or producer of: *Herman Kahnsciousness*; *Understanding Understanding* (with Humphry Osmond); *Is Today Tomorrow?—A Synerjistic Collage About Alternative Futures*; *I Seem To Be a Verb* (with Buckminster Fuller); *The Medium is the Massage* and *War and Peace in the Global Village* (with Marshall McLuhan); *The Radical Therapist*—Vols. One and Two; *The Uncle Sam Papers*; *Community Sex Information Guide*; *What Every Child Should Know*; *A World Without—What Our Presidents Didn't Know*; *Cosmic Perspective* (with Carl Sagan).

"It won't be a Buck Rogers kind of space epic."
— **Robert O'Brien,** president, M-G-M, who constantly supported production of *2001: A Space Odyssey,* even when it went $4,500,000 beyond the original budget.

"A movie studio is the best toy a boy ever had."
— **Orson Welles**

"The screen is a magic medium. It has such power that it can retain interest as it conveys emotions and moods that no other art form can hope to tackle." — **Stanley Kubrick**

Stanley Kubrick, left, and Arthur C. Clarke.

" 'My dear Rikki,' Karellen retorted, 'it's only by *not* taking the human race seriously that I retain what fragments of my once considerable mental powers I still possess.' " —from *Childhood's End,* by **Arthur C. Clarke**

"*2001: A Space Odyssey* is about man's past and future life in space. It's about concern with man's hierarchy in the universe, which is probably pretty low. It's about the reactions of humanity to the discovery of higher intelligence in the universe. We set out with the deliberate intention of creating a myth. The Odyssean parallel was in our minds from the beginning, long before the film's title was chosen." — **Arthur C. Clarke**

"I don't like to talk about *2001* much because it's essentially a nonverbal experience. Less than half the film has dialogue. It attempts to communicate more to the subconscious and to the feelings than it does to the intellect. I think clearly that there's a basic problem with people who are not paying attention with their eyes. They're listening. And they don't get much from listening to this film. Those who won't believe their eyes won't be able to appreciate this film." —**Stanley Kubrick**

Stanley Kubrick, left, and
Arthur C. Clarke.

. . . and there were other views:

"Are you coming to my party tomorrow?"

The cost of construction of the 200-inch Hale telescope at Palomar and the cost of production of the out-of-sight motion picture *2001: A Space Odyssey*, produced and directed by Stanley Kubrick, were about the same: $10,500,000.00.

The divorce rate at the Cape Kennedy missile-launch center is said to be the highest in the nation, but who's divorcing whom?

Bob Dylan: "Just because you like my stuff doesn't mean I owe you anything."

I have seen Stanley Kubrick's musical comedy (*2001*) every day since it opened in Manhattan nearly two years ago, and I can hardly wait to see it today. The first time I saw *2001* I was sure it was a put-on. It is, after all, riddled with humor; Kubrick is, after all, well known for tongue-in-cheek; the universe is, after all (it must be; look at the front page of *The New York Times* any day), a cosmic joke, and wasn't this motion picture *about* the universe?

I am now convinced that the film is the best.

Every time I see it, I re-love that sexy love scene in the car . . . Leonard Rossiter maneuvering his whiskey glass . . . the stars exploding in an abandoned corset factory in Manhattan.

André Breton: "Everything leads us to believe that there exists a certain point of the intelligence at which life and death, the real and the imaginary, the past and the future . . . cease to be perceived as opposites."

Arthur C. Clarke: "M-G-M doesn't know it yet, but they've footed the bill for the first $10,500,000.00 religious film." (Clarke says he's been on Atlantis. Recently.)

Kubrick: "It's hard to convey a film's unique qualities in its advertising. The sense of what a movie is like quickly gets around."

The word got around. The ads didn't convey the mindtaking, the breathtaking experience that is *2001*—the many reasons everyone should see it, and would like to see it. The title *2001: A Space Odyssey* may even have been misleading. The medium *is* the message.

2001 is an astonishing visual *tour de force*. (There are more murders in it than there were by Bonnie and Clyde on-screen.)

"Hush" was the key word during production. As in, "Let's keep those secrets right here in the office, eh fellows." "Hush" was the key word during the movie itself. As in, "I don't suppose you have any idea what the damned thing is?" "Hush" continues to be the key word about the box office. "You know, Jerry, sir, we never give out those figures."

The rule of *Variety*'s thumb is that a production of this magnitude must recoup two and one-half times its production nut to break even; in this case, at least $25,000,000.00. (Clarke says that he and Kubrick are laughing all the way to the bank.)

For the box-office hit *Dr. Strangelove*, Kubrick had been voted Best Director by the New York Film Critics Circle. "Don't laugh," he said at Trader Vic's, "but I'm fascinated with the possibility of extraterrestrials."

Clarke was contacted in Ceylon, and responded: INTERESTED IN WORKING WITH ENFANT TERRIBLE STOP CONTACT MY AGENT STOP WHAT MAKES KUBRICK THINK I'M A RECLUSE?

Once upon a time (which would have made a provocative title for the film), Stanley Kubrick and Arthur C. Clarke—two of the best we have—set out to show the reactions of humanity to the discovery of the existence of higher intelligences in the universe. It turned out to be classified information.

Kubrick: "If it can be written, or thought, it can be filmed." Oh that it were.

Wyndham Lewis: "The artist is always engaged in writing a detailed history of the future because he's the only person aware of the nature of the present." H. Marshall McLuhan: "Knowledge of this simple fact is now needed for human survival." McLuhan's Fuller Nietzsche.

Kubrick: "There's a new beauty afoot." (Terrific ten-year-old girl on her way home from the sixth grade: "You know, current events take up too much time.")

Leonard Cohen: "God is alive, magic is afoot. Magic is alive, God is afoot."

Celebrating the start of the third millennium, Kubrick made a motion picture that's a joy to look at, one that could be projected endlessly on a museum gallery wall. The Guggenheim in NYC! He wanted to make a motion picture about an event that might occur within the lifetime of most of today's filmgoers — an encounter between us and them. (It is probable that the encounter has already taken place.)

The film's "star," HAL, a computer, was right when he said that it was human error that was endangering the Jupiter mission. (Look at *The Times* front page again.) HAL had been overprogrammed for mission enthusiasm and success. He became oversensitive to the human element.

(To her indefatigable father after three grueling days of sightseeing in Washington, terrific ten-year-old, sensory-overloaded girl in the Smithsonian Institution: "I'll walk through the exhibits with you, but I won't look.")

We are all machines. (What happened to your lunch?)

We have met the enemy and we are theirs.

Getting there was all the fun.

In *2001*:

The brilliant, absolutely brilliant, acting — a Kubrick touchstone since *The Killing* (Timothy Carey, Sterling Hayden, Elijah Cook, Marie Windsor). Here, William Sylvester, Dan Richter, Keir Dullea, Gary Lockwood, Douglas Rain, Leonard Rossiter, Vivian Kubrick.

The brilliant, absolutely brilliant, use of music: "The Blue Danube," a stroke of genius. Khatchaturian's "Gayne Ballet Suite." Ligeti (who successfully sued for having had his music distorted). ("The Blue Danube" was also performed in Dullea's *The Hoodlum Priest*.)

The brilliant, absolutely brilliant, dialogue: "A woman's cashmere sweater has been found . . . Sorry I'm late . . . I don't know. What do you think? . . . Deliberately buried, eh." Please think about it.

The brilliant, absolutely brilliant, sound effects: Breathing. Laughter and chatter of the extraterrestrials examining the astronaut in a room in his mind. More information than words.

I don't like movies — and I only see the ones I've already seen. *2001* may be the first motion picture that may be called a motion picture, that could have been produced only in the medium.

"Dear 15-Year-Old Miss Stackhouse, of North Plainfield, N.J.: Yours is perhaps the most intelligent speculation I've read on *2001*." Signed/Stanley Kubrick. (See page 201.)

At one time, the director thought that his film would run about an hour. And then, the special effects started to take hold. Magic *was* afoot. (See ninety-six-page picture section.)

And so, The Dawn of Man was made — and they called it, okay, *2001: A Space Odyssey*. It started where *Dr. Strangelove* had left off. At the territorial imperative. "Mein Führer, I can walk, I can walk."

It is said that *2001: A Space Odyssey* — "Some sort of great film!" agreed *The New Yorker* — is about the first contact with a mysterious intelligence. Have you looked at your air-conditioner lately?

(This book was produced with the help of the film's principals and many other friends: Edward Rosenfeld, Eric Norden, Carole Livingston, Joan Feinberg, and Stephan Chodorov.)

"Elena, you're looking wonderful."

Would you believe . . . .

A stellar cataclysm filmed
in an abandoned corset
factory in Manhattan?

Three feet long?

Source of illumination
for "the sun" had to be
11 stops overexposed?

A Moon bus two feet long?

Thirteen inches in diameter?

"Hi, everybody. Nice to be back with you."

Little did Arthur C. Clarke know in 1950 that his latest short story, "The Sentinel," would be the basis, fifteen years later, for a $10,500,000.00 motion-picture production.

THE SENTINEL*

Arthur C. Clarke

THE NEXT TIME you see the full moon high in the south, look carefully at its right-hand edge and let your eye travel upward along the curve of the disk. Round about two o'clock you will notice a small, dark oval: anyone with normal eyesight can find it quite easily. It is the great walled plain, one of the finest on the Moon, known as the Mare Crisium—the Sea of Crises. Three hundred miles in diameter, and almost completely surrounded by a ring of magnificent mountains, it had never been explored until we entered it in the late summer of 1996.

Our expedition was a large one. We had two heavy freighters which had flown our supplies and equipment from the main lunar base in the Mare Serenitatis, five hundred miles away. There were also three small rockets which were intended for short-range transport over regions which our surface vehicles couldn't cross. Luckily, most of the Mare Crisium is very flat. There are none of the great crevasses so common and so dangerous elsewhere, and very few craters or mountains of any size. As far as we could tell, our powerful caterpillar tractors would have no difficulty in taking us wherever we wished to go.

I was geologist—or selenologist, if you want to be pedantic—in charge of the group exploring the southern region of the Mare. We had crossed a hundred miles of it in a week, skirting the foothills of the mountains along the shore of what was once the ancient sea, some thousand million years before. When life was beginning on Earth, it was already dying here.

The waters were retreating down the flanks of those stupendous cliffs, retreating into the empty heart of the Moon. Over the land which we were crossing, the tideless ocean had once been half a mile deep, and now the only trace of moisture was the hoarfrost one could sometimes find in caves which the searing sunlight never penetrated.

We had begun our journey early in the slow lunar dawn, and still had almost a week of Earth-time before nightfall. Half a dozen times a day we would leave our vehicle and go outside in the space suits to hunt for interesting minerals, or to place markers for the guidance of future travelers. It was an uneventful routine. There is nothing hazardous or even particularly exciting about lunar exploration. We could live comfortably for a month in our pressurized tractors, and if we ran into trouble, we could always radio for help and sit tight until one of the spaceships came to our rescue.

I said just now that there was nothing exciting about lunar exploration, but of course that isn't true. One could never grow tired of those incredible mountains, so much more rugged than the gentle hills of Earth. We never knew, as we rounded the capes and promontories of that vanished sea, what new splendors would be revealed to us. The whole southern curve of the Mare Crisium is a vast delta where a score of rivers once found their way into the ocean, fed perhaps by the torrential rains that must have lashed the mountains in the brief volcanic age when the Moon was young. Each of these ancient valleys was an invitation, challenging us to climb into the unknown uplands beyond. But we had a hundred miles still to cover, and could only look longingly at the heights which others must scale.

We kept Earth-time aboard the tractor, and precisely at 22:00 hours the final radio message would be sent out to Base and we would close down for the day. Outside, the rocks would still be burning beneath the almost vertical sun, but to us it would be night until we awoke again eight hours later. Then one of us would prepare breakfast, there would be a great buzzing of electric razors, and someone would switch on the shortwave radio from Earth. Indeed, when the smell of frying sausages began to fill the cabin, it was sometimes hard to believe that we were not back on our own world—everything was so normal and homely, apart from the feeling of decreased weight and the unnatural slowness with which objects fell.

It was my turn to prepare breakfast in the corner of the main cabin that served as a galley. I can remember that moment quite vividly after all these years, for the radio had just played one of my favorite melodies, the old Welsh air "David of the White Rock." Our driver was already outside in his space suit,

nspecting our caterpillar treads. My assistant, Louis Garnett,
was up forward in the control position, making some belated
ntries in yesterday's log.

As I stood by the frying pan, waiting, like any terrestrial
housewife, for the sausages to brown, I let my gaze wander
dly over the mountain walls which covered the whole of the
outhern horizon, marching out of sight to east and west below
he curve of the Moon. They seemed only a mile or two from
he tractor, but I knew that the nearest was twenty miles away.
On the Moon, of course, there is no loss of detail with distance
– none of that almost imperceptible haziness which softens
nd sometimes transfigures all far-off things on Earth.

Those mountains were ten thousand feet high, and they
climbed steeply out of the plain as if ages ago some subter-
anean eruption had smashed them skyward through the molten
rust. The base of even the nearest was hidden from sight by
he steeply curving surface of the plain, for the Moon is a very
ttle world, and from where I was standing the horizon was
nly two miles away.

I lifted my eyes toward the peaks which no man had ever
climbed, the peaks which, before the coming of terrestrial life,
ad watched the retreating oceans sink sullenly into their
raves, taking with them the hope and the morning promise of a
world. The sunlight was beating against those ramparts with a
lare that hurt the eyes, yet only a little way above them the
tars were shining steadily in a sky blacker than a winter mid-
ight on Earth.

I was turning away when my eye caught a metallic glitter
igh on the ridge of a great promontory thrusting out into the
ea thirty miles to the west. It was a dimensionless point of
ght, as if a star had been clawed from the sky by one of those
ruel peaks, and I imagined that some smooth rock surface
was catching the sunlight and heliographing it straight into my
yes. Such things were not uncommon. When the Moon is in
er second quarter, observers on Earth can sometimes see the
reat ranges in the Oceanus Procellarum burning with a blue-
white iridescence as the sunlight flashes from their slopes and
eaps again from world to world. But I was curious to know
what kind of rock could be shining so brightly up there, and I
climbed into the observation turret and swung our four-inch
telescope round to the west.

I could see just enough to tantalize me. Clear and sharp in
he field of vision, the mountain peaks seemed only half a mile
way, but whatever was catching the sunlight was still too
mall to be resolved. Yet it seemed to have an elusive symmetry, and the summit upon which it rested was curiously flat.
stared for a long time at that glittering enigma, straining my

eyes into space, until presently a smell of burning from the galley told me that our breakfast sausages had made their quarter-million-mile journey in vain.

All that morning we argued our way across the Mare Crisium while the western mountains reared higher in the sky. Even when we were out prospecting in the space suits, the discussion would continue over the radio. It was absolutely certain, my companions argued, that there had never been any form of intelligent life on the Moon. The only living things that had ever existed there were a few primitive plants and their slightly less degenerate ancestors. I knew that as well as anyone, but there are times when a scientist must not be afraid to make a fool of himself.

"Listen," I said at last, "I'm going up there, if only for my own peace of mind. That mountain's less than twelve thousand feet high — that's only two thousand under Earth gravity — and I can make the trip in twenty hours at the outside. I've always wanted to go up into those hills, anyway, and this gives me an excellent excuse."

"If you don't break your neck," said Garnett, "you'll be the laughingstock of the expedition when we get back to Base. That mountain will probably be called Wilson's Folly from now on."

"I won't break my neck," I said firmly. "Who was the first man to climb Pico and Helicon?"

"But weren't you rather younger in those days?" asked Louis gently.

"That," I said with great dignity, "is as good a reason as any for going."

We went to bed early that night, after driving the tractor to within half a mile of the promontory. Garnett was coming with me in the morning; he was a good climber, and had often been with me on such exploits before. Our driver was only too glad to be left in charge of the machine.

At first sight, those cliffs seemed completely unscalable, but to anyone with a good head for heights, climbing is easy on a world where all weights are only a sixth of their normal value. The real danger in lunar mountaineering lies in overconfidence; a six-hundred-foot drop on the Moon can kill you just as thoroughly as a hundred-foot fall on Earth.

We made our first halt on a wide ledge about four thousand feet above the plain. Climbing had not been very difficult, but my limbs were stiff with the unaccustomed effort, and I was glad of the rest. We could still see the tractor as a tiny metal insect far down at the foot of the cliff, and we reported our progress to the driver before starting on the next ascent.

Inside our suits it was comfortably cool, for the refrigeration units were fighting the fierce sun and carrying away the body heat of our exertions. We seldom spoke to each other, except to pass climbing instructions and to discuss our best plan of ascent. I do not know what Garnett was thinking, probably that this was the craziest goose chase he had ever embarked upon. I more than half agreed with him, but the joy of climbing, the knowledge that no man had ever gone this way before, and the exhilaration of the steadily widening landscape gave me all the reward I needed.

I don't think I was particularly excited when I saw in front of us the wall of rock I had first inspected through the telescope from thirty miles away. It would level off about fifty feet above our heads, and there on the plateau would be the thing that had lured me over these barren wastes. It would be, almost certainly, nothing more than a boulder splintered ages ago by a falling meteor, and with its cleavage planes still fresh and bright in this incorruptible, unchanging silence.

There were no handholds on the rock face, and we had to use a grapnel. My tired arms seemed to gain new strength as I swung the three-pronged metal anchor round my head and sent it sailing up toward the stars. The first time it broke loose and came falling slowly back when we pulled the rope. On the third attempt, the prongs gripped firmly and our combined weights could not shift it.

Garnett looked at me anxiously. I could tell that he wanted to go first, but I smiled back at him through the glass of my helmet and shook my head. Slowly, taking my time, I began the final ascent.

Even with my space suit, I weighed only forty pounds here, so I pulled myself up hand over hand without bothering to use my feet. At the rim I paused and waved to my companion, then I scrambled over the edge and stood upright, staring ahead of me.

You must understand that until this very moment I had been almost completely convinced that there could be nothing strange or unusual for me to find here. Almost, but not quite; it was that haunting doubt that had driven me forward. Well, it was a doubt no longer, but the haunting had scarcely begun.

I was standing on a plateau perhaps a hundred feet across. It had once been smooth—too smooth to be natural—but falling meteors had pitted and scored its surface through immeasurable eons. It had been leveled to support a glittering, roughly pyramidal structure, twice as high as a man, that was set in the rock like a gigantic, many faceted jewel.

Probably no emotion at all filled my mind in those first few seconds. Then I felt a great lifting of my heart, and a strange, inexpressible joy. For I loved the Moon, and now I knew that the creeping moss of Aristarchus and Eratosthenes was not the only life she had brought forth in her youth. The old, discredited dream of the first explorers was true. There had, after all, been a lunar civilization—and I was the first to find it. That I had come perhaps a hundred million years too late did not distress me; it was enough to have come at all.

My mind was beginning to function normally, to analyze and to ask questions. Was this a building, a shrine—or something for which my language had no name? If a building, then why was it erected in so uniquely inaccessible a spot? I wondered if it might be a temple, and I could picture the adepts of some strange priesthood calling on their gods to preserve them as the life of the Moon ebbed with the dying oceans, and calling on their gods in vain.

I took a dozen steps forward to examine the thing more closely, but some sense of caution kept me from going too near. I knew a little of archaeology, and tried to guess the cultural level of the civilization that must have smoothed this mountain and raised the glittering mirror surfaces that still dazzled my eyes.

The Egyptians could have done it, I thought, if their workmen had possessed whatever strange materials these far more ancient architects had used. Because of the thing's smallness, it did not occur to me that I might be looking at the handiwork of a race more advanced than my own. The idea that the Moon had possessed intelligence at all was still almost too tremendous to grasp, and my pride would not let me take the final, humiliating plunge.

And then I noticed something that set the scalp crawling at the back of my neck—something so trivial and so innocent that many would never have noticed it at all. I have said that the plateau was scarred by meteors; it was also coated inches deep with the cosmic dust that is always filtering down upon the surface of any world where there are no winds to disturb it. Yet the dust and the meteor scratches ended quite abruptly in a wide circle enclosing the little pyramid, as though an invisible wall was protecting it from the ravages of time and the slow but ceaseless bombardment from space.

There was someone shouting in my earphones, and I realized that Garnett had been calling me for some time. I walked unsteadily to the edge of the cliff and signaled him to join me, not trusting myself to speak. Then I went back toward that circle in the dust. I picked up a fragment of splintered rock and tossed it gently toward the shining enigma. If the pebble had vanished at that invisible barrier, I should not have been surprised, but it seemed to hit a smooth, hemispheric surface and slide gently to the ground.

I knew then that I was looking at nothing that could be matched in the antiquity of my own race. This was not a building, but a machine, protecting itself with forces that had challenged Eternity. Those forces, whatever they might be, were still operating, and perhaps I had already come too close. I thought of all the radiations man had trapped and tamed in the past century. For all I knew, I might be as irrevocably doomed as if I had stepped into the deadly, silent aura of an unshielded atomic pile.

I remember turning then toward Garnett, who had joined me and was now standing motionless at my side. He seemed quite oblivious to me, so I did not disturb him but walked to the edge of the cliff in an effort to marshal my thoughts. There below me lay the Mare Crisium — Sea of Crises, indeed — strange and weird to most men, but reassuringly familiar to me. I lifted my eyes toward the crescent Earth, lying in her cradle of stars, and I wondered what her clouds had covered when these unknown builders had finished their work. Was it the steaming jungle of the Carboniferous, the bleak shoreline over which the first amphibians must crawl to conquer the land — or, earlier still, the long loneliness before the coming of life?

Do not ask me why I did not guess the truth sooner — the truth that seems so obvious now. In the first excitement of my discovery, I had assumed without question that this crystalline apparition had been built by some race belonging to the Moon's remote past, but suddenly, and with overwhelming force, the belief came to me that it was as alien to the Moon as I myself.

In twenty years we had found no trace of life but a few degenerate plants. No lunar civilization, whatever its doom, could have left but a single token of its existence.

I looked at the shining pyramid again, and the more I looked, the more remote it seemed from anything that had to do with the Moon. And suddenly I felt myself shaking with a foolish, hysterical laughter, brought on by excitement and overexertion: For I had imagined that the little pyramid was speaking to me and was saying, "Sorry, I'm a stranger here myself."

It has taken us twenty years to crack that invisible shield and to reach the machine inside those crystal walls. What we could not understand, we broke at last with the savage might of atomic power and now I have seen the fragments of the lovely, glittering thing I found up there on the mountain.

They are meaningless. The mechanisms — if indeed they are mechanisms — of the pyramid belong to a technology that lies far beyond our horizon, perhaps to the technology of paraphysical forces.

The mystery haunts us all the more now that the other planets have been reached and we know that only Earth has ever been the home of intelligent life in our Universe. Nor could any lost civilization of our own world have built that machine, for the thickness of the meteoric dust on the plateau has enabled us to measure its age. It was set there upon its mountain before life had emerged from the seas of Earth.

When our world was half its present age, *something* from the stars swept through the Solar System, left this token of its passage, and went again upon its way. Until we destroyed it, that machine was still fulfilling the purpose of its builders; and as to that purpose, here is my guess.

Nearly a hundred thousand million stars are turning in the circle of the Milky Way, and long ago other races on the worlds of other suns must have scaled and passed the heights that we have reached. Think of such civilizations, far back in time against the fading afterglow of Creation, masters of a universe so young that life as yet had come only to a handful of worlds. Theirs would have been a loneliness we cannot imagine, the loneliness of gods looking out across infinity and finding none to share their thoughts.

They must have searched the star clusters as we have searched the planets. Everywhere there would be worlds, but they would be empty or peopled with crawling, mindless things. Such was our own Earth, the smoke of the great volcanoes still staining the skies, when that first ship of the peoples of the dawn came sliding in from the abyss beyond Pluto. It passed the frozen outer worlds, knowing that life could play no part in their destinies. It came to rest among the inner planets, warming themselves around the fire of the Sun and waiting for their stories to begin.

Those wanderers must have looked on Earth, circling safely in the narrow zone between fire and ice, and must have guessed that it was the favorite of the Sun's children. Here, in the distant future, would be intelligence; but there were countless stars before them still, and they might never come this way again.

So they left a sentinel, one of millions they scattered throughout the Universe, watching over all worlds with the promise of life. It was a beacon that down the ages patiently signaled the fact that no one had discovered it.

Perhaps you understand now why that crystal pyramid was set upon the Moon instead of on the Earth. Its builders were not concerned with races still struggling up from savagery. They would be interested in our civilization only if we proved our fitness to survive—by crossing space and so escaping from the Earth, our cradle. That is the challenge that all intelligent races must meet, sooner or later. It is a double challenge, for it depends in turn upon the conquest of atomic energy and the last choice between life and death.

Once we had passed that crisis, it was only a matter of time before we found the pyramid and forced it open. Now its signals have ceased, and those whose duty it is will be turning their minds upon Earth. Perhaps they wish to help our infant civilization. But they must be very, very old, and the old are often insanely jealous of the young.

I can never look now at the Milky Way without wondering from which of those banked clouds of stars the emissaries are coming. If you will pardon so commonplace a simile, we have set off the fire alarm and have nothing to do but to wait.

I do not think we will have to wait for long.

"I must say you guys have come up with something."

The New Yorker magazine published four articles
on 2001: *A review of the film, a review of the book,
a Profile of Stanley Kubrick, and the following "Talk
of the Town" article when Kubrick and Clarke were
well into preproduction discussion and writing.*

BEYOND THE STARS*

Jeremy Bernstein

To MOST PEOPLE, including us, the words "science-fiction
movie" bring up visions of super-monsters who have flames
shooting out of at least one eye while an Adonislike Earthman
carries Sylvanna, a stimulating blonde, to a nearby spaceship.
It is a prospect that has often kept us at home. However, we
are happy to report, for the benefit of science-fiction buffs
—who have long felt that, at its best, science fiction is a splendid
medium for conveying the poetry and wonder of science—that
there will soon be a movie for *them*. We have this from none
other than the two authors of the movie, which is to be called
Journey Beyond the Stars—Stanley Kubrick and Arthur C.
Clarke. It is to be based on a forthcoming novel called *Journey
Beyond the Stars*, by Arthur C. Clarke and Stanley Kubrick.
Mr. Clarke and Mr. Kubrick, who have been collaborating on
the two projects for over a year, explained to us that the order
of the names in the movie and the novel was reversed to stress
Mr. Clarke's role as a science-fiction novelist (he has written
dozens of stories, many of them regarded as modern science-
fiction classics) and Mr. Kubrick's role as a moviemaker (his
most recent film was *Dr. Strangelove*).

Our briefing session took place in the living room of Mr.
Kubrick's apartment. When we got there, Mr. Kubrick was
talking on a telephone in the next room, Mr. Clarke had not
yet arrived, and three lively Kubrick daughters—the eldest is

eleven—were running in and out with several young friends. We settled ourself in a large chair, and a few minutes later the doorbell rang. One of the little girls went to the door and asked, "Who is it?" A pleasantly English-accented voice answered, through the door, "It's Clarke," and the girls began jumping up and down and saying, "It's Clark Kent!"—a reference to another well-known science-fiction personality. They opened the door, and in walked Mr. Clarke, a cheerful-looking man in his forties. He was carrying several manila envelopes, which, it turned out, contained parts of *Journey Beyond the Stars*. Mr. Kubrick then came into the room carrying a thick pile of diagrams and charts, and looking like the popular conception of a nuclear physicist who has been interrupted in the middle of some difficult calculations. Mr. Kubrick and Mr. Clarke sat down side by side on a sofa, and we asked them about their joint venture.

Mr. Clarke said that one of the basic problems they've had to deal with is how to describe what they are trying to do. "Science-fiction films have always meant monsters and sex, so we have tried to find another term for our film," said Mr. C.

"About the best we've been able to come up with is a space Odyssey—comparable in some ways to the Homeric *Odyssey*," said Mr. K. "It occurred to us that for the Greeks the vast stretches of the sea must have had the same sort of mystery and remoteness that space has for our generation, and that the far-flung islands Homer's wonderful characters visited were no less remote to them than the planets our spacemen will soon be landing on are to us. *Journey* also shares with the *Odyssey* a concern for wandering, exploration, and adventure."

Mr. Clarke agreed, and went on to tell us that the new film is set in the near future, at a time when the Moon will have been colonized and space travel, at least around the planetary system, will have become commonplace. "Since we will soon be visiting the planets, it naturally occurs to one to ask whether, in the past, anybody has come to Earth to visit us," he said. "In *Journey Beyond the Stars*, the answer is definitely yes, and the Odyssey unfolds as our descendants attempt to make contact with some extraterrestrial explorers. There will be no women among those who make the trip, although there will be some on Earth, some on the Moon, and some working in space."

Relieved, we asked where the film was to be made, and were told that it would be shot in the United States and several foreign countries.

"How about the scenes Out There?" we inquired.

Mr. Kubrick explained that they would be done with the aid of a vast assortment of cinematic tricks, but he added emphatically that everything possible would be done to make each

scene completely authentic and to make it conform to what i
known to physicists and astronomers. He and Mr. Clarke fee
that while there will be dangers in space, there will also b
wonder, adventure, and beauty, and that space is a source o
endless knowledge, which may transform our civilization in th
same way that the voyages of the Renaissance transformed th
Dark Ages. They want all these elements to come through i
the film. Mr. Kubrick told us that he has been a reader o
science-fiction and popular-science books, including Mr
Clarke's books on space travel, for many years, and that he ha
become increasingly disturbed by the barrier between scientifi
knowledge and the general public. He has asked friends basi
questions like how many stars there are in our galaxy, he wen
on, and has discovered that most people have no idea at all
"The answer is a hundred billion, and sometimes they stretc
their imaginations and say maybe four or five million," he saic

Speaking almost simultaneously, Mr. Clarke and Mr. Ku
brick said that they hoped their film would give people a rea
understanding of the facts and of the overwhelming implica
tions that the facts have for the human race.

We asked when the film will be released.

Mr. Kubrick told us that they are aiming for December, 196
and explained that the longest and hardest part of the job wi
be designing the "tricks," even though the ones they plan to us
are well within the range of modern cinematic technology.

When we had been talking for some time, Mr. Clarke sai
he had to keep another appointment, and left. After he ha
gone, we asked Mr. Kubrick how *Dr. Strangelove* had been re
ceived abroad. It had been shown all over the world, he tol
us, and had received favorable criticism everywhere excep
oddly, in Germany. He was not sure why this was, but though
it might reflect the German reliance on our nuclear strengt
and a consequent feeling of uneasiness at any attempt to mak
light of it. He said that his interest in the whole question o
nuclear weapons had come upon him suddenly, when it struc
him that here he was, actually in the same world with the hy
drogen bomb, and he didn't know how he was learning to liv
with that fact. Before making *Dr. Strangelove*, he read widel
in the literature dealing with atomic warfare.

We said goodbye shortly afterward, and on our way out
phrase of J. B. S. Haldane's came back to us: "The Univers
is not only stranger than we imagine; it is stranger than we *ca*
imagine."

"I know I've never completely freed myself of the suspicion that there are some extremely odd things about this mission."

Kubrick's original plan was to open 2001 with a ten-minute prologue (35mm film, black and white) — edited interviews on extraterrestrial possibilities with experts on space, theology, chemistry, biology, astronomy.

Kubrick says that he decided after the first screening of 2001 for M-G-M executives, in Culver City, California, that it wasn't a good idea to open 2001 with a prologue, and it was eliminated immediately.

Partially edited transcripts of interviews follow.

Academician A.I. Oparin
Director, A.N. Bach Institute of Biochemistry
Academy of Sciences of the U.S.S.R., Moscow

The origination of life is not an extraordinary event, a lucky circumstance, as has been a general concept until quite recently; it is an inevitable phenomenon, part and parcel of the universal evolution. In particular, our terrestrial form of life is a result of the evolution of carbonic compounds and multimolecular systems formed in the process of this evolution.

Could similar phenomena occur on other celestial bodies? We can observe the initial stages of evolution everywhere on various celestial objects. There can be no doubt of the existence of highly molecular complex organic substances on such objects as the Moon or Mars. Even if these substances could not be formed on those planets, they could be brought there by falling meteorites.

For evolution to have taken place on Earth, large expanses of water were necessary, which we could not observe and did not even expect to find on the Moon or Mars.

However, in the process of evolution of these planets, at the initial stage, these planets, for instance, Mars, could be more rich in water, and life could have emerged there along the same lines as on the Earth, and, having once emerged, it could develop and adjust to those severe, I would say unbearable for human beings, conditions existing on these celestial objects.

We possess, so to say, a single copy of the Book of Life, that of terrestrial life, while the knowledge of other forms of life could tell us about our past and, what's more, it could supply us with many clues as to our future. The discovery of new forms of life superior to ours would immensely enrich our culture and expedite our development.

Thus, human venture into space, direct perception of the solar system and, in particular, of Earth-type planets will add much to our perception of life and its development.

I doubt if we can seriously talk of any visits to the Earth from outer space that took place in the past. It is still the sphere of science fiction more than that of science. Of course, science fiction is fine in its own right; however, we should in all honesty say that the boundaries of our knowledge are but too far from the point where we could seriously discuss this problem without having any evidence whatsoever of communications of this nature.

Doubtless, a great number of complex and highly developed forms of the evolution of matter are to be found in the limitless expanse of the universe. But it is in no way imperative that we call these forms "life" or consider them such, as they differ in principle from our terrestrial form of life. It is my opinion that should we come across such phenomena in the process of our increasing space effort, we can work out some name other than "life" for them.

We can hardly expect to find anywhere in space human beings or living organisms morphologically similar to those of our terrestrial world. I presume the highly organized forms that may be found elsewhere in the universe are completely different in their appearance, which does not, however, rule out the possibility of finding intelligent life of a new type, other than our terrestrial life. Taking into consideration a great number of planetary systems within our galaxy alone, there exists a strong probability of finding one or several planets similar to our own. However, the development of life is such a complex process that, even in this case, full coincidence of the forms of life on these duplicated planets with our terrestrial form of life is hardly possible. These forms may be very close; however, certain distinctions will be observed.

Dr. Harlow Shapley
Paine Professor of Practical Astronomy Emeritus
Harvard University, Cambridge, Massachusetts

Q: *Dr. Shapley, what arguments mitigate against there being life on planets other than Earth?*

The thought is rather clear that we aren't going to have life in our solar system, because of the temperature problem. We can't have life without it being metabolic or metabolism-working — and it's not going to work if the water is all frozen or steamed away. We need water in a liquid state, and that we don't think we have much of in this solar system, and so that is the argument that mitigates having life as we know life, as we practice life, in this solar system. But there are a lot of other systems which we could have life on. In fact, it would do for me to point out that our studies of the number of galaxies and the number of stars in galaxies in all lead us to the conclusion that there must be something like ten to the twentieth — at least ten to the twentieth power stars: ten to the twentieth, that's a pretty big number, but if you write down one and put twenty zeros after it that would be the way it would look if you were expressing it in numbers. Well, that's a whole lot of stars, and suppose we say that only one in a billion, one in a thousand million, is suitable for life, we'd still have a tremendous number — we would have a hundred thousand million galaxies and stars that might harbor life. If only one in a million were comfortable, we would still have an enormous amount of life.

We are peripheral — I like to use that word. I mean we are on the edge; we are not in the center of a galaxy, we are not important in a galaxy, we're just here.

Of course, we ought to define life, shouldn't we — we should define life — and many people take shots at it, but I think the simplest one is to say that life is an activity of replication of macro-molecules. The macro-molecules, when they divide up, are self-replicating and represent what we would call life metabolic operations.

On Mars the conditions are so poor that I would not want to gamble that we are going to find life — but we are going to send apparatus out toward the vicinity of Mars — we are going to make a lot of photographs; we are going to do a bit of thinking on the subject and we may come to the conclusion that Mars probably does have a low form of operation that we call metabolic life—could be . . .

If one of my graduate students twenty-five years ago had said, "I want to write or study on the origin of life," I would have asked him to close the door as he went out and do it quickly, because you didn't do that then; it wasn't proper, especially for the young, to commence speculating in a big way about the origin of life or even the size of the universe.

There is a little point that we are now getting brave enough to discuss, and that is cosmic evolution. My idea about cosmic evolution is that everything that we can name—material or immaterial—evolves and changes with time. It goes from simple to more complex, or moves away.

We had novae, you see, for that evolutionary step from hydrogen into helium, burning hydrogen fuel into helium ash; and now we realize that in the novae we have temperatures that will take us further up this sequence of atoms.

We now know how the elements evolve. Well, if the elements evolve that way and biology evolves that way and the stars and the galaxies evolve that way, we might as well go the whole distance—say there is a cosmic evolution. The whole works evolve with time. Time is a factor in the matter—I don't know what the end is going to be. Some people ask, "What will happen when we run out of this fuel?" . . . I don't know the answer to that.

Whence came the hydrogen out of which the universe has developed . . . we don't know the answers—well, it may come from twists in the space time. Maybe a source we are building on. Okay, I say, who is the twister?

Life is going to appear where the chemical conditions are right: well, they are right now, on the surface of this planet, but back a few thousand million years ago, when the Earth was cooling off and rocks would be too hot, the life that could get started there would not have some of the necessary elements.

It would have methane and ammonia and water vapor and hydrogen gas and maybe one other. Those were the kind of elements of molecules that were on the surface of the Earth when life began. But now we can have those same elements in a laboratory.

Out in space, of course, you have electrical discharges from lightnings and, let us say, at the primal atmospheres . . . and you have these that I have just named—ammonia, methane, water vapor, hydrogen gas. You had those out in space, but we can have them in the laboratory.

That is what Stanley Miller, under the guidance of Harold Urey and some of the rest of us, put our oars in, what we could do also on the surface of the Earth. And so we set up a laboratory in Chicago that had just those things. . . . We didn't have any lightning from outer space, but we could put in electric discharges, which we did. Stanley Miller one day told me, he could see that his apparatus was showing something pink in what was otherwise a transparent gaseous medium. He let it run for a week. At the end of that week it was decidedly pink. And then he stopped his experiment and analyzed what he had done. He had used the same machinery that omnipotence—if there be such—could use, and we used it and he tested it and he used the new techniques that we don't know much about—mainly chronographic analysis—and what happened? He analyzed it and found he had amino acids, and that was one of the big jumps . . . I would say it was one of the best experiments of the last ten years.

First, just two or three, and then, at the end of the year, all twenty of the commonly accepted amino acids were found in this University of Chicago laboratory experiment. And that, of course, is a tremendous thing . . . a step toward life, because amino acids are what proteins are made of, and proteins are what human beings are made of. So we found out how to do those things, and since then we don't need to appeal to the Almighty, I mean, to the supernatural, or to miracles for the origin of life. We know the tricks of how it can be done. How it undoubtedly was done on this peripheral planet in this one solar system and probably elsewhere.

Who is—what is, aware? Is a dog aware of himself . . . is a fish aware of himself . . . is this amoeba of mine aware? It knows that one thing is edible and digestible, and another is not. So intelligence, to me, is just a matter of degree.

Francis J. Heyden, S.J.
Professor & Head of Dept. of Astronomy
Georgetown University
Washington, D.C.

Now, as far as religion is concerned, I do not know of any

eleventh commandment that says: "Thou shalt not talk to any-one off the face of the Earth." As a matter of fact, though, this would be a big problem. I can understand where we would re-ceive a message from some place out in space, but to talk back to them and exchange ideas, that I would say is close to physi-cally impossible for the present, because all our communication is done by means of electromagnetic radiation, which travels at the speed of light. So that even if someone on a planet near the closest star were to send a message to us, it would take four-and-a-half years from the time he said "hello" there until we heard it here; by the time we answered "glad to hear from you" and "how are you?" it would be four-and-a-half years before he got our answer. So you see, it would take quite a lifetime just to have a very casual passing of the time of day.

If it doesn't look like man at all and it is intelligent, we could communicate with it and have an exchange of ideas. I do not know whether we would call it man or not. We don't call angels men, but all through the Old Testament we have had constant references to certain angels who are pure spirits — who have been messengers of God to men.

On this question of the meaning of religion in exploration of life outside of our own Earth — whether that life be on one of the planets in space, or whether it be on even some star in a solar system all of its own, we would only have one question that would come up and that would be the question of the fall of Adam and Eve and the inheritance that we have gotten from that fall. These people probably never had an Adam and Eve who ran into trouble in Paradise and got thrown out. Possibly they are in what the philosophers and theologians of the Mid-dle Ages referred to as the state of pure nature, meaning that they do not have the darkened intellects and the weakened wills that we have, and therefore if we met them we would probably meet some of the finest guides and consultants and intelligent people that we could ever run into. It would be most beneficial for us. On the other hand, if the fall of Adam and Eve had been repeated, we might meet some people that would benefit by the same fruits of the redemption that we do, who would under-stand us, and speak almost the same language. But this is all speculation.

A being anywhere in space is a creature of God. So that if you even meet some living thing on the most distant galaxy, it would be a creature created by the same God that made us all.

In some respects, I suspect that eventually we may know, too, that we have the same biological or vital laws throughout the whole universe.

God can be known by any intelligent being. It is the belief of the philosophers, starting with Aristotle, and those who preceded him even, that an intelligent man looking at the wonders of nature — studying them, either from the standpoint of science or admiring them simply from the standpoint of beauty, with order and variety, to them . . . will come to the realization that there is a supreme being, or a God. On the other hand, we know from the Bible that God has revealed Himself to mankind on this Earth in a very, very special way, in order to help us appreciate Him more and more, or to come to know Him better. Now, as far as other beings in space are concerned, if they are intelligent they will know God the way a scientist would know Him — or the way Aristotle and other great philosophers down through the ages have instructed us that we can argue from the conditions of things in this world to the existence of a supreme being. Since we are intelligent, we would understand that God who made us is also intelligent. But we might not know whether or not these people have as full an understanding of God as we have through Revelation until we found out what form of Revelation was given to them.

What could man learn from contacting extraterrestrial intelligence? First of all, the extraterrestrial might know more than we do. We might get answers to a lot of things; but it would depend on whether or not we could contact him directly and not wait for the long time-lag between question and answer, perhaps as long as a couple of hundred years. On the other hand, he might be just giving out information, and as we gathered it in and interpreted it, we would be advancing our own reservoir of knowledge in any field that he happened to be communicating to us. In addition to that, I would say this: that the satisfaction of knowing that there is someone else out in space, who is able to communicate by intelligent signals, is a great advance in our own knowledge — and that helps us, I think, to appreciate the position that we have in this universe and our own role in the universe.

It is sometimes suggested to me that possibly there is a conflict over investigating whether or not there are intelligent beings somewhere else than on this Earth. People very often feel that we have been put here on this Earth to stay, and that is where we are going to stay, and that space is God's locker — we are not supposed to pry into it. I do not believe that; after all, we do have the psalm that says, "The Heavens tell of Thy Glory, O God" and also, as a philosopher, we have the urge to learn as much as we can. We have restless minds as well as bodies. Minds that are always inquiring into things, to learn how they are made . . . how they work . . . what they are; and there is nothing in all of Revelation that is against learning more and more. As a matter of fact, I think myself that the man with what I call "scientific faith" is much more at rest in his soul than one who is just satisfied with what he knows from reading the scriptures.

There has always been the attitude among believers as far back as we go in the history of religion that God is in His Heaven — God is above. One reason for that, of course, is that we are conscious that we don't see God face-to-face here on this Earth, and we have been accustomed to the beauties of, let us say, a sunset. If you stand looking at the sun as it sets, this beautiful panorama in the sky, something like Shelley's "In the golden glory of the setting sun, o'er which clouds are brightening" — and so on — I can see where a person might want to make that a sort of a shrine for himself. I can see and understand the idea of a sun worshiper . . . just from that; and I think that it is because of that we are inclined to place the residence of all divinity in space or up in the Heavens above: because there is so much beauty and so much wonderment there that we do not understand. But again, as one having scientific faith, I know that God is everywhere and that God is as much in my little finger as he is in the most distant star.

There is a great conservatism among some people who feel we are not supposed to pry into, let us say, the mysteries of space. This is, of course, against all of the efforts of astronomers from time immemorial who have tried to know more and more about the stars and about the planets and the laws of their motion. What a tremendous achievement it was when, first of all, Johannes Kepler found from observational data the three laws of planetary motion, and having approached his goal from observational data, he was followed about two generations later by Isaac Newton, who started out with a theory, and from his theory of gravitation derived the same three laws that Kepler had gotten from observation. This is a real scientific advance. I do not think anyone in the world is ashamed of it. As a matter of fact, putting a satellite in orbit about the Earth in this generation — and I think we do live in a wonderful generation of discovery — was an achievement of a dream that Isaac Newton had. Isaac Newton suggested that we put a cannon on top of a high mountain and fire a projectile parallel to the direction of the gravity of the Earth at such a speed that the cannonball would go in orbit about the Earth. No one would say that we have done wrong by launching artificial satellites. We have actually achieved something that is worth all the money that we have put into the space effort at present. The weather satellite and communications satellites are examples. Now if we are to go further in our investigations of space, I do not think that we are going to violate any law of God. I don't think any conservatism on the part of people should have any influence on us.

The origin of life on the Earth is a question that . . . I do not know if it is ever going to be solved. On the humorous side, we have some people who think that it evolved from some garbage that was left behind after the crew of a spaceship stopped here one time, had a picnic, and then departed for another planet. Other people believe that life started after a molecule had been developed to a certain degree of complexity, so that it would support life such as DNA. This happened after the conditions for life, such as the right temperature, and other chemical requirements, such as free oxygen and water, were formed. Then, somehow or other, a pre-life germ or some sort of impulse started the life process going, and you had your very simple cells gradually becoming complicated animals. Eventually, out of it all, came the body of an animal that God decided to give a human soul and call man. This is all right if you want to believe in that form of evolution, as long as you remember that the human soul that we have is not something that evolved out of a chemical test tube, or whatever you had in the early stages of development of the Earth. We know that life did not always exist on this Earth — we know that living forms have changed and do change over long periods of time on the surface of the Earth . . . but, all we do have is a brief history of *homo sapiens*, of the intelligent man. We do not know exactly where he came from, how long he has really been here.

Gerald Feinberg
Professor of Physics, Columbia University
New York

I think men will travel to the stars sooner or later; the factors that will decide this are that some men want to, and that even today we can think of ways in principle by which it can be accomplished. Some scientists have said that the stars are too far away for us to ever reach them. But distance by itself doesn't mean anything. Distance is equal to speed multiplied by time, and if relativity and the amount of energy available keep us from traveling too fast, we can always try to extend the amount of time we have available. There are various ways we could do this. One is by extending the human life span, which would be a good idea for other reasons, also. Another would be by some kind of suspended animation for the travelers, either by lowering their body temperature, or by some kind of chemicals which decrease the rate of metabolism. Already some scientists are working on methods like this. So I think that sooner or later it is pretty likely that some men from Earth will travel to other planetary systems.

I think that in a million years the human race would be able to do anything one can think of right now, that doesn't specifically violate the laws of nature; and, perhaps, many things that we think of as violating the laws of nature. So, by extension, I would say that some other form of intelligent life, which is already a million years ahead of us, would be able to do all of those different things.

Some of the things that such an intelligent race might do would be astronomical changes, like making their planets move differently, or perhaps even arranging them into some kind of geometrical array which had some value for whatever their purposes were. I think they would also do a great deal to reshape their own biology. Even if a race is much more intelligent than we are, it's unlikely that they would have reached any kind of perfection: so one of the things I foresee an intelligent race wanting to do is to make itself even better than it is. I think we'll do that to ourselves sooner or later, and I expect that another race would do the same thing.

It is a little surprising that if there are superintelligent races around, we haven't seen some indication of them. One possibility is that they had visited us, say half a million years ago, when there probably wasn't anybody around to know that we'd been visited. But the Earth has been around for a very long time, and man, at least in his present form, has been here only one ten thousandth or so of the life of the Earth, so that the chances that we would have been visited while we were able to recognize it is pretty small.

We're just beginning to get some idea of how we can manipulate the genetic pattern to influence the functions of living cells. If we can do that, then I think it should be possible to produce human beings who can also think better and faster than we can. In fact, I think it's a very exciting prospect that fairly soon there'll be some kind of intellectual relationship between men and machines, in which each of us contributes those aspects of thought that we can do best. I think this is something very much in the cards, and something which I myself am looking forward to with a great deal of interest.

But I don't think that the outlook for electronic machines is so poor, either. There are many advantages that electronic machines have over biological systems—one is that the rate at which information flows within them is many, many times faster; the information flows at near the speed of light. Within human beings, the nerve impulses flow at a few hundred feet a second, which is many, many orders of magnitude slower. I think that difference in itself gives the machines a very great advantage, and I see no reason why that advantage can't be put into use. But I think that both developments will come.

I think there may be some trouble in deciding when a machine is conscious. An intelligent machine wouldn't necessarily think the same way that human beings do—in fact, that I think is very unlikely.

But the fact that two systems don't operate the same way doesn't mean that you can't recognize some kind of functional relation between what they do: what criterion we will use for deciding that a particular creature, if I can call it that, is conscious—I don't know. I think there are going to be some interesting philosophical questions involved in making that choice.

Human psychology is a hard enough subject. Robot psychology I think is right now an impossible subject to speculate against. But I suspect that it may be easier to treat the mental diseases of machines than of people.

You might have one computer acting as psychiatrist to another one. I would hope that the superintelligent machine isn't literally mankind's last invention. Some people have worried that we might invent these machines, and then they might decide that human beings were unnecessary for the proper order of things. I don't think that's what's going to happen myself. For one thing, as far as I can see, machines are unmotivated, even if they are superintelligent; their motivations have to be provided from the outside, presumably by us, and, therefore, even if after we made the superintelligent machines, they then start improving themselves or inventing new things, these will be as much our inventions as theirs. I think it all depends how you look at it.

I think one problem which is connected both with intelligent machines and with biologically improving human beings is—do we want to do it? Even if it becomes technically possible to make intelligent machines or supermen, we still have to decide what purpose it will serve.

I can imagine the human race might decide that it doesn't want to make these creatures.

I don't think that until now mankind ever has refused to do something really important that was technically possible for it. There have been some irreversible changes in man's way of life in the past: such as the introduction of agriculture eight thousand years ago, or the introduction of industrialization about two hundred years ago. They just came about in the natural progression of technology and science. I think that the difference now is that we can foresee, if only by twenty or thirty years, the fact that some of these decisions are going to have to be made. And I think as long as we can foresee this, we should at least think about whether we want to do it.

F.C. Durant, III
Assistant Director, Astronautics
National Air and Space Museum, Smithsonian Institution
Washington, D.C.

It is hard to imagine that life could exist on this planet knowing that literally billions of stars exist, and the presumption of billions and billions of planets that revolve about them.

I believe the search for extraterrestrial life is certainly one of the most exciting kinds of exploration that could be accomplished, if it is done in a logical and scientific manner.

Radio observation, both passive and active, appears to be one of the more logical types of exploration underway, and I would presume that this is certainly a valid approach.

I think the mind boggles at the impact of discovery by man of an extraterrestrial civilization, or just extraterrestrial life in some form of development. Yet it is something which I think we will someday face. I think it will have the effect of bringing men closer together, certainly on our own planet. I suggest at that moment national boundaries might mean very much less.

As to the possibility that the Earth has been visited by extraterrestrial life — sometime in the past — I know of no reports that would lead me to be convinced, or feel, that this is so; and yet it would be utterly ridiculous to say that it has not occurred at some time — hundreds, thousands, or even millions of years ago

I know of no reports where there were signals which have been received from beyond the solar system; that have been received in any way which can be construed as coming from intelligent beings.

The problem of conceiving the level of capability, technology and the development of life that is millions of years old, or intelligent life that has been intelligent for millions of years, simply staggers one's imagination. It is very difficult even to begin to conceive of the degree of communication that might be direct ... the interests, pleasures, if you will, of such life.

Should man make contact with extraterrestrial intelligence very much more advanced than our own, it would be hoped that some type of friendly relations might be able to be established. The next step, it would seem to me, would be to be able to learn from such intelligence, presuming communication is established. If their intelligence is too far advanced, of course, one just doesn't know, it might be that we would not even be considered important enough to bother about.

The possibilities of utilizing machine intelligence, advanced computer systems with memory circuits, in the future are, I think, immense. Surely as man develops more complex machine intelligence, he will learn to instruct such machines to perform routine acts; teach them how to make simple judgments. This is as far as one can predict, based on today's technology. It would be foolish not to expect that as machines progress, the capability to make more and more complex decisions — eventually perhaps approaching those of intelligent man — would follow. It is even possible to imagine that more rational decisions might be made by a machine eventually than by man, which brings up the interesting possibility of turning over certain State decisions to the machines. However, this again is more than a decade away, which I think is the limit that anyone can predict these days.

I can imagine the possibilities that advanced forms of machinery at some time in the future might feel pain, pleasure — have emotional response. If it was found that by adding to computer design counterparts of man's own experience and emotions some value was obtained, then machinery simulating such emotions and sensory perceptions might be deemed desirable and built.

Certainly, if man develops machines that have sensory perceptions and emotional response — machines, that, if you will, feel pain and pleasure — then it is reasonable to assume that they may become upset or have neuroses as man does today. Certainly, I could imagine that certain machines eventually might even require rest periods and an opportunity to reconsider their reactions. What we're talking about really, now, is considering the possibility of building something that acts very much like man. I think there is another approach — in attempting to build something that does not have perhaps the weaknesses of man.

I don't believe that there are any ceilings or limits to man's capability, given the technical tools to accomplish it. In other words, I do not believe man will ever stop exploring space. He will go farther, longer even perhaps with colony transportation, reproducing and raising whole new generations, exploring the universe. I do not myself accept that there is necessarily a limitation to traveling at the speed of light. Of course, we move at such a very small fraction of the speed of light, we do not know the future. There are evidences, of course, that one cannot approach more than a certain percentage of the speed of light, but I do not necessarily accept that there are not ways of traveling faster than the speed of light. I have no idea whatever how to do it any more than I would have an idea right now how one could in any way avoid the forces of gravity, and yet, in my opinion, the possibility exists . . . In my mind it is a possibility that could occur, that would be just as miraculous and magical as perhaps modern solid-state electronics — or solid-state physics — would have been to scientists of 1869. I say that things might be possible, although I do not have the foggiest notion how they may be accomplished. Such discoveries will probably appear just as magical to us today as a transistor radio or solid-state physics would have seemed to Thomas Edison. We could no more understand as we sit here today their accomplishment, and yet these are things that I do believe will occur . . . in the next year, decade, or later. But I believe they will eventually happen.

Jeremy Bernstein
Professor of Physics
Stevens Institute of Technology, Hoboken, N.J.
Staff Member, The New Yorker

One of the most impressive things that a quest into extraterrestrial life can lead to — if we ever discover intelligent civilizations and communicate with them — is to try to learn from them how they have dealt with death — what forms death has had for them.

The entire argument that attempts to generalize from our history in the solar system to what goes on in other planetary systems is really based on the notion that the evolution of our solar system is not in any way unique. This is, of course, from an exact point of view, impossible to establish. We simply do not know enough yet to state whether our solar system is or is not unique. What we do know is that there must be billions of other planetary systems. We know that there are stars that have planets — we even know that some of these planets are comparable n size to our own Jupiter—and therefore we are sure that there must be billions of planets in the universe, but all the rest of it s a conjecture which is based on probability.

The real future of space travel lies in making use of nuclear explosive propulsion systems, making use of the energy from controlled nuclear bombs. Therefore it has seemed to me that the ime in which a civilization will learn to do really significant pace travel and the time at which they will learn about atomic nd hydrogen bombs would probably be about the same time. Then the question is whether it is possible for a civilization to exist that is sophisticated enough to survive its own technology. We don't really know whether we are going to survive our own technology, and at least it's one gloomy possibility that very civilization that has come up to the nuclear technological left-stick has not been able to survive its own technology.

The lesson of modern biology is that the distinction between iving and nonliving material is almost arbitrary. And so it is ossible that one would be able to make machines biologically, n test tubes rather than in an electronics factory, and then it vill be almost an arbitrary question as to whether one wants to all such objects machines or living animals.

think one of the most interesting aspects of the exploration of he Moon and, later on, of Mars will be its archaeology—if any: ecause of the low atmosphere, if anybody had visited the Moon r had left Mars at an earlier time, the remains should be extremely well-preserved, since there is nothing much in those tmospheres to have corroded them. But there is really no evidence at all that the Earth was visited at some prior time by xtraterrestrials, although hope springs eternal.

t was assumed up until the experiments of Pasteur that life ould evolve spontaneously from nonliving matter, although it was usually assumed at the same time that man had divine origin—well, of course, if man had divine origin, then the question f extraterrestrial life can no longer be discussed in a scientific ay—it becomes rather an arbitrary one. But Pasteur's experiments appeared to him to prove that life could not be generated om nonliving matter, which he took to be a triumph for science. Well, if life cannot be generated from nonliving matter, ien life can only generate itself, and so you are led to an infinite regress where all hope of scientific explanation of the origin of life becomes impossible. So it is only with Darwin and is successors that the problem of generating life from nonliving matter has been reexamined, and therefore the thought that iere might be extraterrestrial life is in a certain sense a rather modern thought and rests very much on the blurring of distinctions between living and nonliving matter.

I think it is generally and rather naïvely assumed that extraterrestrial life will be benign. That there will be philosopher-kings reigning in the cosmos. Professor Freeman Dyson of the Institute for Advanced Study at Princeton made the point that if we detect signs of extraterrestrial life, what we'll detect first will really be advanced technologies. We will detect signals generated by some very advanced technological system, and it is by no means clear that a civilization capable of such advances in technology is going to be a very benign civilization. The more technological our own civilization becomes in many ways the worse it becomes, and one could imagine terrible civilizations with a very high degree of technology.

One might hope that a civilization which has been going for hundreds of thousands of years might have worked out all of its aggressions and internal problems, but I think it is just as likely to have blown itself off the face of the Earth. I don't know — that's one of the fascinating things that either we or our descendants will learn.

Freeman J. Dyson
Professor of Physics, The Institute for Advanced Study
Princeton University

I don't believe that electronic machinery is going to go very much further than it is now. This is, of course, something that we'll find out in the course of time. I may be completely wrong, but there seem to be some natural limitations on what one can do with electronics, which fall very short of what the human mind can do, so I would not believe that anybody with existing types of electronic machinery could build anything that resembles a human mind. But, on the other hand, I would say when we learn how to use biological techniques ourselves, and to build machines with biological materials, then it will be very different. Then it may well be possible to go far beyond anything we have at the moment, and we shall probably be able to create intelligence, and whether we will call that machine intelligence or not is of course a matter of words. I think it will not look like an electronic computer, but it will look much more like a living organism.

I know the biologists are in general very optimistic concerning the things they are going to do — they believe they are on the threshold of great things. I'm not able to judge independently, but I would think it's very likely.

It seems to me clear that we could turn the galaxy upside down if we wanted to, within a million years; there's nothing in the world of physics at least that would prevent us from doing that. There may be some good reasons for not doing it, and there may be good reasons why other intelligent species are not doing it.

I would have expected, if there existed any highly developed race of technological beings, that looking for them would be like looking for evidence of life on Manhattan Island — that they would have transformed the whole surroundings completely. Evidently they haven't done this for some reason — if they exist.

We don't see any traces of them when we look in the sky, and this is peculiar. If an Indian from four hundred years ago were to come into New York harbor, he might not understand what he sees, but he would at least notice there is something there.

If you look at the way our brains operate, we are subject to all kinds of problems merely because we can't remember things, we can't learn things fast and efficiently. There are many practical limitations that we're subject to which one imagines one could overcome if one knew how to do it; so one could hope to improve our brains to the point where we could learn many languages and understand everything that is known in science, and in general be much more competent mentally than we are at present. And one hopes one could do this without radically changing our moral standards and our personalities. But, of course, it's very likely that all kinds of unforeseen effects would appear at the same time, perhaps including new forms of neurosis — so it's a game which one has to play extremely carefully; but I have no doubt whatever it's going to be played. In some ways I'm excited at the prospect and in other ways afraid.

Q: *Some physicists have suggested that some subnuclear particles are actually other subnuclear particles moving backwards in time, and so we might be able to travel backwards in time, too.*

I don't believe this makes any sense: the flow of time is again something that is fairly well understood in the physical sense. The fact that time has a definite direction of flow is a consequence of the fact that we are living beings and that we take in information and make use of it in accordance with certain definite physical and mathematical principles. I don't believe this has much to do with subnuclear particles. The fact that you can talk in a sensible way about particles traveling backwards in time does not mean that we should ever be able to travel backwards in time or that we could imagine other beings to travel backwards in time. This is just a confusion of language.

Q: *What parts of the physical universe are not understood?*

The greatest area of ignorance is in the area of very high energies, where most of the exciting developments in physics are
being made at the moment. This is the world of small particles
crashing into each other at very high energies and producing
other particles. . . . All these things are not at all well understood and are very exciting to scientists just for that reason.

I think it's not only legitimate to start looking for signs of intelligence in the universe, it's also extremely important, and it's
something which should be done much more intensively than it
ever has been done. Up to now we have only looked for about a
month at a couple of stars. That is all, and nothing more has
been done. I hope very much that this search will be revived and
made into a routine operation, and that it will be taken more and
more seriously as time goes on. It clearly is an extremely important question to decide whether or not there are other intelligences in the universe, and it would have profound consequences if one found any positive evidence. Even though I'm
very skeptical as to whether we shall find positive evidence, I'm
all the more anxious that we should try.

It's impossible to foresee what the consequences would be—
which we have absolutely no way of imagining. I don't remember
who it was who said that any alien form of life would not only
be stranger than we imagine but would be stranger than we can
imagine: and this is profoundly true. So, what would be the consequences, we can't imagine, either. Even if we had no communication but merely observed passively what was going on, we
would probably see all kinds of things that are totally unex-
pected and different from things that we see normally, and
this would certainly make big changes in our picture of things—
probably big changes in our view of ourselves, in our view of our
place in the world in general.

I don't believe that anything will ever go faster than light. This
is a basic limitation; it means that travel from one star to another will always take a long time—and therefore it will not be
like going to visit one's family in the next town. This limitation
of the velocity of light is, I believe, quite fundamental—and I'm
happy about it. I think it makes space travel much more interesting, that one can go to places that are remote not only in
space but also in time. But I believe there are very few other
limitations. It's not difficult to imagine methods of propelling
oneself with nuclear energy which go at some fraction of the
speed of light—some few percent perhaps of the speed of light—
and I believe in time one probably will get up fairly close to

the speed of light; but this we don't understand yet how to do.

The solar system as a whole is very accessible. I would think within a hundred years we could probably be traveling around the solar system fairly freely. If you take nuclear energy and — for example — a system of propulsion using electricity and nuclear energy generators and plasma jets, you can imagine fairly efficient and economical transportation around the solar system within a hundred years. Anything beyond that, of course, is a vastly more difficult proposition and would certainly take more than a hundred years.

I think that one of the interesting questions is whether we can make colonies in the solar system within the foreseeable future — whether the human race is going to spread out in many different parts of the solar system. I believe we shall, but of course, I have no means of telling where or how. We don't yet know enough about the places that might be suitable — any more than Columbus knew what he was getting into when he sailed out from Spain. But, one place which I think looks very promising is the comets. Most science-fiction writers concentrate on planets, but it may be that the most interesting places for life to settle are the comets. In the solar system there are ten planets, and there are probably several millions or several billions of comets; a comet might be very suitable as a place to start a colony; it is made of materials that are familiar to us — water, carbon, nitrogen, and oxygen, just the materials one needs for living plants and animals. And the comets have the great advantage that there are a great many of them, and it would probably be easy to establish small colonies, given a certain degree of technical development that we don't yet have.

F.D. Drake
Associate Director, Center for Radiophysics and Space Research
Chairman, Department of Astronomy
Cornell University, Ithaca, N.Y.

The reasons why one believes there is intelligent life elsewhere is based on a body of knowledge which we have accumulated — this includes particularly the vast number of stars that exist in the universe, some one hundred million, million stars; the fact that most of these are like our Sun; the fact that we believe the existence of planetary systems is a very common thing in the universe; and, lastly, that the development of life on planets is not a difficult thing but rather something that occurs very easily when conditions are appropriate.

I think we are not capable of predicting what the capabilities would be of a civilization even a thousand years ahead of our own—perhaps not even a hundred years ahead of our own.

I think it's clear that life will go through an evolutionary cycle everywhere. This is forced upon life—because no matter what planet life appears upon, there is going to be a limited supply of sunlight and therefore a limited supply of food—and this inevitably leads to a competition between species for this limited food supply—leading to the development of species that are capable of competing better for the available food. Now, it is more controversial as to whether intelligence is an inevitable result of this evolution. Some people believe it may not always appear in the course of evolution. However, if one examines the fossil record—the history of life on Earth—one sees that only one characteristic has continuously developed and improved throughout the history of life, and that is intelligence. Sure enough, animals have tried different numbers of legs—we've had six and eight legs and a hundred-legged things—we've had enormous creatures, such as the dinosaurs, and little ones; we've had winged creatures—everything has been tried. The only thing that has persisted and continuously developed is intelligence, and this argues strongly that intelligence will appear everywhere where life evolves.

There are no reasonable arguments that would lead us to believe that we are the only abode of life in the universe.

One cannot rule out the possibility that life on Earth was carried to Earth from elsewhere on a small meteorite or as some kind of a spore—in fact, there is a theory that this is how life came to Earth, called the Panspermia theory. However, it is very unlikely that this happened because the environment of space is so rigorous. Anything traveling across space is bombarded with cosmic rays, ultraviolet radiation, in such an intensity that anything— any life as we know it—would be destroyed over the eons of time that are required for transport across space. For these reasons, we think it unlikely that life was carried across space from one planet to another.

As to whether Earth has ever been visited by another intelligent species, we can compute that the chances of this happening are very small. Making some rather poor estimates, one can guess that this might happen at best once every ten thousand years or so, so that we should not expect frequent visits from other planets; by the same token we cannot rule them out. Now if they happened thousands of years ago all evidence of it has been destroyed. One thing does seem certain, and that is that we have never found yet on Earth any clear-cut evidence of an extraterrestrial visit.

Our planet is extremely easy to observe from elsewhere. It is partially cloud-covered at times; however, the clouds and the haze of the atmosphere do not present any serious hindrance to the observation of Earth. The satellites and such that surround our Earth present no problems at all to anything which attempts to observe the Earth from outside.

It is possible that radio signals of extraterrestrial origin are arriving at the Earth at the present time with an intensity which is detectable with existing equipment. We cannot say for sure that this is happening, and equally we cannot decide whether other civilizations are intentionally sending us such signals. There may be signals that other civilizations are using for their own purposes which are arriving at Earth. However, this is a very exciting and tantalizing thought, to realize that at this very moment perhaps detectable radio signals from other civilizations are passing right through this room.

Now there are people who believe it might be dangerous to answer. Perhaps they will attack us. Perhaps we are the finest beef animals they have ever discovered. But the fact is, and this is something we should understand right now, that we already transmit enough radio waves into space that we can be detected if they want to detect us. We cannot keep our presence secret if other civilizations really want to find us, so we might as well try to answer back. It is no use trying to avoid the issue.

It has been said that our relationship to a civilization that might detect us is about the same as the relationship of a Neanderthal man to our civilization. That is, we would understand and comprehend as little as would a Neanderthal man placed in one of our major cities today.

There is a possibility that there exists on Earth an artifact from an extraterrestrial visit. Now we have estimated that at the very best—under the best conditions—one would not expect a visit from another civilization, an actual landing, more often than once in many thousands of years. Now we would expect that such a visit would leave behind an artifact, because otherwise no evidence of such a visit would be left to the intelligent beings that might come along later. Such landings might leave artifacts. However, as you can see from the fact that they would come so infrequently, the number of such artifacts would be very small, and they would be buried perhaps now in archaeological ruins or what have you. Only a great deal of excavation and good luck combined could lead us to such an artifact.

One can't really be sure whether one would detect the extraterrestrial nature of such an artifact. However, another civilization would probably go to great pains to make it clear that the object was of extraterrestrial origin. So I suspect that we would recognize it as extraterrestrial. We have to date found no artifact that could be construed as being of extraterrestrial origin. This is the prime evidence against the idea that UFOs, for instance, are spaceships from another civilization.

There are a number of examples of cave drawings—ancient scrolls, tablets, and so forth which have very provocative drawings, which appear in some cases to be drawings of creatures in spacesuits—and people have wondered if perhaps these are records of a visit from an extraterrestrial civilization. However, to date no one has been able to give convincing evidence that this is the proper explanation—and, by the same token, in each case a completely natural, non-extraterrestrial explanation can be provided.

Fred L. Whipple
Director, Smithsonian Institution Astrophysical Observatory
Phillips Professor of Astronomy
Harvard University, Cambridge, Massachusetts

With regard to learning about extraterrestrial life, of course, our first move is to go to the planets and study them, as we are now planning—the National Aeronautics and Space Administration's program—that's the first move. Now if we wish to consider the possibility of proving that there are intelligent living beings on other planets, it seems unlikely that this could happen in our solar system. The evidence that has accumulated with regard to the more likely planets is discouraging. Therefore, they will have to live on planets about stars, and all stars are physically very distant. Now, there is the possibility of just listening for them. People have generally assumed that intelligent creatures somewhere are so anxious to make their presence known, or to communicate, that they spend huge fractions of their resources, at least, huge resources, in powerful transmitters that could transmit for tens, hundreds, or thousands of light years into space on the vague hope that somebody will answer them. Now this type of communication I think is highly unlikely. I would suspect that although all cultures might not be like ours, there have to be some practical limitations for survival, and they are not going to spend great resources in this type of effort. But what might happen is that one will find a planetary system in which there are several inhabitable planets—two or more at least—and that then they will establish trade and communication. If we could locate such a system in which we lay very nearly on the plane of their mutual orbits or somewhere near that plane, then there might be a chance that we would pick up communication signals when two or more planets were properly aligned to send a signal in our direction. Now, whether this is worth listening for or not is a real question in my mind, whether the chances are high enough that we can ever detect such communication in such a reasonable period of time.

The question of the endeavor to send men into space and the changes of attitude that have taken place in astronomy represent a practical situation. Twenty-five years ago, I certainly, for one, and a great many other friends of mine who were interested in the possibilities of life in other parts of the universe, put a great deal of thought into the possibility of man going into space. I remember the exact day when I became certain that this would happen—this was back in 1944, twenty-two years ago, when the first V-2 was launched, albeit on a very hapless mission. Nevertheless, at that time my long-anticipated thought that we would go into space became in my mind a certainty. I don't know how many other people thought in the same fashion. I would say for most of my life the expectation that man would go into space had been very real in the minds of many scientists. On the other hand, this had no practical aspect or application at a time when the technical possibilities had not been developed. There was no chance of exploiting a technology then. Now, since the V-2 in 1944, it has been quite clear that it is technically possible to do this, and the question has been just how soon.

This problem of man in space versus instruments in space is, of course, a difficult one. The question really revolves about the practical costs and the resources that we can invest in such matters. My own attitude has been that it is possible to send man into space. I believe that any culture or country, or even person for that matter, who sees a challenge to cross a new frontier, but who doesn't accept the challenge and attempt to cross the frontier, is going decadent. I think we have to consider and plan definitely for man in space as well as for unmanned instrumentation in space.

With regard to sending man into deep space versus instruments into deep space—again, resources are the more important factor. I would be rather satisfied in studying Jupiter, for example, simply to send unmanned instruments. On the other hand, the landing of a man on the satellites of Jupiter could lead to some very exciting results. Then if one carries his imagination a bit farther into the future, visualizes the availability of almost infinite energy sources, stronger materials, and better technology, we might be able to put man down inside the thick atmosphere of Jupiter under high gravity. There he could conceivably make discoveries that the instruments might miss. Also, in this case, it might be extremely difficult getting information back by radio. It might be necessary to return something.

When it comes to the problem of the complexity of a life that we may or may not find on some other terrestrial planets, I speak with great conservatism. The older I get, the more I find that negative statements tend to be dangerous. It is quite true that the evidence, say, on Mars, suggests that you wouldn't expect very large organisms, and this is very probably true. When one considers possibilities, he should speak very carefully, because it is quite possible that below the surface of Mars there might live sizable living organisms and, even conceivably but extremely unlikely, intelligent organisms. We are not sure enough in the case of Venus to state with absolute positivism that somewhere there isn't a habitable area. So, I would say there is some chance that a paleontologist might be needed somewhere in the solar system.

Colonization in the solar system is at the present time in the dream stage. But I would say that if huge power sources such as the hydrogen fusion process become readily controllable and generally available, we could think very seriously of supplying an atmosphere for Mars or sustaining one on the Moon, if water is available there. In the case of Venus, I suspect that it may be impossible to do, although there has been some suggestion of altering the atmosphere by biological techniques, or possibly by other chemical techniques. One should not rule that out completely for the long run. I rather feel that the Moon, too, is one of the bodies that is less likely to become, shall we say, economically feasible for colonization, because of the difficulty of maintaining an atmosphere. The motions of the molecules will enable them to escape from the low gravity of the Moon too rapidly. On the other hand, the Moon offers some great opportunities for astronomy, particularly radio astronomy on the back side, away from man-made radio noise. This can be done without an atmosphere, and surely will be done sometime.

Can we travel faster than light? It is fair to say, on the basis of all the physics that we know today, it is impossible. The relativity limit for ions and electrons is proven by our large accelerators. We, ourselves, are made of ions and electrons. Therefore, we cannot travel faster than the velocity of light. It is a difficult argument to beat.

My point of view on people traveling through space to other stars is rather negative, at least for a long time. It is an extremely expensive process in terms of physical resources, and it demands a goal-directed activity of such magnitude that I really question that it happens very frequently. I am sure attempts of this sort must have been made in galactic time, and may well be made by man if he survives for a few more centuries.

Philip Crosbie Morrison
*Department of Physics, Massachusetts Institute of Technology
Cambridge, Massachusetts*

Life could not be static—it has to evolve, in an effort to maintain itself under changing circumstances and in an effort to extend itself, to take advantage of more and more ways of making a living.

We don't know enough about the evolutionary process to say whether or not it has any inevitable results. We have the evidence before us that intelligence, manipulation of the environment, is one way, a successful way, of making a living. It appears to me that wherever life can find a way to do that, it will eventually manage to do so; but to say we *know* that it will is, I think, a mistake. It might be inevitable, but we do not know that.

The issue about the evolution of intelligence is, I think, simply this one: the evolution of intelligence is a very rapid matter, and the evolution of environmental control which depends upon it is still more rapid. The history of life on Earth is at least three or four billion years old, yet it is only within millions of years at the outside that primate forms of the sort we recognize being able to manipulate the environment extensively came into being; this is one part in a thousand or one part in two thousand. Therefore, even if the ages of the evolutionary patterns on different planets were similar to our own—I think they will be—I don't think they would be very much older—that is not the way to look at it. The point is that the scale of evolution is so long compared to that special part of the scale which is the evolution of environmental control, that unless they started with absolute synchronism (which is absurd—there is no reason for them to synchronize, to start from a word "go" everywhere), then the natural drift will provide very great gaps in time, gaps in time very large compared to one part in a thousand. Say, one part in ten—that is still not a very large fraction; but that one part in ten would be a thousand times the entire life span of our species, and many thousands of times the entire life span of our civilizations. The point is that the growth of intelligence and environmental control are enormously rapid things on a cosmic scale. After all, agriculture is only ten thousand years old, and this ten thousand years, suppose that had started five hundred thousand years ago. There is no question of it: it would have taken about ten or maybe twenty or perhaps even thirty thousand years to evolve from agriculture, say, to industry; but then there are the other two hundred thousand years in the presence of industrial technique — that's only a difference of one percent in the whole skipping of the time pattern. I think it a very strong argument that if there are a dozen patterns of intelligent life, half a dozen would be way ahead of us and half a dozen would either not have evolved at all — if that is not too much of a contradiction — or be well behind.

Talking about organisms of the size we are, anywhere between dozens of centimeters and a few meters, I think those organisms will never be able to dispose of anything much more than a few planets' energy. Now, that's a lot of energy, and it is enough to make a great many changes in the surround, but I don't think it will enable them to change stars very much or to change galaxies appreciably — not to make a park out of a galaxy — to make a park out of a planet, yes, quite easily; to double-deck the Earth — quite easily; to occupy the oceans — to travel from space to communicate — that would be no trouble at all; we will do that ourselves. But to move planets around, or to enclose the sun with a shell, or modulate the sun and make it send out signals — I am rather skeptical about that. It could be . . . but I take conservative views . . . I wouldn't like to extrapolate that far.

Whether we should send or listen for signals from extraterrestrial life is an engineering question, a question of engineering expediency. I believe that it is not sensible to send; it is a more difficult task; we should listen for a time comparable to the time that technologies improve vastly . . . and we haven't been doing that long enough. I think maybe in decades or centuries we should start sending, on the grounds of perhaps everybody is waiting for the first word. That is a conceivable situation: but much more likely we are simply rather amateur about the whole matter . . . It is very much more difficult to build a transmitter than it is to build a receiver. Everybody can own a receiver in his house, but very few people own powerful transmitters. So, from that analogy we should listen sensibly for a long time until we are convinced that it is very hard to do better — and then we can try sending.

So far, I know of only three possibilities that anyone has suggested — perhaps four — the fourth being rather unlikely: radio in the thousand-megacycle region; optical light using coherent laser light in a blacked-out line of a common element; then high-energy gamma rays; and, finally, neutrinos. Of all of these, I still think much the most practical is the thousand-megacycle radio. You recognize that that's where nature makes the least interference, and this is one basis for our saying that it's rational. The noise is least in the radio channel.

I think that there is no reason at all for the position that says that there is great fear, great anxiety about answering some signal we might hear. I admit the conceivable position that these people take, namely that they might be hostile persons, hostile beings.

The task of doing physical damage is so much heavier over the distance of space, so much heavier than the task of making yourself known by signals, that if they are capable of doing physical damage, they already know about us. The fact that they are sending a signal would be the best sign to me that they really want to make intellectual contact and not something voracious or hostile. If those fellows can do it, they're so far ahead they don't ask for you to talk. It is as though we had to worry about ants signaling. If you saw an ant signal at you, would you be more likely to step on him or to step on the other ants who didn't show any signs of such intelligence?

If the time comes, and I suspect someday it will come, and we do learn about some external community, I suppose this would be one of the greatest sources of new thought, in the deepest framework of human thought, that we would have had—comparable, I should say, but greater than, the discovery of ancient times in the Nineteenth Century, when men began to realize that human history was much longer than they had thought. Or perhaps comparable to the intercourse between Medieval Europe and China which restored to them the vision of a new and great world that they had lost sight of since the Fall of Rome; something of that sort, and probably still more pervasive in many ways which it would be impossible for me to detail—affecting, I think, all kinds of thought, from the most austerely moral and philosophical down to the severely practical.

I'm kind of caustic about man's space flight—I think it's a mistake, so I don't think that manned space flight can do anything that unmanned space flight cannot do. It is mainly a symbolic thing, like exploring the South Pole. People always wanted to do that. I'm not against that, mind you, but I haven't myself thought through what the steps are, because I'm not much interested in that kind of physical exploration—adventure—and so on. Naturally, I would like to see it. I watch with excitement the flights on television; I think it's a great spectator sport; I approve of it in that sense, but it's not much more than that. We can do just as well with servo links as the astronauts can do, and a lot more safely. I think perhaps the first time when a justification for sending people out into space will appear is once we are doing complicated investigations so far away that the linkage time to bring the signal back to Earth is an appreciable problem for the motion of the vehicles, and that is perhaps as close as Jupiter, but not closer. The Moon—I don't think there is any great problem—anything we have to react to within a couple of seconds to the Moon is going to wreck the apparatus anyhow—I don't think a man will do much better—and the cost of development seems to me out of all proportion. The risk to the individuals. I would rather see a remote control from an office table. I'm sure that people can build it now. You go down, do your job in Houston, and spend eight hours being on the Moon—that is to say, you see and you feel just what you would see and feel if you were on the Moon. You have apparatus on the Moon that is responding to your hands and to your eyes and giving you the same signal—and you work at it eight hours and go home and someone else comes and takes eight hours; nobody is ever in trouble; if the circuit goes bad, if you cannot fix it with the repair apparatus, which you can control and have there, then you cannot fix it. That's the way it is—no one's dead, though. It's cheaper because you don't have to supply the air and the water and all that stuff that the poor astronaut needs. I really think that astronautics is a kind of daring symbolic thing, and I am very proud of it. I admire the people who do it, but, from a scientific point of view, it has no great claim on my interests.

I believe that there is a complex of arguments—none of them certain, all of them, I admit, open to some question—but their tendency is to lead in one direction, namely: that flight over large distances, compared to interstellar distances, is impossible or next to impossible—that is to say, so prohibitively difficult compared to what you can gain by other channels that it will never be undertaken, except again possibly for some symbolic reason, such as the way in which statesmen fly. The head of the one state goes to see the head of another, and once there he doesn't spend much time doing that; he travels, sees the country, shakes hands, goes back home again, representing some kind of rapprochement, some detente. I could well imagine that being mounted over a very long period for two communities that have been in contact for hundreds of years. They finally exchange one party just to make that gesture of community. But as a casual thing or even as a serious exploration venture, I don't think it is very sensible. I think that machines will do better than man. Man should stay home and work and enjoy himself—but not go out into space, I believe, except for the occasional, the odd fellow who will do this.

You see, I think that interstellar communication also is most likely to be only one way—in terms of the lifetime of any one individual. That doesn't bother me. Consider Greek society. It's hard to imagine a single body of knowledge more influential for the formation of the ideas in the Western world than Greek society. There are one or two others—say, the religious traditions of the Testaments—but apart from that it certainly is Athenian society. Now no European from Renaissance times up to our time ever had any hope of having a two-way communication with Socrates, or Pericles, or Phidias, or anybody else. That did not prevent us from gaining enormously from that body of manuscript and art that we have. That is the way I think we will regard the communications that come from space —I don't think that we are going to find them so close that we can get answers to our questions, except with great effort, preparing to wait for centuries. I do not believe in travel faster than time.

Norman Lamm
Rabbi, The Jewish Center, New York
Erna Michael Professor of Jewish Philosophy
Yeshiva University, New York

Judaism has throughout the ages generally confined itself to the problem of man as the sole concern of God in this world. As a result, there has come about the idea that man is the purpose of the entire universe. This has been a rather general tendency, and never formally incorporated in Jewish doctrine. However, one of the very greatest of all Jewish thinkers, perhaps the most eminent Jewish philosopher of all times, Moses Maimonides — who flourished about eight hundred years ago—strongly opposed "anthropocentrism," the view that man is the purpose of all creation. He maintained that man may be the superior creature on Earth, but he need not therefore be considered the purpose of the universe. In fact, he is not necessarily the most advanced being in the world. According to his approach, Judaism today can welcome with a remarkable openness the idea that intelligent races, even more intelligent than man, exist elsewhere.

As an individual, I think there probably is extraterrestrial life, and this belief is something that I would want to investigate theologically and religiously. But it is not something that monopolizes my thoughts or attention. My concerns, and I think the concerns of man on Earth, should be primarily the perennial problems of human existence. I think there is a great deal of truth in the man who asked the question, "Do you think there is intelligent life on Earth?"

I think that if we should ever come into contact with an extra-terrestrial highly intelligent race much older than our civilization that the primary lessons of the greatest significance we would learn from them would not be technological. If there is a civilization that has lasted that long, then by the very fact of its survival it has indicated that it has learned certain secrets of social justice and harmony and the ability for individuals to get along without killing themselves off on a large scale. I think that will be the main thing we can learn from them. I am less excited about the possibility of learning purely theological information from an older and more advanced civilization.

I am committed very deeply and very personally as a believing Jew to the idea of Revelation. This, however, does not preclude a Revelation to intelligent beings elsewhere, because the Jewish belief is that man, as the Bible taught, was created in the image of God. This means that man shares something with the Creator. This sharing may be interpreted as intelligence, as an ethical inclination, or as a creative ability. There is nothing in our tradition that insists that Earth-man uniquely shares these faculties with his Creator.

The fact that most religions have located God as residing, as it were, in Heaven I don't think has any real relevance to the possibility that at one time extraterrestrial creatures visited the Earth by parachuting out of Heaven. In the Bible itself the term *shamayim*, or Heaven, as the dwelling place of God is meant purely metaphorically. When the Bible speaks of God residing in Heaven, it is used as a metaphor — because when one looks upward, one is overwhelmed by the vastness of space. The philosopher Immanuel Kant said that when he beheld the starry Heavens he was overwhelmed, and religious feelings were indeed in him; similarly, when he beheld the moral order within man.

Now in the Bible itself, in the sixth chapter of Genesis, there is a rather mysterious reference to the "Sons of God" who marry the "Daughters of Men"; and then a reference to something called *Nephilim*, which means, as it has been translated, "The Giants." Whereas a good part of Jewish explanation and exegesis maintains that this was simply a race of strong men, there were certain Jewish sources — such as Philo in ancient Egypt and Josephus, the Jewish general and historian — who saw in this a reference to a mysterious kind of race, which, I suppose, in contemporary terms might be described as an extraterrestrial race.

Man must be ethical because God, too, is ethical. In the same manner we ought to imitate God in being creative. Judaism has always maintained that man is the co-creator of the universe; that God created the world unfinished, as it were, and gave it over to man, endowed with intelligence and instincts and technological inclinations, to finish the world and to improve it — to make it livable and habitable. Therefore, if man can, as it were, imitate God technologically with lifeless stuff, then there is no reason to assume that he has not been given the same grant of sovereignty to create life itself. This is, too, the imitation of God — provided, of course, that man remembers that it is his task to *imitate* but not to *impersonate* God.

One of our great difficulties is: who is to say that the physician, or the scientist, or anyone who has a Ph.D. and is in control of certain processes, has a right to determine the future of anyone's, or anything's, life and death. Man is monkeying around with his environment. He is monkeying around with himself as well. He is changing himself.

It is quite possible that whereas on Earth the period of prophecy has ended, and direct revelations of God to man have not occurred for many, many centuries, that nevertheless, on some other planet, God not only has revealed Himself more directly but is at present in a state of a more direct dialogue with its intelligent inhabitants. There is no reason, according to the Jewish perspective, why this should not be so.

We are other-worldly only to the extent that we believe that there is another kind of nonphysical existence in the presence of God; but we do not therefore deny this world. That is why the Jewish tradition has always had such an affirmative and positive attitude toward science and technology — when it is used creatively and constructively. It is in keeping with this tradition that I, as a Jew, am immensely concerned about the possibilities of life elsewhere. If such life is discovered, this will in all likelihood make man feel more humble, but it will not humiliate him. On the contrary, those of us who have a religious commitment will feel that our horizons — religiously — have been expanded by discovering that God is greater than even our most profound theologians and thinkers have ever imagined Him to be. "For the Lord is great above all His works" is a verse from our Bible that holds true now, and that I suspect we will learn is even more true as our knowledge of the cosmos advances and progresses.

"Replace alpha echo three-five unit prior to failure."

Jeremy Bernstein's Profile of Stanley Kubrick appeared in The New Yorker *when* 2001 *was still in production.*

PROFILE: STANLEY KUBRICK* .

Jeremy Bernstein

...IT WAS THE BUILDING of the Berlin Wall that sharpened Kubrick's interest in nuclear weapons and nuclear strategy, and he began to read everything he could get hold of about the bomb. Eventually, he decided that he had about covered the spectrum, and that he was not learning anything new. "When you start reading the analyses of nuclear strategy, they seem so thoughtful that you're lulled into a temporary sense of reassurance," Kubrick has explained. "But as you go deeper into it, and become more involved, you begin to realize that every one of these lines of thought leads to a paradox." It is this constant element of paradox in all the nuclear strategies and in the conventional attitudes toward them that Kubrick transformed into the principal theme of *Dr. Strangelove.* The picture was a new departure for Kubrick. His other films had involved putting novels on the screen, but *Dr. Strangelove,* though it did have its historical origins in "Red Alert," a serious nuclear suspense story by Peter George, soon turned into an attempt to use a purely intellectual notion as the basis of a film. In this case, the intellectual notion was the inevitable paradox posed by following any of the nuclear strategies to their extreme limits. "By now, the bomb has almost no reality and has become a complete abstraction, represented by a few newsreel shots of mushroom clouds," Kubrick has said. "People react primarily to direct experience and not to abstractions; it is very rare to find anyone who can become emotionally involved with an abstraction. The

longer the bomb is around without anything happening, the
better the job that people do in psychologically denying its
existence. It has become as abstract as the fact that we are all
going to die someday, which we usually do an excellent job of
denying. For this reason, most people have very little interest
in nuclear war. It has become even less interesting as a problem
than, say, city government, and the longer a nuclear event is
postponed, the greater becomes the illusion that we are constantly building up security, like interest at the bank. As time
goes on, the danger increases, I believe, because the thing becomes more and more remote in people's minds. No one can
predict the panic that suddenly arises when all the lights go out
—that indefinable something that can make a leader abandon
his carefully laid plans. A lot of effort has gone into trying to
imagine possible nuclear accidents and to protect against them.
But whether the human imagination is really capable of en-
compassing all the subtle permutations and psychological vari-
ants of these possibilities, I doubt. The nuclear strategists who
make up all those war scenarios are never as inventive as reality,
and political and military leaders are never as sophisticated as
they think they are."

Such limited optimism as Kubrick has about the long-range
prospects of the human race is based in large measure on his
hope that the rapid development of space exploration will
change our views of ourselves and our world. Most people who
have thought much about space travel have arrived at the somewhat ironic conclusion that there is a very close correlation
between the ability of a civilization to make significant space
voyages and its ability to learn to live with nuclear energy. Unless there are sources of energy that are totally beyond the ken
of modern physics, it is quite clear that the only source at hand
for really elaborate space travel is the nucleus. The chemical
methods of combustion used in our present rockets are absurdly
inefficient compared to nuclear power. A detailed study has been
made of the possibilities of using nuclear explosions to propel
large spaceships, and, from a technical point of view, there is
no reason that this cannot be done; indeed, if we are to transport really large loads to, say, the planets, it is essential that it
be done. Thus, any civilization that operates on the same laws
of nature as our own will inevitably reach the point where it
learns to explore space and to use nuclear energy about simultaneously. The question is whether there can exist any society
with enough maturity to peacefully use the latter to perform the
former. In fact, some of the more melancholy thinkers on this
subject have come to the conclusion that the earth has never
been visited by beings from outer space because no civilization

has been able to survive its own technology. That there *are* extraterrestrial civilizations in some state of development is firmly believed by many astronomers, biologists, philosophers, physicists, and other rational people — a conclusion based partly on the vastness of the cosmos, with its billions of stars. It is presumptuous to suppose that we are its only living occupants. From a chemical and biological point of view, the processes of forming life do not appear so extraordinary that they should not have occurred countless times throughout the universe. One may try to imagine what sort of transformation would take place in human attitudes if intelligent life should be discovered elsewhere in our universe. In fact, this is what Kubrick has been trying to do in his latest project, *2001: A Space Odyssey*, which, in the words of Arthur C. Clarke, the co-author of its screenplay, "will be about the first contact" — the first human contact with extraterrestrial life.

It was Arthur Clarke who introduced me to Kubrick. A forty-eight-year-old Englishman who lives in Ceylon most of the time, Clarke is, in my opinion, by all odds the best science-fiction writer now operating. (He is also an accomplished skin diver, and what he likes about Ceylon, apart from the climate and the isolation, is the opportunities it affords him for underwater exploration.) Clarke, who is highly trained as a scientist, manages to combine scientific insights with a unique sense of nostalgia for worlds that man will never see, because they are so far in the past or in the future, or are in such a distant part of the cosmos. In his hands, inanimate objects like the sun and the Moon take on an almost living quality. Personally, he is a large, good-natured man, and about the only egoist I know who makes conversation about himself somehow delightful. We met in New York a few years back, when he was working on a book about the future of scientific ideas and wanted to discuss some of the latest developments in physics, which I teach. Now I always look forward to his occasional visits, and when he called me up one evening two winters ago, I was very happy to hear from him. He lost no time in explaining what he was up to. "I'm working with Stanley Kubrick on the successor to *Dr. Strangelove*," he said. "Stanley is an amazing man, and I want you to meet him." It was an invitation not to be resisted, and Clarke arranged a visit to Kubrick soon afterward.

Kubrick was at that time living on the upper East Side, in a large apartment whose décor was a mixture of [his wife] Christiane's lovely paintings, the effects of three rambunctious young children, and Kubrick's inevitable collection of cameras, tape recorders, and hi-fi sets. (There was also a short-wave radio, which he was using to monitor broadcasts from Moscow, in order to learn the Russian attitude toward Vietnam. Christiane once said that "Stanley would be happy with eight tape recorders and one pair of pants.") Kubrick himself did not conform at all to my expectations of what a movie mogul would look like. He is of medium height and has the bohemian look of a riverboat gambler or a Rumanian poet. (He has now grown a considerable beard, which gives his broad features a somewhat Oriental quality.) He had the vaguely distracted look of a man who is simultaneously thinking about a hard problem and trying to make everyday conversation. During our meeting, the phone rang incessantly, a messenger arrived at the door with a telegram or an envelope every few minutes, and children of various ages and sexes ran in and out of the living room. After a few attempts at getting the situation under control, Kubrick abandoned the place to the children, taking me into a small breakfast room near the kitchen. I was immediately impressed by Kubrick's immense intellectual curiosity. When he is working on a subject, he becomes completely immersed in it and appears to absorb information from all sides, like a sponge. In addition to writing a novel with Clarke, which was to be the basis of the script for *2001*, he was reading every popular and semi-popular book on science that he could get hold of. . . .

I next saw Kubrick at the end of the summer in London, where I had gone to a physicists' meeting and where he was in the process of organizing the actual filming of *2001*. I dropped in at his office in the M-G-M studio in Boreham Wood, outside London, one afternoon, and again was confronted by an incredible disarray — papers, swatches of materials to be used for costumes, photographs of actors who might be used to play astronauts, models of spaceships, drawings by his daughters, and the usual battery of cameras, radios, and tape recorders. Kubrick likes to keep track of things in small notebooks, and he had just ordered a sample sheet of every type of notebook paper made by a prominent paper firm — about a hundred varieties — which were spread out on a large table. We talked for a while amid the usual interruptions of messengers and telephone calls. . . .

Clarke and Kubrick spent two years transforming ["The Sentinel"] into a novel and then into a script for *2001*, which is concerned with the discovery of the sentinel and a search for traces of the civilization that put it there — a quest that takes the searchers out into the far reaches of the solar system. Extraterrestrial life may seem an odd subject for a motion picture, but at this stage in his career Kubrick is convinced that any idea he is really interested in, however unlikely it may sound, can be transferred to film. "One of the English science-fiction writers once said, 'Sometimes I think we're alone, and sometimes I think we're not. In either case, the idea is quite staggering,'" Kubrick once told me. "I must say I agree with him."

By the time the film appears, early next year, Kubrick estimates that he and Clarke will have put in an average of four hours a day, six days a week, on the writing of the script. (This works out to about twenty-four hundred hours of writing for two hours and forty minutes of film.) Even during the actual shooting of the film, Kubrick spends every free moment reworking the scenario. He has an extra office set up in a blue trailer that was once Deborah Kerr's dressing room, and when shooting is going on, he has it wheeled onto the set, to give him a certain amount of privacy for writing. He frequently gets ideas for dialogue from his actors, and when he likes an idea he puts it in. (Peter Sellers, he says, contributed some wonderful bits of humor for *Dr. Strangelove*.)

In addition to writing and directing, Kubrick supervises every aspect of his films, from selecting costumes to choosing the incidental music. In making *2001*, he is, in a sense, trying to second-guess the future. Scientists planning long-range space projects can ignore such questions as what sort of hats rocket-ship hostesses will wear when space travel becomes common (in *2001* the hats have padding in them to cushion any collisions with the ceiling that weightlessness might cause), and what sort of voices computers will have if, as many experts feel is certain, they learn to talk and to respond to voice commands (there is a talking computer in *2001* that arranges for the astronauts' meals, gives them medical treatments, and even plays chess with them during a long space mission to Jupiter. "Maybe it ought to sound like Jackie Mason," Kubrick once said), and what kind of time will be kept aboard a spaceship (Kubrick chose Eastern Standard, for the convenience of communicating with Washington). In the sort of planning that NASA does, such matters can be dealt with as they come up, but in a movie everything is immediately visible and explicit, and questions like this must be answered in detail. To help him find the answers, Kubrick has assembled around him a group of thirty-five artists and designers, more than twenty special-effects people, and a staff of scientific advisers. By the time the picture is done, Kubrick figures that he will have consulted with people from a generous sampling of the leading aeronautical companies in the United States and Europe, not to mention innumerable scientific and industrial firms. One consultant, for instance, was Professor Marvin Minsky, of M.I.T., who is a leading authority on artificial intelligence and the construction of automata. (He is now building a robot at M.I.T. that can catch a ball.) Kubrick wanted to learn from him whether any of the things that he was planning to have his computers do were likely to be realized by the year 2001; he was pleased to find out that they were.

Kubrick told me he had seen practically every science-fiction film ever made, and any number of more conventional films that had interesting special effects. One Saturday afternoon, after lunch and two rapid chess games, he and Christiane and I set out to see a Russian science-fiction movie called *Astronauts on Venus*, which he had discovered playing somewhere in North London. Saturday afternoon at a neighborhood movie house in London is like Saturday afternoon at the movies anywhere; the theater was full of children talking, running up and down the aisles, chewing gum, and eating popcorn. The movie was in Russian, with English subtitles, and since most of the children couldn't read very well, let alone speak Russian, the dialogue was all but drowned out by the general babble. This was probably all to the good, since the film turned out to be a terrible hodgepodge of pseudo science and Soviet propaganda. It featured a talking robot named John and a talking girl named Masha who had been left in a small spaceship orbiting Venus while a party of explorers—who thought, probably correctly, that she would have been a nuisance below—went off to explore. Although Kubrick reported that the effects used were crude, he insisted that we stick it out to the end, just in case.

Before I left London, I was able to spend a whole day with Kubrick, starting at about eight-fifteen, when an M-G-M driver picked us up in one of the studio cars. (Kubrick suffers automobiles tolerably well, but he will under almost no circumstances travel by plane, even though he holds a pilot's license and has put in about a hundred and fifty hours in the air, principally around Teterboro Airport; after practicing landings and takeoffs, flying solo cross-country to Albany, and taking his friends up for rides, he lost interest in flying.) Boreham Wood is a little like the area outside Boston that is served by Route 128, for it specializes in electronics companies and precision industry, and the M-G-M studio is hardly distinguishable from the rather antiseptic-looking factories nearby. It consists of ten enormous sound stages concealed in industrial-looking buildings and surrounded by a cluster of carpenter shops, paint shops, office units, and so on. Behind the buildings is a huge lot covered with bits and pieces of other productions—the façade of a French provincial village, the hulk of a Second World War bomber, and other debris. Kubrick's offices are near the front of the complex in a long bungalow structure that houses, in addition to his production staff, a group of youthful model-makers working on large, very detailed models of spacecraft to be used in special-effects photography; Kubrick calls their realm "Santa's Workshop." When we walked into his private office, it seemed to me that the general disorder had grown even more chaotic since my last visit. Tacked to a bulletin board were some costume drawings showing men dressed in odd-looking, almost Edwardian business suits. Kubrick said that the drawings were supposed to be of the business suit of the future and had been submitted by one of the innumerable designers who had been asked to furnish ideas on what men's clothes would look like in thirty-five years. "The problem is to find something that looks different and that might reflect new developments in fabrics but that isn't so far out as to be distracting," Kubrick said. "Certainly buttons will be gone. Even now, there are fabrics that stick shut by themselves."

Just then, Victor Lyndon, Kubrick's associate producer (he was also the associate producer of *Dr. Strangelove* and, most recently, of *Darling*), came in. A trim, athletic-looking man of forty-six, he leans toward the latest "mod" styling in clothes, and he was wearing an elegant green buttonless, self-shutting shirt. He was followed by a young man wearing hair down to his neck, a notably non-shutting shirt, and boots, who was introduced as a brand-new costume designer. (He was set up at a drawing table in Santa's Workshop, but that afternoon he announced that the atmosphere was too distracting for serious work, and left; the well-known British designer Hardy Amies was finally chosen to design the costumes.) Lyndon fished from a manila envelope a number of shoulder patches designed to be worn as identification by the astronauts. (The two principal astronauts in the film were to be played by Keir Dullea, who has starred in *David and Lisa* and *Bunny Lake Is Missing*, and Gary Lockwood, a former college-football star and now a television and movie actor.) Kubrick said that the lettering didn't look right, and suggested that the art department make up new patches using actual NASA lettering. He then consulted one of the small notebooks in which he lists all the current production problems, along with the status of their solutions, and announced that he was going to the art department to see how the drawings of the moons of Jupiter were coming along.

The art department, which occupies a nearby building, is presided over by Tony Masters, a tall, Lincolnesque man who was busy working on the Jupiter drawings when we appeared. Kubrick told me that the department, which designs and dresses all sets, was constructing a scale model of the Moon, including the back side, which had been photographed and mapped by rocket. Looking over the Jupiter drawings, Kubrick said that the light in them looked a little odd to him, and suggested that

Masters have Arthur Clarke check on it that afternoon when he
came out from London.

Our next stop was to pick up some papers in the separate
office where Kubrick does his writing—a made-over dressing
room in a quiet part of the lot. On our way to it, we passed an
outbuilding containing a number of big generators; a sign reading "DANGER!—11,500 VOLTS!" was nailed to its door.
"Why eleven thousand five *hundred*?" Kubrick said. "Why not
twelve thousand? If you put a sign like that in a movie, people
would think it was a fake." When we reached the trailer, I could
see that it was used as much for listening as for writing, for in
addition to the usual battery of tape recorders (Kubrick writes
rough first drafts of his dialogue by dictating into a recorder,
since he finds that this gives it a more natural flow) there was a
phonograph and an enormous collection of records, practically
all of them of contemporary music. Kubrick told me that he
thought he had listened to almost every modern composition
available on records in an effort to decide what style of music
would fit the film. Here, again, the problem was to find something that sounded unusual and distinctive but not so unusual as
to be distracting. In the office collection were records by the
practitioners of *musique concrète* and electronic music in general, and records of works by the contemporary German composer Carl Orff. In most cases, Kubrick said, film music tends
to lack originality, and a film about the future might be the ideal
place for a really striking score by a major composer.

We returned to the main office, and lunch was brought in
from the commissary. During lunch, Kubrick signed a stack of
letters, sent off several cables, and took a long-distance call
from California. "At this stage of the game, I feel like the coun-
terman at Katz's delicatessen on Houston Street at lunch hour,"
he said. "You've hardly finished saying 'Half a pound of corned
beef' when he says 'What else?,' and before you can say 'A
sliced rye' he's saying 'What else?' again."

I asked whether he ever got things mixed up, and he said
rarely, adding that he thought chess playing had sharpened his
naturally retentive memory and gift for organization. "With
such a big staff, the problem is for people to figure out what they
should come to see you about and what they should *not* come
to see you about," he went on. "You invariably find your time
taken up with questions that aren't important and could have
easily been disposed of without your opinion. To offset this,
decisions are sometimes taken without your approval that can
wind up in frustrating dead ends."

As we were finishing lunch, Victor Lyndon came in with an
almanac that listed the average temperature and rainfall all

over the globe at every season of the year. "We're looking for a cool desert where we can shoot some sequences during the late spring," Kubrick said. "We've got our eye on a location in Spain, but it might be pretty hot to work in comfortably, and we might have trouble controlling the lighting. If we don't go to Spain, we'll have to build an entirely new set right here. More work for Tony Masters and his artists." (Later, I learned that Kubrick did decide to shoot on location.)

After lunch, Kubrick and Lyndon returned to a long-standing study of the spacesuit question. In the film, the astronauts will wear spacesuits when they are working outside their ships, and Kubrick was very anxious that they should look like the space-suits of thirty-five years from now. After numerous consultations with [Frederick] Ordway and other NASA experts, he and Lyndon had finally settled on a design, and now they were studying a vast array of samples of cloth to find one that would look right and photograph well. While this was going on, people were constantly dropping into the office with drawings, models, letters, cables, and various props, such as a model of a lens for one of the telescopes in a spaceship. (Kubrick rejected it because it looked too crude.) At the end of the day, when my head was beginning to spin, someone came by with a wristwatch that the astronauts were going to use on their Jupiter voyage (which Kubrick rejected) and a plastic drinking glass for the Moon hotel (which Kubrick thought looked fine). About seven o'clock, Kubrick called for his car, and by eight-thirty he had returned home, put the children to bed, discussed the day's events with his wife, watched a news broadcast on television, telephoned Clarke for a brief discussion of whether nuclear-powered spacecraft would pollute the atmosphere with their exhausts (Clarke said that they certainly would today but that by the time they actually come into use somebody will have figured out what to do about poisonous exhausts), and taken out his chess set. "How about a little game?"...

On December 29, 1965, shooting of the film began, and in early March the company reached the most intricate part of the camerawork, which was to be done in the interior of a giant centrifuge. One of the problems in space travel will be weight-lessness. While weightlessness has, because of its novelty, a certain glamour and amusement, it would be an extreme nuisance on a long trip, and probably a health hazard as well. Our physical systems have evolved to work against the pull of gravity, and it is highly probable that all sorts of unfortunate things, such as softening of the bones, would result from exposure to weightlessness for months at a time. In addition, of course, nothing stays in place without gravity, and no normal activity is possible unless great care is exercised; the slightest jar can send you hurtling across the cabin. Therefore, many spacecraft designers figure that some sort of artificial gravity will have to be supplied for space travelers. In principle, this is very easy to do. An object on the rim of a wheel rotating at a uniform speed is subjected to a constant force pushing it away from the center, and by adjusting the size of the wheel and the speed of its rotation this centrifugal force can be made to resemble the force of gravity. Having accepted this notion, Kubrick went one step further and commissioned the Vickers Engineering Group to make an actual centrifuge, large enough for the astronauts to live in full time. It took six months to build and cost about three hundred thousand dollars. The finished product looks from the outside like a Ferris wheel thirty-eight feet in diameter and can be rotated at a maximum speed of about three miles an hour. This is not enough to parallel the force of gravity — the equipment inside the centrifuge has to be bolted to the floor — but it has enabled Kubrick to achieve some remarkable photographic effects. The interior, eight feet wide, is fitted out with an enormous computer console, an electronically operated medical dispensary, a shower, a device for taking an artificial sunbath, a recreation area, with a ping-pong table and an electronic piano, and five beds with movable plastic domes — hibernacula, where astronauts who are not on duty can, literally, hibernate for months at a time. (The trip to Jupiter will take two hundred and fifty-seven days.)

I had seen the centrifuge in the early stages of its construction and very much wanted to observe it in action, so I was delighted when chance sent me back to England in the early spring. When I walked through the door of the *2001* set one morning in March, I must say that the scene that presented itself to me was overwhelming. In the middle of the hangarlike stage stood the centrifuge, with cables and lights hanging from every available inch of its steel-girdered superstructure. On the floor to one side of its frame was an immense electronic console (not a prop), and, in various places, six microphones and three television receivers. I learned later that Kubrick had arranged a closed-circuit-television system so that he could watch what was going on inside the centrifuge during scenes being filmed when he could not be inside himself. Next to the microphone was an empty canvas chair with "Stanley Kubrick" painted on its back in fading black letters. Kubrick himself was nowhere to be seen, but everywhere I looked there were people, some hammering and sawing, some carrying scripts, some carrying lights. In one corner I saw a woman applying makeup to what appeared to be an astronaut wearing blue coveralls and leather boots. Over a loudspeaker, a pleasantly authoritative English voice — belonging, I learned shortly, to Derek Cracknell, Kubrick's first assistant director—was saying, "Will someone bring the Governor's Polaroid on the double?" A man came up to me and asked how I would like my tea and whom I was looking for, and almost before I could reply "One lump with lemon" and "Stanley Kubrick," led me, in a semi-daze, to an opening at the bottom of the centrifuge. Peering up into the dazzlingly illuminated interior, I spotted Kubrick lying flat on his back on the floor of the machine and staring up through the viewfinder of an enormous camera, in complete concentration. Keir Dullea, dressed in shorts and a white T shirt, and covered by a blue blanket, was lying in an open hibernaculum on the rising curve of the floor. He was apparently comfortably asleep, and Kubrick was telling him to wake up as simply as possible. "Just open your eyes," he said. "Let's not have any stirring, yawning, and rubbing."

One of the lights burned out, and while it was being fixed, Kubrick unwound himself from the camera, spotted me staring openmouthed at the top of the centrifuge, where the furniture of the crew's dining quarters was fastened to the ceiling, and said, "Don't worry—that stuff is bolted down." Then he motioned to me to come up and join him.

No sooner had I climbed into the centrifuge than Cracknell, who turned out to be a cheerful and all but imperturbable youthful-looking man in tennis shoes (all the crew working in the centrifuge were wearing tennis shoes, not only to keep from slipping but to help them climb the steeply curving sides; indeed, some of them were working while clinging to the bolted-down furniture halfway up the wall), said, "Here's your Polaroid, Guv," and handed Kubrick the camera. I asked Kubrick what he needed the Polaroid for, and he explained that he used it for checking subtle lighting effects for color film. He and the director of photography, Geoffrey Unsworth, had worked out a correlation between how the lighting appeared on the instantly developed Polaroid film and the settings on the movie camera. I asked Kubrick if it was customary for movie directors to participate so actively in the photographing of a movie, and he said succinctly that he had never watched any other movie director work.

The light was fixed, and Kubrick went back to work behind the camera. Keir Dullea was reinstalled in his hibernaculum and the cover rolled shut. "You better take your hands from under the blanket," Kubrick said. Kelvin Pike, the camera operator, took Kubrick's place behind the camera, and Cracknell called for quiet. The camera began to turn, and Kubrick said, "Open the hatch." The top of the hibernaculum slid back with a whirring sound, and Keir Dullea woke up, without any stirring, yawning, or rubbing. Kubrick, playing the part of the solicitous computer, started feeding him lines.

"Good morning," said Kubrick. "What do you want for breakfast?"

"Some bacon and eggs would be fine," Dullea answered simply.

Later, Kubrick told me that he had engaged an English actor to read the computer's lines in the serious dramatic scenes, in order to give Dullea and Lockwood something more professional to play against, and that in the finished film he would dub in an American-accented voice. He and Dullea went through the sequence four or five times, and finally Kubrick was satisfied with what he had. Dullea bounced out of his hibernaculum, and I asked him whether he was having a good time. He said he was getting a great kick out of all the tricks and gadgets, and added, "This is a happy set, and that's something."

When Kubrick emerged from the centrifuge, he was immediately surrounded by people. "Stanley, there's a black pig outside for you to look at," Victor Lyndon was saying. He led the way outside, and, sure enough, in a large truck belonging to an animal trainer was an enormous jet-black pig. Kubrick poked it, and it gave a suspicious grunt.

"The pig looks good," Kubrick said to the trainer.

"I can knock it out with a tranquilizer for the scenes when it's supposed to be dead," the trainer said.

"Can you get any tapirs or anteaters?" Kubrick asked.

The trainer said that this would not be an insuperable problem, and Kubrick explained to me, "We're going to use them in some scenes about prehistoric man."

At this point, a man carrying a stuffed lion's head approached and asked Kubrick whether it would be all right to use.

"The tongue looks phony, and the eyes are only marginal," Kubrick said, heading for the set. "Can somebody fix the tongue?"

Back on the set, he climbed into his blue trailer. "Maybe the company can get back some of its investment selling guided tours of the centrifuge," he said. "They might even feature a ride on it." He added that the work in the machine was incredibly slow, because it took hours to rearrange all the lights and cameras for each new sequence. Originally, he said, he had planned on a hundred and thirty days of shooting for the main scenes, but the centrifuge sequences had slowed them down by perhaps a week. "I take advantage of every delay and breakdown to go off by myself and think," he said. "Something like playing chess when your opponent takes a long time over his next move."

At one o'clock, just before lunch, many of the crew went with Kubrick to a small projection room near the set to see the results of the previous day's shooting. The most prominent scene was a brief one that showed Gary Lockwood exercising in the centri- fuge, jogging around its interior and shadow-boxing to the ac- companiment of a Chopin waltz—picked by Kubrick because he felt that an intelligent man in 2001 might choose Chopin for doing exercise to music. As the film appeared on the screen, Lockwood was shown jogging around the complete interior cir- cumference of the centrifuge, which appeared to me to defy logic as well as physics, since when he was at the top he would have needed suction cups on his feet to stay glued to the floor. I asked Kubrick how he had achieved this effect, and he said he was definitely, absolutely not going to tell me. As the scene went on, Kubrick's voice could be heard on the sound track, rising over the Chopin: "Gain a little on the camera, Gary! . . . Now a flurry of lefts and rights! . . . A little more vicious!" After the film had run its course Kubrick appeared quite pleased with the results, remarking, "It's nice to get two minutes of usable film after two days of shooting."

Later that afternoon, I had a chance to see a publicity short made up of some of the most striking material so far filmed for *2001*. There were shots of the space station, with people look- ing out of the windows at the Earth wheeling in the distance; there was an incredible sequence, done in red, showing a hostess on a Moon rocket appearing to walk on the ceiling of the spaceship; there was a solemn procession of astronauts trudging along on the surface of the Moon. The colors and the effects were extremely impressive. . . .

"This mission is too important for me to allow you to jeopardize it."

Stanley Kubrick stated a goal of the production: "Solving the previously unsolved problem of making special effects look completely realistic. I had to invent new techniques all the time. We ran through 205 special-effects shots. The last ones were arriving in Hollywood as the negative printing was being done."

A four-man operations room was set up to coordinate the activities of the 106-man production unit.

Douglas Trumbull and Con Pederson, Special Photographic Effects Supervisors, discussed the special effects:

COMPLETION often involved the addition of many different elements which may have included miniature projection, stars, Earth or Jupiter, the sun, and quite often the addition of a second model matched in scale and motion to the first, such as the Orion spacecraft approaching the space station or the pod moving relative to the Discovery spacecraft. All of the movements and exposures of the additional elements would be keyed to match the first original photography of the main model shooting.

Throughout the shooting, meticulous care was taken to keep track of minute details concerning camera movement, speed, shutter speed, and exposure. Thousands of rolls of Polaroid film were used to check basic exposures and lighting setups; they were filed for reference. In addition, every single separate element was wedge-tested for exposure, running the gamut from several stops overexposed to no exposure at all, in increments of one-quarter of a stop. At the end of each take, each element would be rewedged. Every take of every element that went before the cameras was meticulously wedged and checked against previous and subsequent wedges to ascertain that lighting conditions, color, temperatures, etc., remained absolutely constant throughout.

One of the most interesting aspects of this complex combination of models, matted stars, Earth, Moon, sun, etc., was that few if any of these shots were preplanned or designed in ad-

vance. Each shot merely grew from its first element. Subsequent
elements were added and tested for speed, exposure, movement,
etc., and were accepted or rejected according to their merits for
that shot, with little or no regard to that shot's relationship to
any previous or subsequent shots. In most cases, shots would
be matted, combined, and completed in their entirety, even
though only a few feet or seconds would be used in the final cut
of the film. Although this technique may have seemed wasteful,
time-consuming, and expensive, it was the only way that latitude
could be available in the final cutting of the film. The special
effects could be cut just like live action, in that each particular
action or story-point was covered by a multitude of angles and
shots, each of which was carried to completion.

By the time we got to Jupiter, we started to use football terminology to keep things straight: Kick-off . . . Fourth Down . . .
Strong Side II . . . Punt Return . . . Nearly There . . . Deep Pass.
Then we ran out of that and started getting more oblique. These
were always based on some imagined compositional correlation: Pawnbroker . . . 50 Free Games . . . See How They Run
. . . Vertigo . . . On the Brink. The last two Jupiter shots were
later combined into one long shot called Vertibrink, which
later was extended to add Discovery and was then called
Vertilong.

    Repeated attempts to create a truly believable-looking extra-
terrestrial constantly ran into the Coefficient of Difficulty. We
had to ask ourselves for a definition of what was possible to
depict—it may well be there are many things that simply cannot
be done to a certain standard. The asymptotic curve annihilates
you in the quest for the perfect ion—that is, you can approach
it, get infinitely closer all the time, but never reach it. All the
while the Coefficient of Difficulty is expanding. If only we'd had
a few more years. . . .

*Captions on the following pages were prepared with the as-
sistance of Messrs. Kubrick, Clarke, Trumbull, and Pederson.
(Matte, referred to often, is an optical process used to superimpose scenes over scenes.)*

THE DAWN OF MAN

THE DAWN OF MAN

THE DAWN OF MAN

THE DAWN OF MAN

Arthur C. Clarke: "The film starts right back in the past, in the — let me see — Pleistocene Era. I always have to stop and think which of those eras is which."

And Odysseus returned to Ithaca "just at the rising of that brightest star which heralds the light of the Daughter of Dawn."

Thousands of color still photographs were taken in primordial-looking southwest Africa for background use in M-G-M's Boreham Wood studio near London. (In the middle of Absolutely Nowhere, Africa, the *2001* car ran into an oncoming truck and two of the photographers were injured.)

News report, May 1, 1969: "The age of Man can be placed at four million years by new finds in Africa." Clarke: "In 1965, we set four million years as the Dawn of Man because estimates were progressing steadily backwards and I wanted to be on the safe side. It looks as if they've already caught up with us."

Picture below: Man-ape uses pipe to hold mouth open, so, while breathing, he may relax elastic jaw that tended to close.

Dead horse was painted to look like a zebra. Scene of live leopard with "zebra" was filmed with tranquilizer guns at the ready. Due to horse's stench, leopard and camera crew were unenthusiastic about doing the scene.

"One morning, some 4,000,000 years ago, a mysterious black, rectangular block appears around which the curious man-apes gather."

The artifact originally was to be a tetrahedron. Special Effects Supervisor Con Pederson: "The tetrahedron didn't look monumental or simple or fundamental. It tended to express diminution more than impressive scale. And there would be people who would think of pyramids."

The original plan was to superimpose a hypnotic teaching effect onto the artifact, a pictorial scene of meat-eating apes instructing the man-apes.

Kubrick: "There was never any interest in relating the slab to Stonehenge."

Clarke: "I'm sure Stanley and I talked about Stonehenge, but I can't remember the specific details. I don't know if Stan has been to Stonehenge. I have many times." *Kubrick:* "Too far to go[d?]."

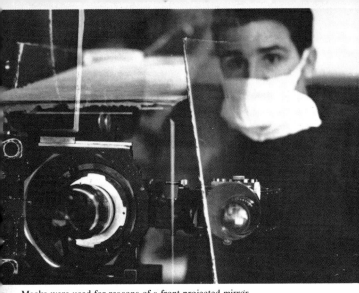

Masks were used for reasons of a front-projected mirror.

During production, five monoliths were used, some three feet long, one twelve feet long.

"After having touched the monolith, a barely conscious reaction occurs in the leader's mind. As he looks out now upon the hostile world, there is already something in his gaze beyond the capacity of any ape. In those dark, deep-set eyes is a dawning awareness — the first intimations of an intelligence which would not fulfill itself for another four million years."

Kubrick: "The idea of a magical alignment of the sun, the Earth, and the Moon, or of Jupiter and its moons, was used throughout the film to represent something magical and important about to happen. I suppose the idea had something to do with the strange sensation one has when the alignment of the sun takes place at Stonehenge."

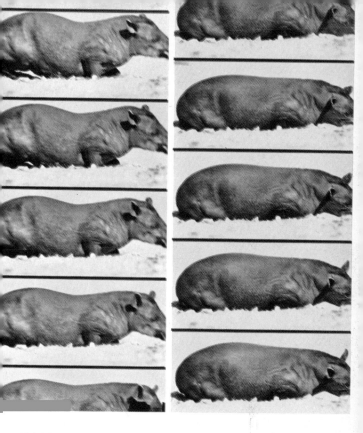

Kubrick goes on location. Animal bone becomes extension of man just outside the studio door. Sky is real.

Apes were actors, mimes, and dancers, except for two baby chimpanzees, which had to be prodded by their trainer to cower with the fake apes. The actors had to have exceptionally thin arms and legs and narrow hips so that when they wore the costumes of hair they wouldn't look bulky and like men stuffed into gorilla suits. It was an extremely complex task to produce apelike masks with delicate articulation for bearing fangs, snarling, eating, drinking. (A company that manufactured artificial limbs was contracted to produce a long-fingered, narrow apelike hand, which could be operated remotely by the actor's hand within the sleeve of the longer arm. This failed to look convincing and was abandoned.) Facial makeup was created by making a plastic substructure skull with hinged jaw. A fine rubber mold was made with the equivalent of skin on the face; hair was added as one would put hair on a wig. Movement in the lips was achieved by having false tongue and false teeth and an arrangement of toggles that the actors could move with their tongues and that allowed the lips to curl left, right, or both directions. The eyes were the actors'; the mask was made right up to the eyelids. Fifteen hundred individually controlled lamps were on the ceiling of sound stage.

A computer program was run to determine how long it would take to get the required number of ape costumes made for actors. Based on all the consecutive versus parallel steps, longest-line items, optimum flow, etc., the answer was nine years. A few minor adjustments were made, and the costumes were made in three months. Arthur C. Clarke: "*2001* did not win the Academy Award for makeup because judges may not have realized apes were actors."

Dan Richter as man-ape leader, Moon-Watcher.

Special projector had to be built for large (8-inch × 10-inch) transparencies. Light reflected on actors was weak enough not to interfere with brilliantly reflecting background screen. Large-scale front projection was *2001* innovation. Usually, transparency projections are thrown from behind screen.

Front-projection screen was 40 feet by 90 feet and covered with highly reflective materials.

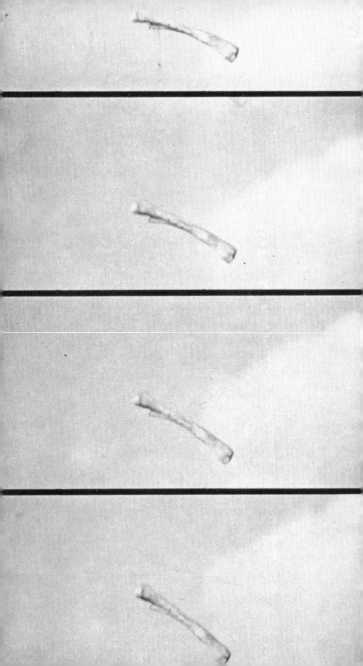

Sunrise on Earth.

Orbiting satellites carrying nuclear weapons make their rounds at end of Twentieth Century. Model was about two feet long.

(Many models designed by Harry Lange were not shown. They included probes with solar panels and various antennae for different missions. They were generally fuselages—cylindrical or faceted—and about three feet long.)

Kubrick: "Don't underestimate the charm of 'The Blue Danube,' played by Herbert von Karajan. Most people under 35 can think of it in an objective way, as a beautiful composition. Older people somehow associate it with a Palm Court orchestra or have another unfortunate association, and generally, therefore, criticize its use in the film. It's hard to find anything much better than 'The Blue Danube' for depicting grace and beauty in turning. It also gets about as far away as you can get from the cliché of space music."

Back-lit Earth was photographed on an animation stand.
Satellite was a still photograph shot on a large horizontal camera.

Orion model was about three feet in length.

Special Effects Supervisor Douglas Trumbull: "Basic construction of models was of wood, fiberglass, plexiglass, steel, brass, aluminum. Fine detailing was made up of special heat-forming, plastic-cladding, flexible metal foils of different textures and thicknesses, and of wire, tubing, and thousands of tiny parts carefully selected from hundreds of plastic model kits, ranging from boxcars and battleships to aircraft and Gemini spacecraft. Cameras could get very close to models with no loss of detail or believability."

Only one screen on Orion, carrying Dr. Heywood Floyd (William Sylvester) to the Moon, was rigged for rear-projection of television film. Dr. Floyd is chairman of the U.S. National Council of Astronauts.

Sleeping Dr. Floyd missed a developing love scene on his tele. Film crew in Detroit made footage of futuristic car and Kubrick in England filmed an actor and actress in dummy seats. Car and couple sequences were spliced and projected onto television screen.

Pen floated on nylon thread, then was glued onto eight-foot-diameter rotating glass for shot of stewardess picking it "out of the air." Film-within-film continues on TV set.

Beginning of shot: Space station in orbit, Earth drifting. Shot from six-inch color transparency on animation stand, moving .0025 of an inch per frame. Stars shot separately to match, then matted to clear all elements in shot. Space station model is six feet long. Orion was photographed from still picture, tail-view, camera tracking away. Its movement was timed and planned to gain slightly on previously filmed space-station movement, a matter of trying a few different speeds until one looked right. It was checked in a theater by using two projectors, one projecting original shot of space station, the other the takes of the Orion. With black backgrounds, this was possible to do without flooding out the screen.

"I think the big mistake in schools is trying to teach children anything, and by using fear as the basic motivation. Fear of getting failing grades, fear of not staying with your class, etc. Interest can produce learning on a scale compared to fear as a nuclear explosion to a firecracker." — **Stanley Kubrick.**

"The most remarkable thing about *2001* is that it is doing so well without any concession to popular taste. Kubrick never once said, 'Let's not let the popcorn set get away.' It's so uncompromising that people realize it deals with much bigger issues than science alone."
— **Arthur C. Clarke.**

"Perhaps it sounds ridiculous, but the best thing that young filmmakers should do is to get hold of a camera and some film and make a movie of any kind at all." — **Stanley Kubrick.**

"As soon as you mention science fiction, most people think of bug-eyed monsters and weird apparitions. There has been little attempt at integrity on the part of filmmakers in dealing with the possibility of extraterrestrial life. This is what makes *2001* so unique, I think. It poses metaphysical, philosophical and even religious questions. I don't pretend that we have the answers. But the questions are certainly worth thinking about." — **Arthur C. Clarke.**

"How could we possibly appreciate the Mona Lisa if Leonardo had written at the bottom of the canvas: 'The lady is smiling because she is hiding a secret from her lover.' This would shackle the viewer to reality, and I don't want this to happen to *2001*." — **Stanley Kubrick.**

"The eye is the window of the soul." — **Leonardo da Vinci.**

Three readout screens are between the pilots of the Orion, preparing to dock with the revolving space station. The center screen is a computer-driven display that simulates in real time the approach to the space-station docking area, much as today's astronauts visually dock their LM with Apollo Command Module by means of radial grid and vertical-horizontal coordinates. Readout was actual filmed simulation of dock-

ing approach; it included guidance corrections. It was made by animation (not by computer graphics): Multiple exposures of graphic representations. Other two readouts are supposed to show a routine cascade of status displays for other systems in Orion. They would be displayed, some believe, largely to reassure the pilot that conditions are "normal"—that the computer really is on pilot's side.

Orion is successfully docked with space station. *2001's* first spoken words, nearly one-half hour after it begins: "Here you are, sir."

Curved space station under construction: three hundred feet long, nearly forty feet high at one end.

Because of space station's slow rotation, centrifugal force would press passengers down against floor with force that gave them sensation of normal weight. U.S. corporations manage Cape Kennedy, and it is expected that they will also be in space.

Picturephone was designed with help of John R. Pierce, of Bell Laboratories, who designed Telstar communications satellite. Original artwork of Earth by John Rose; sections were chosen with variety of glass cloud overlays. Transparencies needed careful exposure to make Earth look like bright object. Earth on a rotating still-transparency projector is seen on large screen in space-station window area. Stanley Kubrick's daughter Vivian played uncredited role of Dr. Floyd's daughter, "Squirt." Footage of Vivian was first made and Sylvester played to her answers. In the scene, the next day was to be her birthday, and she told her father that she wanted a bushbaby as a gift. A scene was photographed, in set resembling Macy's department store, showing purchase of bushbaby, but it was not in final film.

A bushbaby.

Space-station scenes being readied.

Russian space scientists, returning to Earth from Moon, are unable to learn from Dr. Floyd what is causing mysterious action in U.S. sector.

Aries carrying Dr. Floyd from space station to Clavius crater in Moon is a cutout that was animated.

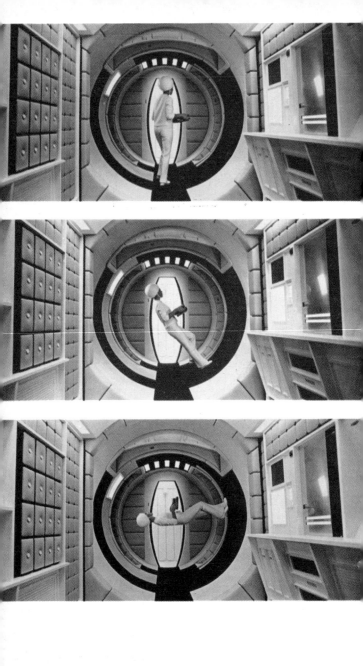

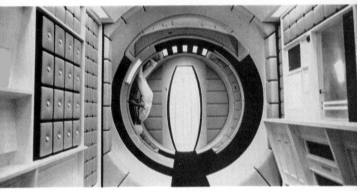

Official M-G-M caption: "Stewardess carrying weightless food tray enters cockpit area of Aries. She walks in Velcro-lined shoes that enable her to cling to Velcro-lined floor in any position, even when she appears to be upside down.

How it was done:
Room in foreground turned — the actress walked a treadmill in separate room in background. Camera was locked to front of set, which rotated 180 degrees. Entire set rotated. Stewardess stayed at bottom, giving appearance of walking on wall. *At right,* exterior view of rotating galley.

Kubrick laid music track over stewardesses' prattle. What they were saying was what audience already knew, that Dr. Floyd was asleep. One of the stewardesses goes to pilot's cabin and reports that Dr. Floyd is asleep. Kubrick decided to lay in more music. Note more films-within-film.

"A number of people thought Floyd went to the planet Clavius. Why they think there's a planet Clavius I'll never know. But they hear him asked, 'Where are you going?', and he says, 'I'm going to Clavius.' With many people—*boom*—that one word registers in their heads and they don't look at fifteen shots of the Moon; they don't see he's going to the Moon." — Kubrick [in conversation with Maurice Rapf].

Technical error is seen when Dr. Floyd sucks his food in zero gravity. Instead of staying in straw, as it would in real zero gravity, food slips back into container. Film's only intentional joke, says Arthur Clarke, is reading of zero gravity toilet instructions.

ZERO GRAVITY TOILET

PASSENGERS ARE ADVISED TO READ INSTRUCTIONS BEFORE USE

1 The toilet is of the standard zero-gravity type. Depending on requirements, system A and/or system B can be used, details of which are clearly marked in the toilet compartment. When operating system A, depress lever and a plastic dalkron eliminator will be dispensed through the slot immediately underneath. When you have fastened the adhesive lip, attach connection marked by the large "X" outlet hose. Twist the silver coloured ring one inch below the connection point until you feel it lock.

2 The toilet is now ready for use. The Sonovac cleanser is activated by the small switch on the lip. When securing, twist the ring back to its initial-condition, so that the two orange lines meet. Disconnect. Place the dalkron eliminator in the vacuum receptacle to the rear. Activate by pressing the blue button.

3 The controls for system B are located on the opposite wall. The red release switch places the uroliminator into position; it can be adjusted manually up or down by pressing the blue manual release button. The opening is self adjusting. To secure after use, press the green button which simultaneously activates the evaporator and returns the uroliminator to its storage position.

4 You may leave the lavatory if the green exit light is on over the door. If the red light is illuminated, one of the lavatory facilities is not properly secured. Press the "Stewardess" call button to the right of the door. She will secure all facilities from her control panel outside. When green exit light goes on you may open the door and leave. Please close door behind you.

5 To use the Sonoshower, first undress and place all your clothes in the clothes rack. Put on the velcro slippers located in the cabinet immediately below. Enter the shower. On the control panel to your upper right upon entering you will see a "Shower seal" button. Press to activate. A green light will then be illuminated immediately below. On the intensity knob select the desired setting. Now depress the Sonovac activation lever. Bathe normally.

6 The Sonovac will automatically go off after three minutes unless you activate the "Manual off" over-ride switch by flipping it up. When you are ready to leave, press the blue "Shower seal" release button. The door will open and you may leave. Please remove the velcro slippers and place them in their container.

7 If the red light above this panel is on, the toilet is in use. When the green light is illuminated you may enter. However, you must carefully follow all instructions when using the facilities during coasting (Zero G) flight. Inside there are three facilities: (1) the Sonowasher, (2) the Sonoshower, (3) the toilet. All three are designed to be used under weightless conditions. Please observe the sequence of operations for each individual facility.

8 Two modes for Sonowashing your face and hands are available, the "moist-towel" mode and the "Sonovac" ultrasonic cleaner mode. You may select either mode by moving the appropriate lever to the "Activate" position.

9 If you choose the "moist-towel" mode, depress the indicated yellow button and withdraw item. When you have finished, discard the towel in the vacuum dispenser, holding the indicated lever in an "active" position until the green light goes on . . . showing that the rollers have passed the towel completely into the dispenser. If you desire an additional towel, press the yellow button and repeat the cycle.

If you prefer the "Sonovac" ultrasonic cleaning mode, press the indicated blue button. When the twin panels open, pull forward by rings A and B. For cleaning the hands, use in this position. Set the timer to positions 10, 20, 30 or 40 . . . indicative of the number of seconds required. The knob to the left, just below the blue light, has three settings, low, medium or high. For normal use, the medium setting is suggested.

10 After these settings have been made, you can activate the device by switching to the "ON" position the clearly marked red switch. If, during the washing operation, you wish to change the settings, place the "manual off" over-ride switch in the "OFF" position. You may now make the change and repeat the cycle.

Moon is transparency of telescopic picture of real Moon, rephoto-
graphed on animation stand. Moon-shuttle Aries is a still photograph of
model two feet in diameter shot on horizontal camera in order to get
the longest track movement as it moves away. Movement of Aries
was made by visualizing its relative movement against background and
translating it simply to a first-and-last frame position. Inset shows
8 × 10 moon plate being photographed on 65mm Oxberry animation
stand.

Two-hundred-forty-thousand-mile trip is ending for Dr. Floyd. Aries is a photograph and window scenes are rear projections. Earth in background shot with
Moon terrain on animation camera, with stars. Background "mastered" and
printed on new negative by horizontal camera at same time camera photographed Aries and automatically masked terrain.

Aries lands in ten-foot-diameter Astrodome — eight three-foot-long, pie-shaped
panels that withdrew "underground." Lights of landing platform were extra-
brilliant tiny bulbs from West Germany.

Dust was raised by air nozzles in rocket motors. Scene was photographed at high
speed to create slow-motion effect.

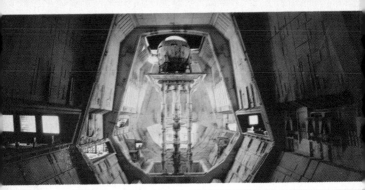

Clavius base airlock with Aries IB descending — a set about fifteen feet deep;
Aries was about two feet in diameter. Several held takes were exposed with the
little rooms and screens together on them; separation masters of airlock scene
were also printed. Scenes "inside" the little glass booths — of people moving
around — were each shot as a separate scene to fit the perspective, full size
on 35mm film, and then successively printed onto the several held takes of
65mm film. Last step was adding airlock scene around them. This was done on
same camera that combined all 35mm "plates," the Lin Dunn Matte camera.

Popular Science magazine: "Kubrick destroyed a mad, mad world with a nuclear bomb orgy at the climax of *Dr. Strangelove*. In *2001*, he resurrects a far
better world in which you find man routinely shuttling to the Moon."

Clavius below: Dr. Floyd apologizes for "cover story created to give
impression there is an epidemic at the base," but says it is necessary in
view of "the discovery," which "may well prove to be among the most
significant in the history of science."

Cutout photo of Moon bus, with rear projection action in windows. Movement was combination of camera pulling back and bus moving laterally along its perspective axis. Camera was tilted slightly so this axis would line up with horizon.

Forced perspective is simple procedure. Visualize a scene with a low horizon—mountains behind hills, etc. Flat picture. Imagine projecting that picture onto a 4-foot × 10-foot card at back of a tilted table, about 6 feet deep. At the back you set up a plane of cardboard and cut out farthest horizon features. Then, a little closer, you set up cutouts of the next nearest features, refocusing projector. Keep doing this until you have little cutouts of the hills, etc., in depth. If it's done right, most of the picture material is in the background. Now you begin to model actual dimensional hills using these cutouts as a rough guide; model conforms to composition you started with, but has actual detailed surfaces so it can be lit from any angle and look real. Difference is that if you look *down* on this 6-foot-deep reconstructed landscape it looks ludicrously squeezed, as though it were originally three times that thick—which it should be; but if it were, one couldn't keep it all in focus like a real landscape.

Sandwiches were passed out on the Moon bus.

Douglas Trumbull, a Special Photographic Effects Supervisor, painting details of tiny Moon base onto large composite photograph of Moon terrain model.

Moon bus cockpit: Two readouts were prepared specially for this view; they were shot in 35mm on animation stand and projected in 16mm from back of set. Moon terrain seen through windows was photographed later and matted in. Moon bus approaches site of monolith found on Moon: Tycho Magnetic Anomaly—One.

Moon bus landing pad and monitor domes. Base was a large model photographed, reduced, and stripped into another picture; holes were drilled for back-lighting.

Moon terrain and miniature Moon base ready for filming.

TMA-1 scene was photographed in early 1966. Lunar terrain model was added a year later. Film vault was set aside for held takes. Exposed film had a synch mark so timed runs could be duplicated. Compositions were registered by clip to film. Pit was 60 feet by 120 feet, and 60 feet deep. Sand was washed, dried, and given color and texture similar to Moon's.

Astronauts enter pit, examine artifact, which emits electronic sound when it is hit fully by sun for first time. (It had been dug up during 14-day lunar night.) It was coincidental that sound was emitted at moment of photography scene. Monolith was sun-powered-triggered device programmed to send to Jupiter message that it had been uncovered. There was no sound on Moon; astronauts heard it in their radio receivers.

Clarke: "2001 is based on the idea that if there are higher life forms in the universe, a higher intelligence, they may have come this way millions of years ago. When they saw no one on Earth at the time, they may have left a burglar alarm to signal them whenever intelligent life arose on Earth. However, the alarm was left not on Earth, but on the Moon. They may not have wanted to hear from us until man had developed enough intelligence to reach the Moon."

"The rate of blood flocculation for everyone suddenly increases rather mysteriously a few minutes before sunrise."
—**Maki Takata, Japanese doctor, in 1940.**

From the novel: "[Dr. Floyd] looked up at the Earth, beginning to wane in the morning sky. Only a handful of the six billion people there knew of this discovery; how would the world react to the news when it was finally released? . . . The political and social implications were immense; every person of real intelligence — everyone who looked an inch beyond his nose — would find his life, his values, his philosophy, subtly changed. . . ."

Stanley Kubrick eyes a plastic mock-up of the high-gain Discovery antenna, scaled to the 15-foot Discovery model. Background: Con Pederson, Special Effects Supervisor, holds a smaller scale antenna as he works on an early Discovery mock-up.

"I do not remember when I got the idea to do the film. I became interested in extraterrestrial intelligence in the universe, and was convinced that the universe was *full* of intelligent life, and so it seemed time to make a film." —**Stanley Kubrick.**

"I never learned anything at all in school and I didn't read a book for pleasure until I was nineteen years old." —**Stanley Kubrick.**

"To be boring is the worst sin of all." —**Stanley Kubrick.**

"The screenplay is the most uncommunicative form of writing ever devised." —**Stanley Kubrick.**

"What I'm after is a majestic visual experience." —**Stanley Kubrick.**

"A filmmaker has almost the same freedom a novelist has when he buys himself some paper." —**Stanley Kubrick.**

"He called up and told me to get him copies of everything that had been written about space, and I mean everything. I did, and he read all of it." —**Roger Caras, Kubrick aide.**

"I think the thing about this film that fascinates — and terrifies — people is that it is a film about reality. It was designed for integrity and honesty." —**Arthur C. Clarke.**

THE HALF-BILLION-MILE JUPITER MISSION

The 700-foot-long spaceship Discovery—a model 54 feet long with a
6-foot-diameter "command module" ball. For long shots, a 15-foot-
long model of Discovery was built. Judith Shatnoff, *Film Quarterly* :
"The Discovery looks like the vertebrae of some extinct reptile as it
speeds through the space night, an image which connects it to that

— EIGHTEEN MONTHS LATER.

bone old Australopithecus africanus hurled into the air." (Others have compared Discovery to a spermatozoon.) Nuclear reactor engines at rear would provide craft's propulsion. (At one time Kubrick considered showing the explosion of atomic bombs as propulsion, which experts have said would be a practical method of propulsion.)

Outside views of centrifuge, which was 38 feet in diameter, 10 feet wide in interior. 16mm projectors were fitted to centrifuge's outside and moved with set. Kubrick: "Centrifuge set was constructed in a steel framework which looked very much like a ferris wheel. Set was made in such a way that it had the structural integrity to preserve itself while the frame was rotated. Actor stayed at the bottom at all times. Camera was attached to set so that when set moved the camera didn't know it. It's a little bit like the relativity thing of somebody walking backwards in a train.

"Camera was on a gimbaled mount, and operator was in a gimbaled seat, with a television finder; as the frame rotated at three miles per hour, the camera was constantly adjusted by the operator to keep actor in the picture. The effect on the screen is that the camera is standing still and the actor is walking up and around the top and down the other side."

Kubrick directed centrifuge scenes by closed-circuit television. Hard hats were worn by non-actors because of exploding light bulbs and falling equipment.

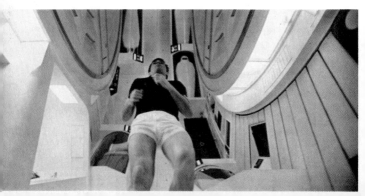

Aboard Discovery were placed three crew members in state of complete artificial hibernation. They were to be awakened when craft entered Jupiter space.
Dr. Ormond G. Mitchell, professor of anatomy, New York University Medical Center, and a *2001* consultant: "Induced hibernation of humans for long periods of time is not only completely feasible but imminent." The Harbor General Hospital, in California, was consulted because of its familiarity with the
deep-freezing of live animals. Mission Commander Dr. Dave Bowman (Keir
Dullea) and his deputy, Dr. Frank Poole (Gary Lockwood), did not know
(but the three "sleeping beauties" knew) that the purpose of the mission was
to locate the source of the radio signal aimed at Jupiter by TMA-1 during
the lunar sunrise.

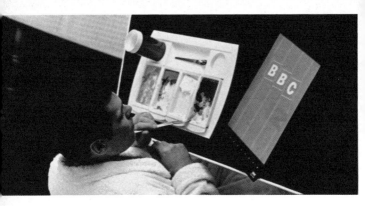

Bowman and Poole eat automatically-produced meals while watching on Newspad earlier-videotaped BBC interviews with themselves. Newspad is a kind of flat portable TV device that could display any type of visual or printed material.

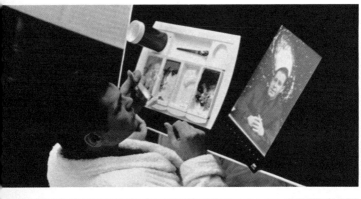

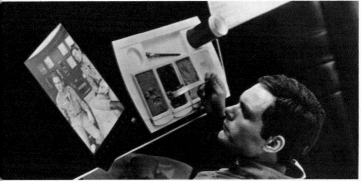

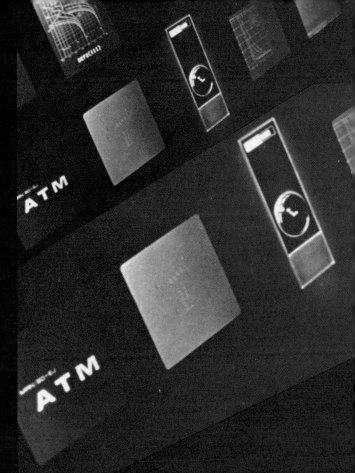

Sixth "member" of crew was red-eyed H.A.L. 9000 computer —
affectionately called HAL, for *h*euristically programmed *a*lgorithmic
computer.

Kubrick: "Many designs for HAL were worked up. Final design took
shape at the last minute, as most things do in a film. You wait as long
as you can to see if anyone comes up with anything better, and you
finally choose what seems best."

Clarke: "The tools the ape-men invented caused them to evolve into
their successor, *homo sapiens.* The tool we have invented *is* our successor. Biological evolution has given way to a far more rapid process—technical evolution. The machine is going to take over."

The actor who delivered HAL's voice was . . . .

Douglas Rain as Pyramus in
A Midsummer Night's Dream.

Douglas Rain as Henry V.

. . . Douglas Rain, Winnipeg-born actor who played a variety of roles for nearly 20 years at Stratford (Ontario) Festival. Rain was originally hired to narrate *2001*, but was asked to record HAL when the narration was struck and Kubrick decided that the original voice of HAL – Martin Balsam's – was too emotional, making the visuals redundant. Kubrick was looking for an unctuous, patronizing, neuter quality – "and Rain was great." Original name for *2001* computer was Athena, goddess of war, wisdom, fertility. Male personality and voice were deemed better.

Rain: "I wrapped up my work in nine and one-half hours. Kubrick is a charming man [he told David Cobb, *Toronto Telegram*]. Most courteous to work with. He was a bit secretive about the film. I never saw the finished script and I never saw a foot of the shooting."

Kubrick: "Maybe next time I'll show Rain in the flesh, but it would be a nonspeaking part, which would perfectly complete the circle."

*Douglas Rain as Sir Toby Belch
in* Twelfth Night.

Douglas Rain.

Bowman inside hublink transition corridor to centrifuge, where Discovery crew spends most of its time in artificial gravity. Hublink rotates, so part of the set had to rotate with it. Camera rotated to give Bowman appearance of being on the rotating part. Part of set on either side of the bearing—the nonrotating part of the ship—was rotating in opposite direction.

Preparing Keir Dullea for hublink sequence. Camera is on rotating mount.

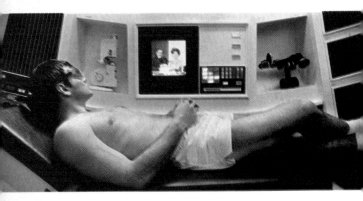

Aboard Discovery are all the comforts of home—and probably more. Pre-recorded televised birthday greeting from home for Poole, receiving simultaneously a sun-ray treatment. Five birth dates are celebrated in *2001*: Man, Dr. Floyd's "darling little daughter," Poole, HAL, star-child. Clarke says that he suggested *2001* subtitle be "Childhood's Beginning." On Sunday, December 20, 1968, from 140,000 miles in space, Apollo astronaut James Lovell radioed a birthday greeting to his mother.

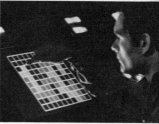

HAL of course whips Poole at chess (in prefilmed game):

POOLE: ". . . queen takes pawn . . ."

HAL: ". . . bishop takes knight's pawn . . ."

POOLE: "Hmmm, lovely move. Rook to king one."

HAL: "I'm sorry, Frank. I think you missed it. Queen to bishop three, bishop takes queen, knight takes bishop, mate."

POOLE: "Yeah, looks like you're right."

HAL played Pentominoes—five-square light game—with Bowman in scene not shown in film. Parker Brothers manufactured Pentominoes, hoping scene would be included.

With the words, "Just a moment, just a moment," HAL announces imminent communications breakdown with Earth due to faulty AE-35 unit in outside antenna.

Mission Control: "Sorry about this little snag, fellows. We'll get this info to you just as soon as we work it out." Kubrick tested dozens of military ground-control landing officers, hiring—over strenuous British Actors Equity objection—Chief Warrant Officer Franklin W. Miller, U.S. Air Force traffic controller stationed in England. Actors did not sound like the familiar mission control voice. Miller remembers working with Kubrick: "He saw that every little detail of personal comfort was at my disposal. I had aspirins if I had a headache, and even lotion when lights offered too much glare. Nothing seemed to be too much trouble. He always put me at my ease. Without realizing it, I once was tapping my foot—a nervous habit—which no one could see beneath the console where I was sitting, but it produced quite a thump on the tape. Instead of asking me to stop tapping, Kubrick got me a blanket, put it under my feet, and I tapped all I wanted to." Miller was transferred to Bangkok after his "perfectly marvelous experience."

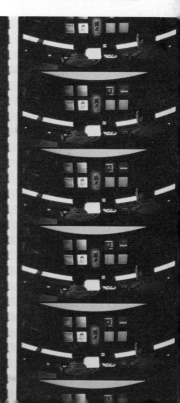

Full-size pod is mounted onto Discovery launching ramp for filming pod-bay sequence. For a maximum depth of field, exposure was 4 seconds per frame and one hour was taken to film pod emerging inch-by-inch from command module. Pod is used for extra-vehicular activities.

Below: Thirteen-inch pod emerges on pod-bay ramp from six-foot-diameter Discovery command module. Kubrick would set up his models, line up the camera, adjust lighting, shoot many different angles, movements, speeds, and takes to cover all conceivable interesting angles and movements.

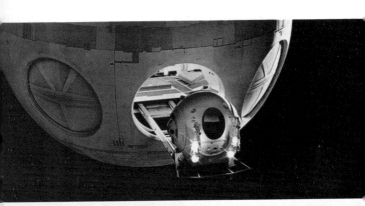

Discovery command module is stationary on a steel pole. Poole in cockpit is seen in rear projection plates added later. Pod is on turntable, mounted on an arm that moved vertically.

Interior of Discovery command module, Lockwood in commander's couch. One of HAL's ubiquitous eyes is surrounded by readout displays. Eight projections.

Drifting stars added after command module and pod were filmed. They were matted for pod onto new negative with the window action.

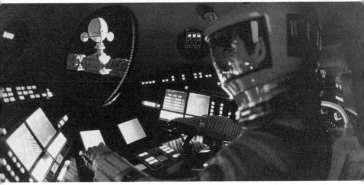

View of the Discovery's antenna was filmed later and matted into pod's window area. Six projections are underway simultaneously on nine-inch screens on one side of Bowman and six-inch screens in front.

Typical effects shot would consist of Discovery on one side, pod on other, figure of astronaut in middle. This meant three masters for Discovery, usually with antenna turning, and requiring a moving matte to eclipse star background, plus three masters for pod, also rotating and requiring a matte, plus single master containing matted stars, shot on animation stand and combined at Technicolor. If astronaut were also on masters, it would be a total of ten records to be duped. Many runs put strain on the black, washing out scene, or flattening it. Tiny figures of astronauts were reductions from 70mm color prints (movie film) projected on a tracking setup — another generation away from the original and more subject to degeneration and grain. Further copying by master could weaken them considerably. Old but costly matte technique of shooting a number of exactly matching motorized takes of the action was employed, and they were held undeveloped. This included test footage to work out the balance of the masters of the rest of the scene, which would be married on the held take of the astronaut, often half a year later. Lab take was processed for a guide, and could be mastered if needed.

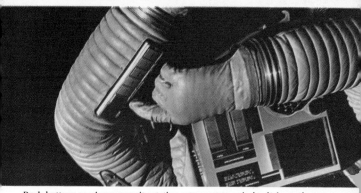

Push-buttons on sleeve permit rotating astronaut to polarize helmet visor against sun. Control for movement was on chest pack.

Bowman maneuvers to antenna system, which keeps Discovery in contact with Earth 500,000,000 miles away.

Full-scale set was used in AE-35 communications unit replacement sequence. Main dish of antenna was about twelve feet and the side dishes were about three and one-half feet.

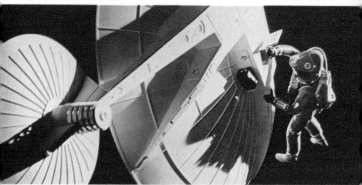

Three-dimensional rotating X-ray in AE-35 checkout sequence on electronic test bench in Discovery pod-bay consisted of 150 differently positioned pictures. Mission Control on Earth using a twin HAL 9000 and Discovery astronauts find nothing wrong with AE-35.

In pod bay were three dummy pods. Two had operational doors and mocked-up interiors. Separate interior pod set was built with instrumentation, controls, readout displays.

Opposite: Last sequence before *2001* intermission: Bowman and Poole in soundproof pod discuss HAL's disconcerting behavior without realizing HAL is reading their lips.

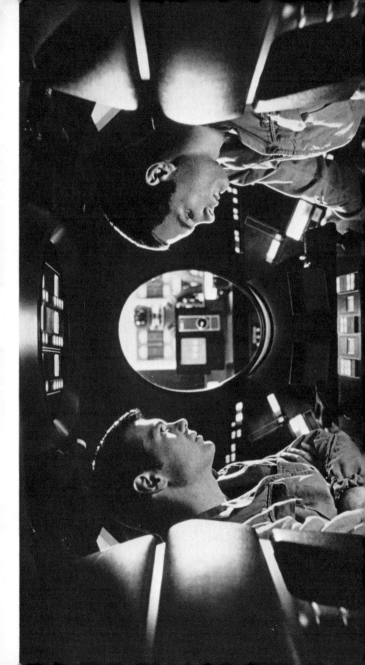

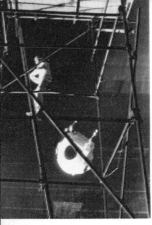

Astronauts decide to reinstall AE-35 unit to continue failure mode analysis. If unit does not fail, says Poole, "that would pretty well wrap it up as far as HAL is concerned, wouldn't it?" While reinstalling the unit, Poole is sent whirling off into space by HAL. Bowman in pod attempts rescue.

Looking through staging that was jump-off platform for stunt man, on wire, portraying Poole's body. Camera moved along floor and shot up. Full-size pod is six feet in diameter. Twelve-inch model was sometimes used.

Poole in weightless condition hanging from ceiling is hauled toward rescue pod piloted by Bowman. Poole was given a spin—his wire harness had pivot joint—and he rotated until he moved into pod arms.

Stunt man spent long sessions hanging upside down and would nearly faint from heat, fatigue, lack of air.

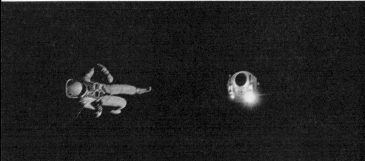

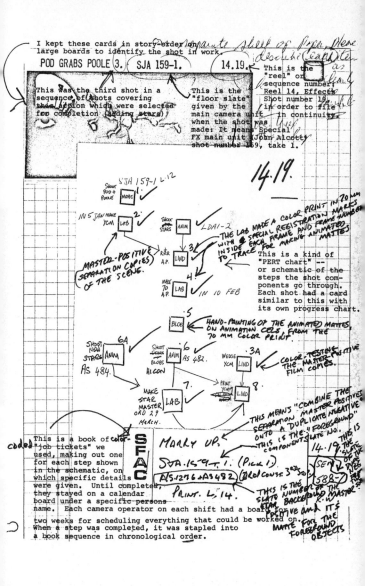

I kept these cards in story-order in large boards to identify the shot in work.

on a separate sheet of paper, please describe each item as clearly

POD GRABS POOLE 3.   SJA 159-1.   14.19.

This was the third shot in a sequence of shots covering the action which were selected for completion (adding stars)

This is the "floor slate" given by the main camera unit when the shot was made. It means Special FX main unit John Alcott shot number 159, take 1.

This is the "reel" or sequence number! Reel 14, Effects. Shot number 19, in order to file in continuity.

14.19.

SHOOT POD + POOLE | MOVIE | 1. SJA 159-1 L.12

IN 5 JAN MAKE YCM | LAB | 2. ✓

MASTER-POSITIVE (SEPARATION COPIES) OF THE SCENE.

SHOOT STARS | ANIM | LDA1-2

THE LAB MADE A COLOR PRINT IN 70 MM WITH SPECIAL REGISTRATION MARKS INSIDE EACH FRAME AND FRAME NUMBERS TO TRACE FOR MAKING ANIMATED MATTES

RRR A.P. | 3.

MAKE TO A.P. | LAB | 4. IN 10 FEB

This is a kind of "PERT chart" -- or schematic of the steps the shot components go through. Each shot had a card similar to this with its own progress chart.

BLOE | 5.

HAND-PAINTING OF THE ANIMATED MATTES ON ANIMATION CELS, FROM THE 70 MM COLOR PRINT.

SHOOT NEW STARS | ANIM | 6A AS 484.

SHOOT STARS + BLOBS HICON | ANIM | 6 AS 482.

WEDGE YCM | LIND | 3A

COLOR-TESTING THE MASTER-POSITIVE FILM COPIES.

MAKE STAR MASTER ORD 29 MARCH. | LAB | 7.

PRINT YCM + MATTE | LIND | 8.

THIS MEANS "COMBINE THE SEPARATION MASTER POSITIVES ONTO A DUPLICATE NEGATIVE" THIS IS THE "FOREGROUND" COMPONENT SLATE NO.

SFAC

MARRY UP.

SJA.159-1. (PICK 1)

AS.1276 + AS.482 (PROD CONT. 3rd Sel.)

PRINT. L. 14.

14.19. THIS IS THE SLATE OF THE YCM

SER | 1588-7 THIS IS THE SLATE NUMBER OF THE BACKGROUND MASTER POSITIVE AND IT'S MATTE FOR THE FOREGROUND OBJECTS

THIS IS THE SLATE NUMBER OF THE STAR BACKGROUND.

coded This is a book of color-coded "job tickets" we used, making out one for each step shown in the schematic, on which specific details were given. Until completed, they stayed on a calendar board under a specific persons name. Each camera operator on each shift had a board two weeks for scheduling everything that could be worked on. When a step was completed, it was stapled into a book sequence in chronological order.

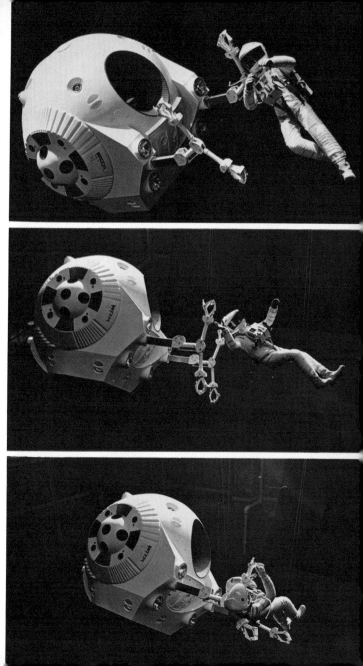

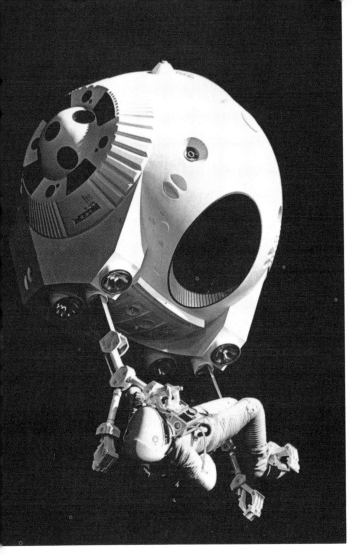

Dummy did not "float" like real human body, so stunt man had to be used in entire sequence. He had to move his arms and legs very slowly to give impression of being limp. Scene was shot at 96 frames per second so that in normal projection at 24 frames per second the slowing-down effect gave it proper space-drift sense. In producing sequence, astronaut had to collide with pod arms many times in many takes, and at twice the impact as the speed indicates in film.

HAL had been programmed to lie if interrogated by Bowman and Poole about true purpose of the mission. In succession, HAL has reported faulty antenna azimuth control unit, murdered Poole, murdered three hibernating astronauts, and now was determined to keep Bowman from reentering ship.

Clarke: "I personally would like to have seen a rationale of HAL's behavior. It's perfectly understandable, and in fact would have made HAL a very sympathetic character; he had been fouled by those clods at Mission Control. HAL was indeed correct in attributing his mistaken report to human error."

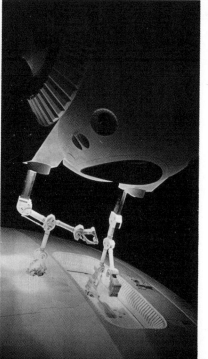

BOWMAN: "Open the pod-bay doors, please, HAL. Hello, HAL, do you read me?"

HAL: "Affirmative, Dave. I read you. . . . This mission is too important for me to allow you to jeopardize it."

Bowman maneuvers pod so he may enter Discovery through air lock. Two pod arms were run by many men at consoles for simultaneous control of actions and fingers, wrist, forearm, elbow, shoulder. Pod interior was maze of servos, actuators, cables.

Kubrick: "Man is said to be the missing link between ape and civilized human being, which you may say is inherent in *2001*, too."

Bowman makes emergency transfer from pod to Discovery air lock through vacuum of outer space. Scene appears to be horizontal, but was filmed vertically. Camera was at bottom of set and Dullea's body hid wires from ceiling. Speeded-up camera gave illusion of explosive action. U.S. Air Force tests with chimpanzees and dog proved that man could live exposed to vacuum for brief time.

Only major accident in production occurred when workman broke his back in fall from top of set of HAL brain room as he tried to catch a toppling light. Set was three stories high. Dullea hung between sheets of perforated metal.

Bowman methodically disconnected HAL's intelligence functions, reducing "him" from sentient being to routine vehicular monitoring device. For all practical purposes, HAL was dead.

"Every time I get through a session with Stanley, I have to go lie down." — **Arthur C. Clarke.**

"How the Solar System Was Won was never a title that was considered." — **Stanley Kubrick.**

"How the Solar System Was Won was our private title. It was exactly what we tried to show." — **Arthur C. Clarke.**

"I would say that *2001* reflects about ninety per cent on the imagination of Kubrick, about five per cent on the genius of the special effects people, and perhaps five per cent on my contribution." — **Arthur C. Clarke.**

Arthur C. Clarke talks about Stanley Kubrick: "Stanley might make a great scientist with his insatiable curiosity. When it comes to filmmaking, he's the best."

Stanley Kubrick on Arthur C. Clarke: "Working with Arthur Clarke gave me the considerable pleasure one gets from being with a friend who has something to say worth listening to. I don't think Arthur has a serious rival about prehistory or the future. As an artist, his ability to impart poignancy to a dying ocean or an intelligent vapor is unique. He has the kind of mind of which the world can never have enough, an array of imagination, intelligence, knowledge, and a quirkish curiosity which often uncovers more than the first three qualities."

"As for the dwindling minority who still don't like it — that's their problem, not ours. Stanley Kubrick and I are laughing all the way to the bank." — **Arthur C. Clarke,** in *Cosmos* magazine.

"Not only will men of science have to grapple with the sciences that deal with man, but — and this is a far more difficult matter — they will have to persuade the world to listen to what they have discovered. If they cannot succeed in this difficult enterprise, man will destroy himself by his halfway cleverness." — **Bertrand Russell.**

Sunrise on Jupiter. Inner moons shown. All shot in animation, stars added later, along with monolith not seen in this illustration. Actual artwork smaller than in photograph. Fine transparencies were taken from large artwork of moons and Jupiter.

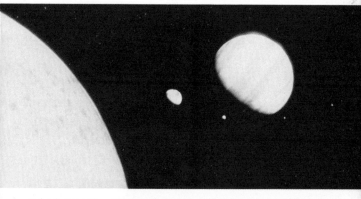

Kubrick: "The trip and the magical alignment of Jupiter and its satellites are the only things in *2001* that don't conform to what is known to physicists and astronomers."

Major concern throughout production was adequate representation of Saturn. After months of unsuccessful attempts at designing Saturn, Kubrick decided that Jupiter might be visually more interesting and possibly easier to produce. More months were spent in an unsuccessful attempt to produce Saturn. Several top London illustrators were then asked to render Jupiter, all without success. Final solution: The Jupiter Machine, a device consisting of an optical scanning technique that transformed flat painted artwork into a perfectly accurate sphere. It took an exposure time of two hours for the device to scan an entire globe onto an 8 × 10 Ektachrome plate, which was later used on animation stand.

Below: Bruce Logan retouches white edge of Jupiter Machine.

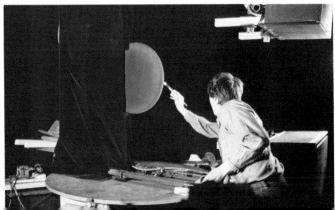

Jupiter was conceived to look vaporous or hazy, although a good part of the
soft edge of it shows in astronomical photographs. This is due to sunlight's at-
tenuation at the limb from the very narrow source angle, owing to its great distance from sun. Jovian atmosphere probably enhances its own soft appearance
because of this diminished back-scatter more from Earthian point of view near
the sun than it would seen lit from the side, a view Earthians cannot have.
Jupiter Machine in operation: 8-inch × 10-inch camera looks through area
between suspended projectors. Two-hour exposures. 8 × 10 Jupiter plates
were airbrushed, phased, and photographed on animation stand.

Jupiter's moons were produced by projecting textural 35mm slides (painted
directly onto 35mm glass slide holder) onto 12-inch diameter opaque white
globe from two sides.

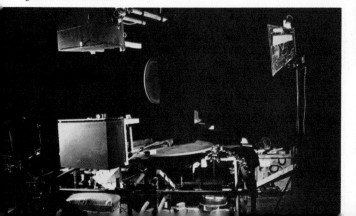

Con Pederson: "Jupiter was selected over Saturn, because to do Saturn meant, in effect, getting a convincing Jupiter first — they are fairly similar — and then finding a way to put rings around it. Best way to do the planet was not the best way to do the rings; they could not be made at same time, as photographic records, like our other planetary images. Putting two separate techniques together into one image would have been quite difficult, though not impossible. Still another technique would be needed to show close-ups of rings. Bear in mind, I'm talking about an image which is really impressively going to convince people. Best matte painter in the world would respect the hazards of concentrating all of viewer's scrutiny on his work."

In Jupiter space, Bowman travels in a pod beyond the infinite.

Readout screens and panel lights are reflected in helmet visor of Bowman seated at pod controls. Screens were miniature rear-projection systems using 16mm film that was reduced from 35mm animation. Symbolic scene for future man surrounded completely by his machinery and the silent reflections of organized energy.

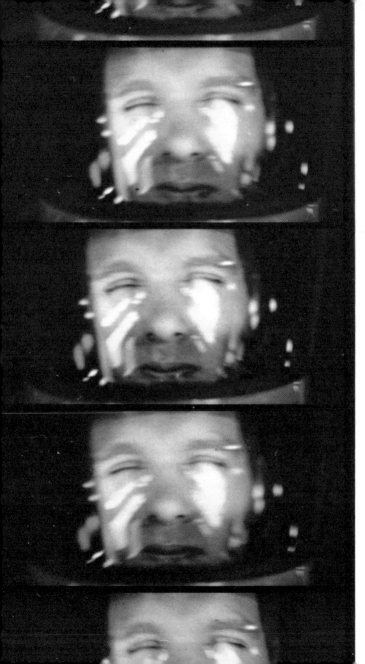

Close-up view of automatic focus on 65mm camera for slit-scan filming. Douglas Trumbull designed slit-scan machine for "light show" through which lone astronaut Bowman travels. Machine could produce two seemingly infinite planes of exposure while holding depth of field from a distance of fifteen feet to one and one-half inches from the lens at an aperture of F/1.8 — with exposures of approximately one minute per frame.

Artist Roy Naisbitt preparing maze of abstract artwork for slit-scan corridor of light effects. This artwork was made up of thousands of high contrast film negatives of op-art paintings, architectural drawings, *moiré* patterns, printed circuits, and electron-microscope photographs of molecular and crystal structures. One effect came out looking like flying carpets, and was quickly grounded.

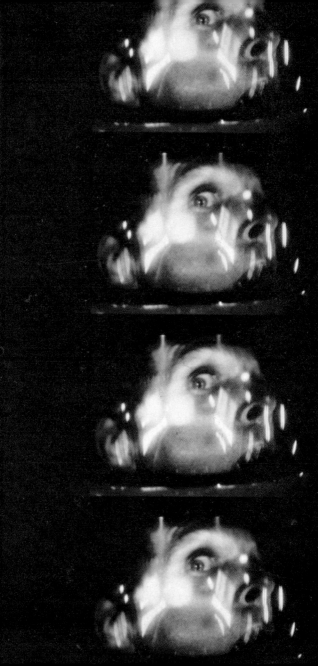

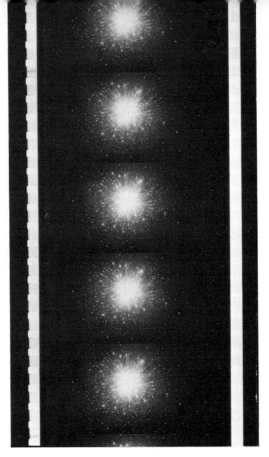

Secret filming at a former corset factory, Broadway and 72nd Street, New York, at very start of project produced exploding galaxy. It was known to staff as "Manhattan project."

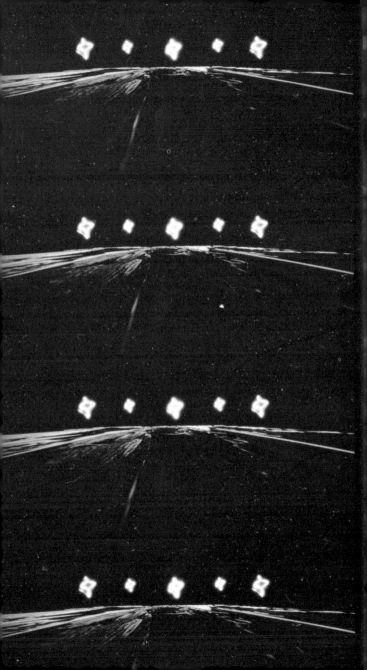

B.G = ET 28.
MINDBENDER   SJA 471-2.4(47)(12)   17.40.

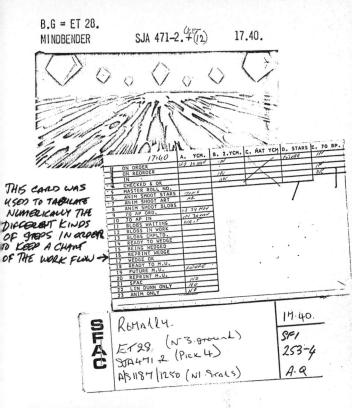

THIS CARD WAS USED TO TABULATE NUMERICALLY THE DIFFERENT KINDS OF STEPS IN ORDER TO KEEP A CHART OF THE WORK FLOW →

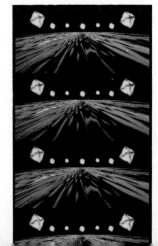

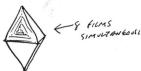

← 8 FILMS SIMULTANEOUSLY

Kubrick's "mind-bender" effect. Slit-scan movie was projected onto multifaced screens mounted on three-foot-high rotated rig—and repeated until seven diamonds appeared.

News report, February 10, 1969: "NASA biochemist reports that laboratory experiments simulating atmosphere of Jupiter suggest that chemical precursors of animal life have evolved on that far planet."

Clouds of interstellar dust and gas were made by interacting chemicals within camera field of size no larger than a paperback book.

Aerial views were made of Hebrides in Scotland and Monument Valley in Arizona, Utah. Best effects over Hebrides were of snow and ice.

Weird views on screen of Hebrides and Monument Valley footage was achieved by using different color filters instead of normal filters in making dupe negative. Months of experimentation developed effects.

Scenes not in *2001*. Dimensional and sculptural extraterrestrials were produced by slit-scan machine. Original script idea was for extraterrestrial resembling Giacometti sculpture. Actor was dressed in skin-tight, all-white costume and photographed using 2:1 anamorphic lens, which made him appear extremely thin when projected without the anamorphic. Result was dull and unconvincing. Another approach: All-black suit with white polka dots. Rubber gargoyle monsters were tried. Near end of production, there was television video feedback technique that produced lifelike, pulsating light images. Some footage was made, but it was too late to incorporate into film. Bowman would have "seen" ETs telepathically.

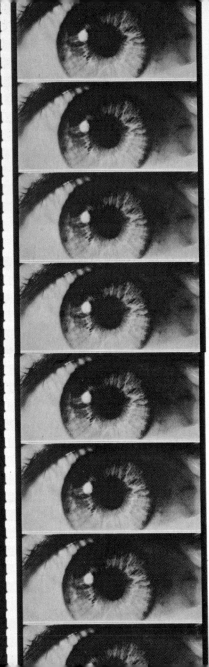

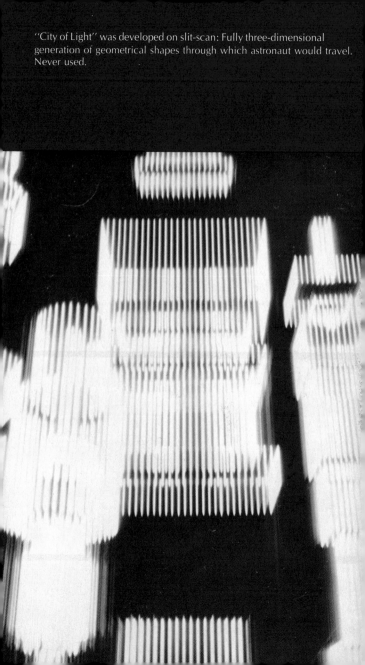

"City of Light" was developed on slit-scan: Fully three-dimensional generation of geometrical shapes through which astronaut would travel. Never used.

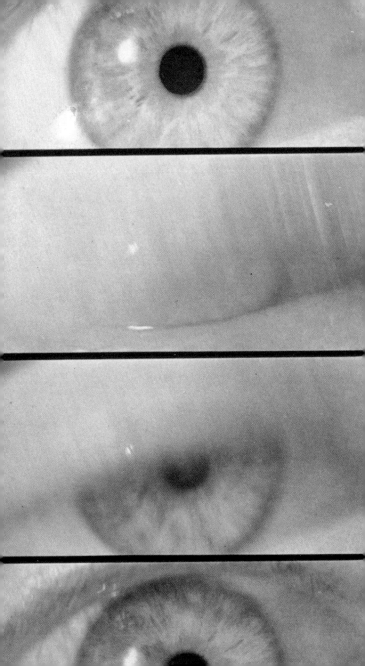

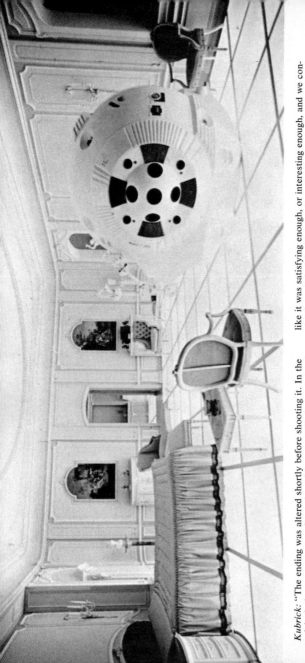

Kubrick: "The ending was altered shortly before shooting it. In the original, there was no transformation of Bowman. He just wandered around the room and finally saw the artifact. But this didn't seem like it was satisfying enough, or interesting enough, and we constantly searched for ideas until we finally came up with the ending as you see it."

From Nietzsche's *Thus Spake Zarathustra*: ". . . one morning Zarathustra got up with the dawn and stepped into the presence of the Sun and thus spake unto him: "Thou great star! What would be thy happiness were it not for those for whom thou shinest? For ten years thou hast come up here to my cave. Thou wouldst have got sick of thy light and thy journey but for me, mine eagle and my serpent . . . Lo! I am weary of my wisdom, like the bee that hath collected too much honey; I need hands reaching out for it. I would fain grant and distribute until the wise among men could once more enjoy their folly, and the poor once more their riches . . . bless me, thou impassive eye, that canst look without envy even upon overmuch happiness. Bless the cup which is about to overflow, so that the water golden flowing out of it may carry everywhere the reflection of thy rapture. Lo! This cup is about to empty itself again, and Zarathustra will once more become a man.'"

Left: Clarke: "I think Keir's breaking the glass was a cinematic gimmick. Stanley was listening to his inner demons at the time and they may have been telling him, 'What's a nice Jewish boy like you doing in a place like this?'"

While breaking of wine glass may have been to keep illusion of reality – Earthian Still Makes Mistakes – breaking of glass at wedding ceremony has long Judaic history, symbolizing destruction of Jerusalem temple in 70 A.D. 2001 could be viewed as marriage of past, present, future.

Thus Spake Zarathustra: "What is the ape to man? A laughing-stock, a thing of shame. And just the same shall man be to the Superman: a laughing-stock, a thing of shame."

Bedroom is a cage, in a human zoo tricked out with artifacts from Bowman's mind to make him feel comfortable while he is investigated and reconstructed by superpowers who are surrealistically presented in strange laughing sounds, an alteration of György Ligeti music. Bowman's life passes in this room, though to him it seems like moments.

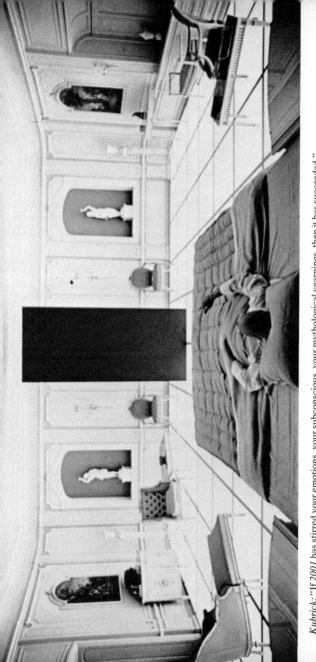

Kubrick: "If 2001 has stirred your emotions, your subconscious, your mythological yearnings, then it has succeeded."

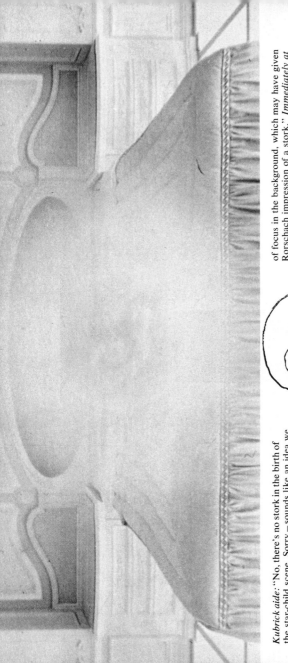

Kubrick aide: "No, there's no stork in the birth of the star-child scene. Sorry — sounds like an idea we should have pursued. Don't know how we missed it. There is a white bust and a couple of paintings out of focus in the background, which may have given Rorschach impression of a stork." *Immediately at left: 2001 artist's sketch of star-child as he sees it in the bubble.*

First footage shot in England was of young naked boy, against black velvet. Much later, young sculptress produced embryonic figure in clay. Fiberglass doll was produced and remotely operated glass eyes were added to head. Final star-child was produced using extremely heavy back light. Completed bubble was white paint airbrushed onto a black card and over which was superimposed movement of the two-and-one-half-foot star-child fetus. Glow of light was also superimposed. Resemblance to Dullea was intentional.

"There before him, a glittering toy no Star-Child could resist, floated the planet Earth with all its peoples."

Only ending that went to shooting-script stage, and was eliminated, was having star-child detonate nuclear weapons orbiting the Earth, as in book version. Consensus: Ending would have been too similar to ending of previous Kubrick film, *Dr. Strangelove*. We won't meet again.

From Arthur C. Clarke's *The Space-Dreamers*, published in 1954: "He rose to leave, thinking he'd preserved his incognito rather well. The stranger gave him a curious little smile and said quietly: 'Good-bye.' He waited until Hassell had gone twenty feet, then called after him in a louder voice: 'And good luck—Ulysses.'"

NO	FT FRS METROCOLOR	DESCRIPTION
1B	47/12	Int. Hotel Bedroom — CS — Elderly man, asleep in bed, as we see it is Bowman — he slowly raises his right hand, pointing with forefinger — then he slowly starts to raise his head from the pillow —
2B	60/5	MLS — Camera shooting down to Bowman lying in bed in f.g., as cube is seen at the end of his bed — Bowman is still raising his hand and head —
3B	75/14	LS — Cube is seen at right, as Bowman is seen in b.g., raising his head and hand —
4B	84/14	MLS — Cube — P.O.V. —
5B	98/8	MS — Bed, with smoky haze over it —
6B	108/15	MCU — Bowman, facing right, in smoky haze —
7B	123/4	MLS. — CAMERA TRUCKS in to cube, as it gradually covers the screen —
8B	192/10	Ext. Space — ELS — Jupiter, rising out of top of frame — curve of moon is entered in right f.g. — star-chid enters in left f.g. —
9B	233/14	MCU — Star-child, in smoke — FADE OUT TO:
10B	244/6	MS — The following Title is Superimposed: THIS FILM WAS DIRECTED AND PRODUCED BY STANLEY KUBRICK
11B	255/10	MS — The following Title is Superimposed: SCREENPLAY BY STANLEY KUBRICK AND ARTHUR C. CLARKE
12B	264/11	MS — The following Title is Superimposed: PRESENTED BY METRO-GOLDWYN-MAYER

NO	FT FRS	DESCRIPTION
13B	273/3	MS — The following Title is Superimposed: IN CINERAMA ®
14B	282/4	MS — The following Title is Superimposed: STARRING KEIR DULLEA
15B	290/12	MS — The following Title is Superimposed: STARRING GARY LOCKWOOD

```
NO  FT ' FRS      DESCRIPTION
16B              MS — The following Titles are Superimposed:
                                 STARRING
                            WILLIAM SYLVESTER
        300/9                DANIEL RICHTER
17B              MS — The following Titles are Superimposed:
                                 FEATURING
                            LEONARD ROSSITER
                            MARGARET TYZACK
                              ROBERT BEATTY
                              SEAN SULLIVAN
        316/0                 DOUGLAS RAIN
18B              MS — The following Titles are Superimposed:
                                   WITH
                     FRANK MILLER     PENNY BRAHMS
                     GLENN BECK       MIKE LOVELL
                     EDWINA CARROLL   EDWARD BISHOP
                     BILL WESTON      ANN GILLIS
        335/14   ALAN GIFFORD     HEATHER DOWNHAM
19B              MS — The following Titles are Superimposed:
                     JOHN ASHLEY      DAVID HINES
                     JIMMY BELL       TONY JACKSON
                     DAVID CHARKHAM   JOHN JORDAN
                     SIMON DAVIS      SCOTT MACKEE
                     JONATHAN DAW     LAURENCE MARCHANT
                     PETER DELMAR     DARRYL PAES
                     TERRY DUGGAN     JOE REFALO
                     DAVID FLEETWOOD  ANDY WALLACE
                     DANNY GROVER     BOB WILYMAN
        360/5     BRIAN HAWLEY     RICHARD WOOD
                                            REEL 10 PAGE 5
20B              MS — The following Title is Superimposed:
                         SPECIAL PHOTOGRAPHIC EFFECTS
                                  DESIGNED
                                    AND
                                  DIRECTED
                                    BY
        370/14               STANLEY KUBRICK
21B              MS — The following Title is Superimposed:
                         SPECIAL PHOTOGRAPHIC EFFECTS
                                 SUPERVISOR
        379/4                 WALLY VEEVERS
22B              MS — The following Title is Superimposed:
                         SPECIAL PHOTOGRAPHIC EFFECTS
                                 SUPERVISOR
        388/5               DOUGLAS TRUMBULL
23B              MS — The following Title is Superimposed:
                         SPECIAL PHOTOGRAPHIC EFFECTS
                                 SUPERVISOR
        396/15                CON PEDERSON
24B              MS — The following Title is Superimposed:
                         SPECIAL PHOTOGRAPHIC EFFECTS
                                 SUPERVISOR
        405/9                  TOM HOWARD
```

NO	FT	FRS	DESCRIPTION
25B			MS — The following Titles are Superimposed:
			PRODUCTION DESIGNED BY
			TONY MASTERS
			HARRY LANGE
		417/2	ERNEST ARCHER
26B			MS — The following Title is Superimposed:
			FILM EDITOR
		425/10	RAY LOVEJOY
27B			MS — The following Title is Superimposed:
			WARDROBE BY
		434/3	HARDY AMIES
28B			MS — The following Title is Superimposed:
			DIRECTOR OF PHOTOGRAPHY
		442/11	GEOFFREY UNSWORTH B.S.C.
29B			MS — The following Title is Superimposed:
			ADDITIONAL PHOTOGRAPHY
		452/2	JOHN ALCOTT

REEL 10 PAGE 6
Corr. 7-10-68

NO	FT	FRS	DESCRIPTION
30B			MS — The following Titles are Superimposed:
			MUSIC BY
			ARAM KHATCHATURIAN
			GAYANE BALLET SUITE
			Performed by the Leningrad
			Philharmonic Orchestra
			Conductor Gennadi Rozhdestvensky
		462/2	Courtesy Deutsche Grammophon
31B			MS — The following Titles are Superimposed:
			MUSIC BY
			GYÖRGY LIGETI
			ATMOSPHERES
			Performed by the Southwest German
			Radio Orchestra
			Conductor Ernest Bour
			LUX AETERNA
			Performed by the
			Stuttgart State Orchestra
			Conductor Clytus Gottwald
			REQUIEM
			Performed by the
			Bavarian Radio Orchestra
		474/5	Conductor Francis Travis
32B			MS — The following Titles are Superimposed:
			MUSIC BY
			JOHANN STRAUSS
			THE BLUE DANUBE
			Performed by the
			Berlin Philharmonic Orchestra
			Conductor Herbert von Karajan
		485/1	Courtesy Deutsche Grammophon

```
NO  FT  FRS      DESCRIPTION
33B              MS — The following Titles are Superimposed:
                               MUSIC BY
                            RICHARD STRAUSS

         494/9              THUS SPAKE ZARATHUSTRA

34B              MS — The following Title is Superimposed:
                          FIRST ASSISTANT DIRECTOR
         502/15               DEREK CRACKNELL

                                         REEL 10 PAGE 7
                                         Corr. 7-10-68

35B              MS — The following Titles are Superimposed:
                          SPECIAL PHOTOGRAPHIC EFFECTS UNIT
                 COLIN J. CANTWELL    BRUCE LOGAN
                 BRYAN LOFTUS         DAVID OSBORNE
                 FREDERICK MARTIN     JOHN JACK MALICK
                          IN TECHNICOLOR ® AND METROCOLOR
                             Approved No. 21197
                     MOTION PICTURE ASSOCIATION OF AMERICA
                                Ars Gratia Artis
                          A Metro-Goldwyn-Mayer Release
                                  (Trademark)
                          A METRO-GOLDWYN-MAYER     .
                                  PRODUCTION
                 The events, characters and firms
                 depicted in this photoplay are
                 fictitious. Any similarity to actual
                 persons, living or dead, or to actual
                 events and firms is purely
         516/11  coincidental.

36B              MS — The following Titles are Superimposed:
                          CAMERA OPERATOR   KELVIN PIKE
                             ART DIRECTOR   JOHN HOESLI
                             SOUND EDITOR   WINSTON RYDER
                                 MAKE-UP    STUART
                                            FREEBORN
                     EDITORIAL ASSISTANT    DAVID DE WILDE
                       SOUND SUPERVISOR     A. W. WATKINS
                           SOUND MIXER      H. L. BIRD
                   CHIEF DUBBING MIXER      J. B. SMITH
                 SCIENTIFIC CONSULTANT      FREDERICK I.
         529/10                             ORDWAY III

37B              MS — The following Title is Superimposed:
         537/15           FILMED IN SUPER PANAVISION®

38B              MS — The following Title is Superimposed:
                          MADE AT MGM BRITISH STUDIOS LTD.
         577/11               BOREHAM WOOD, ENGLAND

39B              MS — The following Title is Superimposed:
                                 THE END
         586/2                                      FADE OUT!

                 FINISH —
```

"Look, Dave. I can see you're really upset about this. I honestly think you should sit down calmly, take a stress pill, and think things over."

The long-awaited preview was on April 1, 1968, before a specially invited audience in New York's Capitol Theater.

Stanley Kubrick, in interview with Maurice Rapf: "I attribute the poor reaction to the audience and to the originality of the film. The film departs about as much from the convention of the theater and the three-act play as is possible. Not many films have departed further than that, certainly not the big films. I don't know why there was such a concentration of nonreceptive people, but there was. The audience that is now seeing 2001 is reported as being 80 percent 35 years or under, down to five years old. I would say the audience at the first preview must have been 90 percent 35 to 60. The preview audience and the paying audience have been two ends of the moviegoing scale."

The original running time of *2001* was two hours and forty-one minutes. "Too long, boring" were chief criticisms heard from people who walked out during the previews and on opening night in New York.

"The basement in the M-G-M building [in New York] where we have our editing facilities was generally crowded during trim sessions," remembers an M-G-M executive. "Lots of people looking for Stanley — big people, little people, fat people, thin people. Stanley's youngest daughter, Vivian, was present during much of the editing. She's a chocolate donut nut — always asking for a chocolate donut. Stanley hated the Sixth Avenue Delicatessen across the street. He said it couldn't make a good outgoing sandwich.

"Stanley was happy over the film's general acceptance and confused and puzzled over the difficulty and lack of understanding that was being reported."

Nineteen minutes were trimmed from the original print. Sequences trimmed were Dawn of Man, Orion, Poole exercising in the centrifuge, and Poole's pod exiting from Discovery. Trimming commenced at four P.M. on April 5, 1968, and the first session did not end until seven A.M. the next day. Work continued at this pace until the trim was completed three days later.

Kubrick has talked on three different occasions about the cuts:

1. "*2001* was not the first picture I have tightened after a couple of previews. *Doctor Strangelove* lost an entire pie-throwing sequence at the end because it seemed excessive, and *Paths of Glory* was trimmed between preview and release."

2. "I made all the cuts in *2001* and at no one's request. I had not had an opportunity to see the film complete with music, sound effects, etc., until about a week before it opened, and it does take a few runnings to decide finally how long things should be, especially scenes which do not have narrative advancement as their guideline. Most of the scenes that were cut were impressions of things and could have been anywhere from four times shorter than they were — or four times longer, depending on how you felt about it."

3. "I just felt as I looked at it and looked at it that I could see places all the way through where I could tighten up, and I took out 19 minutes. I don't believe that the trims made a crucial difference. I think it just affected some marginal people. The people who like it, like it no matter what its length, and the same holds true for the people who hate it."

"I must say you guys have come up with something."

Dear Mr. Kubrick:
I am three and one-half years old.
You're right!

[Name withheld on parents' request]
Champlain, New York

Your film was really great. . . . The real reason for sending this letter is to ask for posters for my bedroom walls. . . . I have a film projector if you have any scenes you didn't use.

P.L. Amodio
Kent, England

YOU MADE ME DREAM EYES WIDE OPEN STOP YOURS IS MUCH MORE THAN AN EXTRAORDINARY FILM THANK YOU
FRANCO ZEFFIRELLI
ROME

I am enclosing my four ticket stubs. I would like my money returned, if for no other reason than as an apology for boring the life out of my family and myself for three hours. When will you learn what the public, that you are always screaming about, has known for years. You cannot cover up mediocrity with obscurity.

Mrs. Patricia Attard
Denver

P.S. The tickets were $2.50 each.

My pupils are still dilated, and my breathing sounds like your soundtrack. I don't know if this poor brain will survive another work of the magnitude of *2001*, but it will die (perhaps more accurately "go nova") happily if given the opportunity. Whenever anybody asks me for a description of the movie, I tell them that it is, in sequential order: Anthropological, camp, McLuhan, cybernetic, psychedelic, religious. That shakes them up a lot.

Jesus, man, where did you get that incredibly good technical advice and information? Whenever I see the sun behind a round sign, I start whistling *Thus Spake Zarathustra*. My kettle-drum impression draws the strangest looks.

> *Robert Higgins*
> *Detroit*

I have had time to see *2001* once, though I do look forward to seeing it again sometime. I remember thinking at the time I saw the picture that it might be worth a chuckle to mention finding a monolith during our Apollo flight. Though I enjoyed the film very much and thought it was a fine piece of work, I was somewhat confused by the meaning of the third part. This was cleared up when I read the book.

> *William A. Anders*
> *Lt. Col., U.S.A.F.*
> *NASA Astronaut*

Being young enough to look forward to 2001 as the prime of my life, I must thank you for giving me a glimpse of what terror and beauty may await us in that year.

> *Bob Wright*
> *Atlanta, Georgia*

I have heretofore been able to resist the urge to write fan letters, but after seeing *2001* for the third time, I can no longer put it off. Please accept the sincere congratulations of a long-time science-fiction fan for a job masterfully done. You've succeeded in pleasing many thousands of people, but, if my personal experience is a reliable indicator, you've mystified many more.

If there's one thing I've learned in my 46 years, it's that I'm no intellectual giant, but I can't believe the plot was *that* hard to understand. Nevertheless, you wouldn't believe some of the interpretations of it I've heard! They range all the way from "There *was* no story. The whole thing was a series of disconnected vignettes just like the early Cinerama spectaculars" to "It was about the Second Coming. Didn't you see the cross formed by the string of planets and that black thing?" One lady (?) even said the show was fine "until they indulged in pornography" by showing the fetus at the end.

At any rate, my minority position has raised a doubt—maybe *I'm* the one who missed the point. It occurs to me that the plot bears a striking resemblance to Arthur Clarke's "Childhood's

End" (my all-time favorite science-fiction story). Perhaps the reason it and *2001* appeal to me so much is because this is the way I choose to think of Mankind—as struggling toward an Ideal, rather than toward the mud-bound materialism I see each day.

> *W.E. (Walt) Churchill*
> *Wichita, Kansas*

I SAW YESTERDAY YOUR FILM AND I NEED TO TELL YOU MY EMOTION MY ENTHUSIASM STOP I WISH YOU THE BEST LUCK IN YOUR PATH

> FEDERICO FELLINI
> ROME

I am a senior at Radcliffe College, majoring in English. *2001* was WOW, FUN, KEEN, NEAT! Congratulations.

> *Jody Adams*
> *Cambridge, Massachusetts*

P.S. *Dr. Strangelove* was great, too.

It was, in short, the best movie I have ever seen. Even though I am considered bright, I could not understand the last part of the movie. Someday when I am older, I hope to get involved in the field of astronautics. Now, I am 13. In 2001, I will be 46 years old. For the time being, could you send me something explaining the end of the movie!

> *Joel Robin Burcat*
> *Philadelphia*

P.S. I did not mean to brag about being bright in the second sentence.

I was relieved during the intermission to overhear numerous couples express their disgust at the picture and to hear it made no sense to others, either. Many people left during the intermission. I have always had a high regard for M-G-M and stayed to the bitter end. My faith in M-G-M has been totally destroyed.

> *Mrs. Elsie M. Gutwald*
> *Lutherville, Maryland*

I suspect that a whole generation of new filmmakers will be shaken up by the experience of your picture. I can envision ideas being tossed away, scripts being burned, and rough cuts being destroyed. Of course I exaggerate. What I really wish to express is my appreciation that perhaps an entirely different way of making pictures has been actualized. It will be, I think, a liberation of sorts for anyone who takes movies seriously.

Alan R. Howard
Columbia Pictures Corp.
Hollywood, California

I am 14 and loved every minute of *2001*. Anybody who says it was dull is an idiot. How can a movie so different, like *2001*, be dull. Oh, well, some people are dumb.

I understand the movie quite well now. It's sort of like a picture reflecting the personality of the painter and at the same time showing beauty and talent. Now that I think of it, a movie such as this could have no other ending.

But the main reason I wrote this letter is because I need help. Now I know you are busy and you are famous, but I hope this doesn't cause you to be a snob. Please take time out to at least scribble a note to me. My friend, Stephen Dilling, and I are going to make a movie. It will be one hour long at the most. It will be about space. We decided to go right to the top, Stanley Kubrick. How much higher could one get? The movie will be called *2001: A Sequel*. We would like to purchase or borrow one spacesuit of any color. We are honest and will take good care of it.

Randy Clower
Duncanville, Texas

Scenes planned for Clower-Dilling production, *2001: A Sequel*

Aho don salad ad fonya dayesu a fau. Bah sood ads fauta basto nod yae. Dteed atod lonat aen aut solom dis, d sae Toody Loo.

Sincerely,
Dan
[Daniel Kiamie
Lawrence, Massachusetts]

P.S. If you think that this letter has *you* baffled, then you should see what *2001* did for me — it was truly a journey into the unknown!

I must tell you it is the worst picture I have ever seen. I have been racking my brain all afternoon trying to figure out the point you were trying to make, and it is beyond my understanding. I think you were trying to tell us something about life, but what it is, I just can't determine. My girlfriend and I watched the audience's reaction as the people were leaving the theater. Some people stared at each other and said nothing, while others laughed. The movie made no sense to me at all. Never before in my 19 years have I left a movie knowing nothing what it was about. Perhaps I just haven't lived long enough to know very much about life, but I should have gotten something from this movie, but I was left with nothing. You wrote and directed a picture far above the understanding of us ordinary people, which makes it a waste of time. *Cue* magazine said it was mentally stimulating and brilliantly conceived, but that doesn't tell us very much. Perhaps the critic himself didn't understand the picture, so he wrote nothing of real value to read.

Therese Kustra
College Point, New York

The only possible human excuse I could think of is that your film was actually directed by HAL 9000. However, I am convinced that "he" would have done much better.

Federico Lang
Buenos Aires

Although I have my doubts that your eyes will ever see this writing, I still have hopes that some secretary will neglect to dispose of my letter and that I may even receive acknowledgment. I have just seen your motion picture and I believe — please, words, don't fail me now — that I have never been so moved by a film — so impressed — awed — etc. The music was absolutely on a zenith. "The Blue Danube" really belonged in some strange way, and the main theme with its building crescendos was more beautiful than John Lennon's "I Am the Walrus," and from me that's a compliment. The story in *Life* magazine, of course, showed the most routine scenes, as *Life* has a tendency to eliminate any overwhelming virtue in a motion picture, and the three best scenes were lumped together and were almost unrecognizable. But lest I run off at the mouth, let me conclude by saying that if the Academy of ill-voted Oscars doesn't give you a multitude of awards in 1969, I will resign from humanity and become a soldier.

Harvey Laser
Palos Verdes Estates, California

May I offer my congratulations for a marvelous picture. Once again you have given us all something to aim at.

Richard Lester
Twickenham Film Studios
Middlesex, England

For the life of me, I cannot understand why the critics (all of which I read when they reviewed the film) haven't stood up and shouted with enthusiasm in their reviews. Sadly, I have come to the conclusion that for so many years films were made for the 12-year-old mind that at last, alas, our critics have emerged with 12-year-old minds. Pity.

A.R. Munnerlyn
New York City

I would like to find out where I can get a spacesuit similar to the one the stewardess wore in *2001*.

Martha Billy
Chattanooga, Tennessee

I just wanted to drop you a note to tell you that my wife and I saw your picture last night, and we were both knocked out by it. It's a fantastic film, and I use that word very deliberately.

Are you going to take a rest, or are you ready for your next picture? We've got a tremendous project that I'd love to talk to you about.

Samuel W. Gelfman
United Artists Corp.
New York City

I have enclosed reviews and publicity material from my appearance at the Maisonette of the St. Regis recently completed.

During my engagement at the Maisonette, I appeared on the *Johnny Carson Show*. Also *To Tell the Truth, Joe Franklin, New Yorker's Metromedia, Cleveland Amory Show*. I am set for the *Merv Griffin Show* September ninth. I also have had a great deal of syndicated nationwide newspaper publicity in connection with my appearance at the Maisonette.

I would very much appreciate your considering me for any casting which you might be contemplating. I would like very much to meet and talk with you at your convenience.

> *Wynne Miller*
> *New York City*

Don't be disappointed by the reviews the film got in New York. No matter how good a picture is, there will be someone who will not like it. I suppose if God were in a motion picture, some critic would say he was a second-rate actor in a third-rate film.

I have been interested in movies ever since I can remember. I collect stills, read books, magazines, etc., on the subject. As a matter of fact, I spent the last $6 I had in my checking account to get a subscription to *The American Cinematographer*. I am now unemployed. The reason, I think, is evident. I don't enjoy any work that I do because the only work I would like to do is in motion pictures. Photography is my only hobby. I once met Vincent Price backstage in a theater, and he told me what I have known all along. No matter how many cinematography schools you go to, you can't get into the union because it is a closed union.

My ambition, as you may have guessed, is to be in motion pictures. I feel that if you do not help me, I will never get into them. So I ask you now:

1. Please send me stills of *2001*.
2. Give me the names of people who can get me into the union.

Please send me a letter of introduction to the American Society of Cinematographers. In this way, I can attend a cinematography school knowing that I will have a better chance than I ever will have of getting into pictures. I ask for your help so that I can be what I want to be in life.

> *William McQuade*
> *Astoria, New York*

2001 is today. Any film is necessarily not only what it is about, but is about when it was made. The past is the present and the future is the present. Any instant in time is a summation of past, present and future. One effect of the increased sophistication of technology — which, in a way, is what *2001* is all about — is the packaging of experience, the synthesis of experience. Going to an event in person and seeing the same event on television are but two levels of the same reality. However, the television experience is synthetic experience. Muzak is synthetic, packaged music. It's music music. A twenty-four-hour Andy Warhol film is about making a film — it has no beginning, middle and end conceptually. It is not an abstraction of time. Real time equals film time. The same concept is analogous to *2001*. Even though set in the "future," it is edited in such a way to make these "unreal" events "real." Editing in *2001* is not used to abstract a sense of time. That's one reason why so many people find *2001* perplexing. They expect things to be tied up in neat little packages for them to experience. They expect their value judgments to be made for them by the film editor, the critic or anyone else who will do it for them. People are afraid of using their own senses to determine their own reality. Technology will, and has done it for them. Anyway, I flew back from Los Angeles on American Airlines last week. Everything on that flight had to do with passing time, not what it was. The plastic, packaged brunch wasn't about food, but about passing forty-five minutes. The Astrovision film *Buona Sera, Mrs. Campbell* wasn't about itself, but about passing two hours. The two channels of Muzakish music were that much more time to be passed. Flying on a transcontinental jet is one thing that *2001* is all about today. And to be able to catch Leroy Anderson and his hundreds of strings on the "classic" music channel for both take-off and landing (different numbers in each case) was eerie and devastating. It transported me right into the set of *2001* — stereo Leroy Anderson on at full volume, trapped in this capsule orbiting through the sky. It was incredible. *2001* is today.

John S. Margolies
New York City

I. *The Freudian Level*: The deep space probe to Jupiter bears an uncanny resemblance to a DNA or RNA strand. To say the least, it appeared to be a male sperm floating in the uterus (blackness of space), destined to rendezvous with the black slab monolith (the vagina), which when the probe (sperm) approaches, the monolith (vagina) suddenly opens up, causing the probe to travel untold millions of miles to another sun (ova), which the space probe (sperm) fertilizes in the Regency room, thus giving birth to the star-child.

II. *The Religious Level*: I felt it was strongly implied that a Force beyond man's own finiteness was controlling things in the picture. The Ubiquitous Infinite—that is, the source of all creation—appeared quite manifest in three particular scenes: (1) The idea of encountering the slab three times—during the Dawn of Man on Earth, on the Moon at the lunar excavation site at Tycho, and near the planet Jupiter—seemed to connote the idea of the Father, Son, and Holy Ghost trilogy; (2) After Dave Bowman has been thrust through the seemingly infinite chute, there is one scene where seven glowing geometric shapes come into view from off-camera; the idea of the number seven, which is a religious symbol oftentimes linked with God, came to mind; (3) Finally, the number seven appears again, this time inside the space pod in the Regency room, where we see Bowman's eye change color seven times—as if to symbolize a revelation he is undergoing or a particular transformation that is happening to him.

Frank L. Bettger
Los Angeles

I would have to say that, in all honesty, the advertising campaign that preceded this picture was, to say the least, *deceitful*; on my family's part, it was not that much of a let-down, because we were not one of the young children who were tricked into believing that this was a science-fiction epic, while all it was was a deep insight into the creation of the universe.

Julian J. Nussbaum
North Miami Beach, Florida

A letter to Stanley Kubrick's father:

My reason for writing is to let you know my reaction to Stanley's *2001* motion picture which I saw a few weeks ago at the Capitol Theater in Manhattan.

Frankly, people who knew I had purchased tickets told me to get a refund. Even from some who had not seen the picture but were persuaded by some aspects of critics' reviews. Refusing to condemn until my evidence was in, I anticipated the screening.

My conclusion is that the entire picture was marvelous. I've spoken to many people and convinced quite a few to see it.

The first portion should not only be seen by everyone, but is especially indicated for biology and anthropology students. If the transformation from anthropoid to *homo sapiens* (in capsule form) outrages the beliefs of Old Testament fundamentalists, that is too bad. In East Africa, Dr. Leakey and his associates have not only found the osteological evidence, but the tools and the presence, one million years ago, of a passive herbivorous type and an aggressive carnivorous group, living side-by-side. We're presented with a true pictorial lesson in Darwinian evolution.

The second portion, centered on the space station and Moon settlement, is an example of a controlled manipulation of the factor of time. Everyone can grasp the Present. Many, the Past (although here, there are many disputes concerning human and nature events). When we deal with time in the future, the question is: is it fantasy? If the story envisages a situation based upon the hard facts of science, space technology, physics, and astronomy, then we are permitted to say that the future described is a projection, even taking into consideration variables. The Moon car, the spaceman's suit, the rotating space station (with its artificial gravity), were described many years ago by Dr. Hermann Oberth (*Man Into Space*, 1957) whose 1922 doctorate thesis was the subject of space travel. Today, research under NASA has proved the basic correctness of those objects and situations pictured in this segment of *2001*.

The third, and final, portion seems to have aroused most passions amongst viewers. The long journey to Jupiter is based upon astronomical known distance. The required time is based upon projected improvements on propellants, and the reduced thrust need from a space station. The suspended animation, monitoring, the computer (HAL), the airlocks are all based upon hard facts of present performance and research. So all that is left is the descent into Jupiter's atmosphere through corridors of color (from changes in electromagnetic effects upon the ions in that atmosphere — a similar effect noticed by American and Russian astronauts, who have reported profound spectrum changes and effects), and the rapid dying and rebirth of man (in the presence of his symbolic suit — The Space Age) and the rebirth, in space (the ovum), in the presence of the onward and upward influence of his evolutionary intelligence (the Vibrating Metallic Bar).

For those adults who cannot enjoy this picture I must agree with the sage who said: "You cannot place pearls before swine."

Well, Jack, I had to get this off my chest. Sally, Sande, and I often speak of you. I'm a grandfather (2x).

Milton B. Schlenoff, D.C.
Riverdale, New York

2001 is one of the few films that catches, in a very understated way, the ominous irony of present-day trends toward an inhuman society, as well as the metaphysical mystery of the universe, which is as clear to thoughtful atheists as it is to truly religious people. I'm afraid neither one of these two aspects of your film was grasped by so many of the critics. The final triumph of your effort resides, perhaps, in the reaction of my hard-boiled, "sophisticated," 14-year-old son, a typical New Yorker who cannot be moved by anything and recently even succeeded in having forgotten that he had seen *The Bicycle Thief*. He was left absolutely speechless by your film and could not recover for several minutes, and then, on Broadway, proceeded to walk in an uptown direction, although we live downtown, in Greenwich Village. Congratulations.

Amos Vogel
Former Director, Film Department
Lincoln Center for the Performing Arts, Inc.
New York City

I have just seen your *Space Odyssey: 2001*. My wife and I drove fifty miles to see it. During the return trip we tried to discuss calmly what we had seen, but we invariably ended up screaming at each other. Had we lived another fifty miles from the theater we might possibly have worked something out—some sort of conclusion that we could have lived with. *Space Odyssey* cost me $5.00—$2.50 for my wife and $2.50 for me. I think, for my $5.00, I am entitled to some answers. First, let me say that I thoroughly enjoyed most of the first half of the movie. I just naturally dig gadgets of a technological nature, and your movie handled them in a nonchalant manner that I found rather appealing. It was only when you started waving that damn black two-by-four all over the screen that I got a little up-tight, as they say. Being a conservative, I found HAL 9000 a little uppity (sp?).

Ansel H. Smith
Monroe, Louisiana

I'm $15\frac{1}{2}$ years old, going into my junior year at John Browne High School in Flushing, and am what is commonly referred to as a movie nut. But the picture I'm most nuts about is your unprecedented masterpiece, *2001: A Space Odyssey*. I saw it for my first time at the Loew's Capitol Theater in New York, and was thoroughly spellbound by the picture I had waited for for three years. I went back to see it again with my brother, who is in the

Air Force, and he will see it again with one of his buddies next week in Washington, D.C., where he is stationed. Since then, I have written a review of *2001* (highly complimentary, of course), which drew raves from my English teacher and will probably be printed in the school social studies magazine next September. I have bought the souvenir book, the soundtrack album, the personality poster advertisement, and have scores of advertisements from magazines and newspapers. I keep a record of reviews that *2001* has received, mostly from New York publications. I am happy to announce that 33 are excellent, which is much more than the reviews that were not so good. The unfairest review I have seen yet is Kathleen Carroll's atrocity in the *New York Daily News*. I'm thoroughly convinced she has absolutely no idea what she's talking about, and I sometimes wonder if she even *saw* the film. I also keep a record of how much money *2001* makes by reading *Variety* every week. Of course, it does not list every theater the picture is playing at, but from the looks of business from the theaters it does list, *2001* is doing, in *Variety* terms, boffo biz. I intend to see the film at least twice more, and take my father and mother with me, because I'm sure it would be a totally new experience for them. I myself have thought of becoming a film director, and if you could possibly find any time in your busy schedule, do you think you could write me a short letter giving me some tips on how to get started in the business? Before I saw *2001* I wrote two other famous directors, but I did not receive a reply from either of them, probably because of their busy schedules. Enclosed is a copy of my review, which I hope you will find enjoyable. I'm not Bosley Crowther, but I do the best I can. Thank you very much for allowing me to use up so much of your time, but I felt I had to write the man whom I consider my idol, and to let him know that I am just one of many who consider this man the best, most inventive director in the film industry.

Michael Singer
Flushing, New York

Few films ask us to think. Since *2001* did, I felt obliged to let you know that I tried to.

I am told that C.G. Jung found dreams to develop in four acts:

— Introduction
— The plot thickens
— Crisis
— Resolution

2001 is a story structured like a dream.

The four acts are announced not by raising and lowering of a curtain but by the appearance four times of knowledge, embodied as a Duranodic slab, like the apple tree of Genesis a phallic symbol, the phallus being the instrument of primary creation, as is knowledge that of intellectual creation.

Introduction — the first appearance of knowledge and its result; the first tool, a weapon, followed by the entire history of man most beautifully pictured as that weapon (tool) rising in the grandeur of a spaceship.

The plot thickens — an overeducated doctor is congratulated on a completely innocuous speech, and he, in turn, congratulates his colleagues on a discovery which took no more initiative than a dog discovering a bone. Knowledge is turned against them. It deafens them. It overwhelms them. So, to discover its origins, they send a ship, captained by a man of humility, calm under pressure, an artist; in short, a hero. Knowledge on board in the form of a computer tries to thwart him. We are not told until the computer is expurgated that it alone knew the purpose of the mission.

Crisis — the hero (*der Held*) arrives at the point of discovery. As we see from the expression on his face, it is a more terrifying experience than his bout with the computer, for, as *we* discover in the final . . .

Resolution — the discovery is not of some strange new world but of himself; the wisdom of age is his rebirth.

But whose dream is it? Yours, of course, but I think you asked yourself if you were so much different from the rest of us and you decided that you were not and so you made a film.

Frederic P. Lyman
Malibu, California

Mr. Kubrick responded:
Thank you for your fascinating note. You are very perceptive, indeed.

You say in effect that a true artist can't be a transcendentalist. I find you to be both. You are a genius and I also expect to (I hope) brush with you in the starry heavens when we are all reposing on our way to becoming (hopefully, again) the energy and spirit that is, do you think, Nietzsche's superman?

Anna Belle Neal
San Francisco

P.S. It's entities like you that give one that pride in being a human being. Pardon me for climbing aboard your bandwagon!

I am bleary-eyed, because Mrs. Lawrence kept me up half the night talking about *2001*.

Her summation (to synopsize a few thousand words): 1) magnificent entertainment, 2) so excitingly thought-provoking.

In discussing the philosophy of the film, she kept repeating, "The beginning is the end, and the end is the beginning."

As a serious, considered analysis, based on thirty-three years in the M-G-M publicity department, I know *2001* will be a blockbuster, one of the most talked-about pictures of many years, and that word-of-mouth will be a tremendous stimulus to the box office for months to come.

> *Edward Lawrence*
> *Los Angeles*

I enjoyed seeing a scientifically accurate description of space life and computers of the future. However, one thing did escape me (as it did all of my friends, many of whom have doctor of philosophy degrees)—the plot. Was there one?

> *Virginia M. Dominick*
> *Cambridge, Massachusetts*

I saw your film and just wanted you to know how beautiful and exciting I found it. Apparently most everybody else does, too, even those few who worry about your ending. For me it was a fascinating, breathtaking experience.

> *Saul Bass*
> *Los Angeles*

I was so impressed, so overwhelmed, so caught-up, so thrilled, so wide-eyed and unable to sleep, so very lifted by *2001: A Space Odyssey*, that I couldn't get over it this morning. It was the most beautiful picture I have ever seen. So beautiful, I nearly drove everyone out of his mind talking about it. Also, so inspired was I, that I wrote the following poem. Movies were created to weave great gossamer traps for the mind to get lost in, but you have created something more beautiful, and I shall leave it at that.

> *Robinson Stockham*
> [*pseudonym for Miss Linda J. Stockham*]
> *Los Angeles*

BEYOND OUR RAINBOWS
(By Miss Stockham)

If the ape had never stood,
Nor the eagle ever soared,
What caves of this world
Would dreams lay dormant in?

If fountains had never weeped,
Nor winds ever blown,
What parched lands of this earth
Would seeds lay still in?

> What fraile creatures;
> What fragile flowers;
> What forlorn valleys
> Would have been lost to nothing,
> If hope had not spermed
> The greater depths
> Of our savage hearts,
> And lifted our souls to the light?

> Who is to know
> But that infinite power
> That lies so far
> Beyond our rainbows.

If meteors had never bruised the sky,
And with red flaming mouths,
Never sought the earth with alien teeth,
Would we have ever known of their existence?

If vapors had never floated on summer airs,
And with casual grace gone to oblivion,
Would we have wondered at our own end,
And at the same time, our initial beginning?

> What fraile creatures;
> What fragile flowers;
> What forlorn valleys
> Would have been lost to nothing,
> If hope had not spermed
> The greater depths
> Of our savage hearts,
> And lifted our souls to the light?

> Who is to know
> But that infinite power
> That lies so far
> Beyond our rainbows.

My reason for writing is to make a rather unusual request. I am at present in the process of decorating my office, and I was very much interested in the "space scenes" in the motion picture. I wonder if it would be possible to get pictures of the "space station" and "moonscape" scenes in the picture. I would prefer 8 × 10 glossy prints, but, as I can have photographs reproduced, I would also be interested in smaller prints, color negatives, or mounted or unmounted slides and film cuttings. Quality lithographed color photographs would also be most welcome.

                                        John H. Lindorfer
                                        Dayton, Ohio

What makes the film provocative is not only because it is like a bolt of lightning in the dark. It is unsettling because of what it illuminates. By soft-pedaling the familiar narrative method that is easily digestible, demonstrable, and arguable, you have produced an unconventional probe of the human condition. As a result, it is as much a tableau of inner space as it is of outer space. It is an abrasive work of modern art that appeals to the eye, the intellect, and the viscera. Like any good poet, you work on the contradictions of the theme. The characters, presumably so far advanced technically, resemble computers. The cold, hard-veined symmetry of outer space accurately mirrors their own barren interiors. How incredibly intelligent is man that he can plummet himself to the stars, and yet how mindless when he programs his own machinery with hatred. Without love, the essential ingredient, the whole show is no more than an Indian rope trick. After having deprived himself of the supports both of myth and religion, modern man puts all his energies into his machinery and finds he has hung himself out on a limb . . . or a spacecraft. If nothing else, the movie prods into life the intuitive conviction that man, himself, is the greatest unknown.

                                        John J. Fox
                                        Brooklyn, New York

It is, at least to me, the first movie to be a true art form. It is one of the few truths I have experienced in my lifetime that has left such a strong impression. I mean *more* than an impression — it is constantly on my mind and has loosened some of my prejudices.

I know that we are incapable of conceiving beyond our world. Maybe we are afraid to and need the security of making everything relate to our small world and small capabilities. I think this shows in our inventions throughout history; for instance, to invent the calendar and the clock when there is no time.

Your movie has given me *many* moments which I seek out in my life — moments of feeling alive.

After your movie, one thought kept coming back into my mind. It is one that I have had many times but which seemed more clear than ever now; how many times must I be born to realize what I am?

> *Solomon Rothman*
> *Leonia, New Jersey*

I know you must think a boy, 14 years old, must be crazy to write a letter to a big producer such as you, but I had to express my thoughts about your recent film. I thought it was great! It's about time somebody made a film about the true science fiction of today. After a while, you get sick of seeing nothing but giant monsters from outer space. It was great. It's been seven weeks since I saw your movie, and I remember the film as well as I know the hangnails on my fingers. Course you know what the critics said. Well, I say down with the critics. They're about as dependable as the Nielsen ratings on television. I thought *2001* was the best film I've seen in the past three years. Please send me some reply from yourself. I get sick from seeing pre-answered letters. They resemble so closely to bills. Also — are you ready for the pitch? Would it be possible for a poor kid to get ahold of some of those great posters of the film?

> *Kim Ellison*
> *Hayward, California*

P.S. Just to see if it's possible to get a letter like this to a producer such as yourself, please write me as soon as possible.

My husband and I are amateur moviemakers, and we have decided to have a star-child in our next movie. But we haven't figured out how to make a star-child and to show it moving, as you did. Could you tell us how to create a star-child? HOLD ON. A GREAT IDEA. If I send you a picture of myself as a baby — I play the star-child, of course — could you find a few moments in your spare time to film a sequence for us? Can't *Napoleon* wait another day?

> *[Name withheld]*

Stanley Kubrick is telling us that man's intelligence is a tool-making intelligence, and that tools take precedence over man. (Even language, which has been considered our highest achievement, is a tool. It is not accidental that there are only forty-three minutes of non-dialogue in this three-hour movie. As we become more and more involved with electronic technology and gadgetry, there will be less and less involvement with language, at least language as we know it.) As to the question of what we are doing with this tool-making intelligence, it would seem Kubrick is telling us we are getting nowhere fast. (I happened to see this movie in Manhattan Island, which is an old, dirty, broken-down tool where the poor people, who allow it, go in circles and dehumanize themselves.)

Kubrick has given us a big, expensive, spectacular joke, and also something of a tragedy, in which man's intelligence, potentially great, is up to nothing.

Kubrick's dissolve from the tool-bone thrown in the sky to a space station in *2001* is not beside the point. Thousands of years of human history were skipped, as if man has not been up to anything except finally making these giant space tools. (IBM will also do away with human history, and humanity may be dismissed in favor of junk.) Not only history, but what happened to language? There is none in the movie. Are we being told language is not important? Perhaps it is not. Most people I know use it only for rudimentary forms of communication, such as "Where is the bathroom?" "I love you," but my cat is just as effective in communicating in spite of his speechlessness. It is said we use language to educate and carry on traditions, but much education is only information, and our traditions are invariably on collision courses. We get propaganda and polemics rather than reasoning. A verbal man such as Stanley Kauffmann has programmed himself to be a reviewer, and, though he has a good movie to verbalize about, he only cranks out a non-review in which he is hung upon words such as *amusing* and *dull*. Except for a few poets who have thrilled us, a few novelists and essayists who may have told us something about our conditions, and a handful of philosophers who have looked into the errors of our forms of knowledge, and versifiers who write the likes of "Daisy, Daisy" to please us, we really have not put language to much use.

Kubrick's fine *2001* seems to be telling us all this. At the end of it, after the mission (our mission) has failed utterly, we see a large, white fetus returning to view the Earth, its oversized eyes almost angelic. How glad we are to be back — and as a little child. Could it be the best thing we have going for us is our infant intelligence, which wonders at the sights, sounds, and touch of the world? We are as children. For us, there may be nothing else.

Truman Brewster
Los Angeles

Ten years ago—when I was sixteen and just beginning to discover the rather splendid world of "serious" music—a friend of mine came dashing into my house with a record album and demanded that I ". . . listen to this!" Patiently, but firmly, I explained to my friend that I was going out soon and could not possibly listen to the entire album. Too late. My friend had placed his record on my turntable and was adjusting the volume on my amplifier. I heard the low, ominous rumbling—the sudden, intensely dramatic pronouncement of a horn—the utter exaltation that is the opening of Richard Strauss' *Thus Spake Zarathustra*.

Ten days ago I was with that same friend and we were listening to that same opening—but this time it was music with sight added—a vision as brilliant as the music—and twice as elative.

I must confess to a feeling of something akin to intimidation—to think that these words might be read by the man responsible for *2001: A Space Odyssey*. I have been an avid and intelligent devotee of motion pictures for almost twenty years—I started early—and I must admit that after leaving the theater showing *2001* I had the definite impression that for the first time in my life I had truly seen a "motion picture." I think that perhaps a hundred years from now people will look back upon those of us who were able to see *2001* with the same awe and envy that I experience when I think of the people who were able to see the first performance of Wagner's *Ring* or Mahler's *Third Symphony*.

In short—I thought *2001* was magnificent. I thought that the implications of *2001* were monumental.

I found *2001* to be your most optimistic film to date. With the exception of *Lolita*, I have enjoyed all of your previous films immensely. It would be difficult to pick my favorite among *The Killing, Paths of Glory*, and *Spartacus*. *Dr. Strangelove* was very depressing—almost as depressing as *2001* was elative. In pondering your films, I find that *Spartacus* was the least stylistic. In fact, in light of *2001*, *Spartacus* becomes somewhat of an enigma. *Spartacus* seems an almost average picture from a man who makes above-average films. However, its "averageness" did not prevent me from seeing it six times. I am speaking of style, because *2001* was so completely stylistic—that is to say, it is the only motion picture ever made that so utterly bears the mark of a single man—of a single mind. Every other motion picture can lead to the speculations—"I wonder what it would have been like if . . . David Lean . . . or William Wyler . . . or . . . Robert Wise had directed it?" That sort of speculation is impossible—and unthinkable—with *2001*.

It is a film of incredible and irrevocable splendor.

Now, on to the implications. For one thing, *2001* has—as no other film ever has—elevated the artistic potentiality of motion pictures to a hitherto undreamed-of level. In a sense, you have not only said "It can be done!" . . . you have "done it!" *2001* does not mark the growth of the art of the cinema; it is the birth of the cinema. People can honestly say that they have never seen anything like it—simply because there never has been anything like *2001*. Ah, but you must know that much better than I!

The major implication inherent in *2001* takes place within the first ninety (?) seconds. Had I not already thought of this implication, I would quite probably now be confined in a rest home suffering from an "elation-caused insanity." About 18 months ago I had an idea. I was thinking about the potentiality of home videotape recorders. It seemed to me that when the day came when HVTRs were available to the general public that there would be a lucrative market for prerecorded videotapes, in much the same way that records and prerecorded stereophonic tapes constitute a lucrative market today. I then thought of the possibilities for the content of these prerecorded VTs. Starting with rock-and-roll, I worked my way up to absolute music. "What if," I thought, "someone wanted to 'see' Beethoven's *Ninth Symphony*?" Would you show them an orchestra and chorus? Or what? Then I thought: "What if someone 'filmed music'?" Then I thought: "What if *I* filmed music?" To make a long story shorter, I then proceeded to read a number of books on photography, buy a small, almost ludicrous super-8mm camera, and put my abstract idea into concrete form. I went out and "filmed" the third movement of Gustav Mahler's *Seventh Symphony*. It worked! It worked beautifully. I was fully aware that I was a rank amateur using a primitive camera that did not even have reflex viewing, and yet upon viewing the final results— about five hours' cutting time was required on my little Sears, Roebuck & Co. editor—I knew beyond any doubt that it worked. Until seeing *2001* I had always thought of filming music in terms of objects existing "naturally" in reality. But it is doubtful that ever in my own lifetime will I be able to "shoot" a natural scene involving three planets. I knew instantly that you had too much reverence for Richard Strauss to tamper with the score— which meant that you had to put the film to the music—and you did—three times!

I have since done a great deal of thinking—and preparing—

about "filmed" music. I have gone so far as to envision a day when there will exist a new kind of artist who is both composer and photographer and who will bring about a new form of art. But that day, I think, is a long way off, but maybe by the year 2001 . . .

I am currently directing my thinking and my mental and financial resources toward the production of several complete symphonies. If I succeed, you will no doubt hear of — or from — me. I would like to succeed if for no other reason than to pay you back for *2001* — to cause you as much elation with my creativeness as you have caused me with yours.

Finally, I would like to comment on some of the aspects of *2001*. My favorite scene is the discovering of the "tool" by the simian. It is the most heroic sequence I have ever encountered. Just the scene alone would have been brilliant — but to show the scene with the music of Strauss was the proverbial "frosting" on the cinematic cake. Also, the changing of the "tool" into a spaceship was brilliant. I was particularly taken with the entire opening sequence — from the glowing eyes of the tiger (?) to that haunting night sequence when the ape-men crowd together for warmth and for the atavistic sense of security such bodily contact must have represented. However, the most devastating part of that scene was the close-up of the eyes — those human, frightened eyes realizing even then that their security was a collective illusion and that the night was fraught with individual danger.

I found the obelisk — slab, or whatever — to be a masterstroke of a leitmotif — especially with Ligeti's voices. And the shots of the obelisk and the sun were hauntingly powerful. The space sequences were, of course, exquisite. After the show, some friends and I debated the "why" of your use of the Strauss waltz. I advanced the theory that several centuries ago three-quarter time was referred to as "perfect time," and that you thought this best described the motion of the universe and man-made objects attempting to imitate and/or conquer that universe. Your incredible sense of humor was particularly noticeable a number of times, but especially in two scenes. In the opening, when one of the simians looks full-face at the camera and growls, and in HAL's rather laconic comment, "I know I've made a number of poor decisions recently . . ." Too much!

At the end of the motion picture, when your name appeared on the screen, I broke into wild applause. The rest of the audience finally caught on, but I must say I was rather disappointed in them. Did they think the film just came into existence? I hope by my applause I made them aware that for the last three hours they had been watching the work of a brilliant man possessing a brilliant mind. I am led to believe that perhaps a number of people don't deserve to see *2001*. But that is a moral issue I shan't go into at this time.

In conclusion, Mr. Kubrick, I thank you for reading my letter and—for ever and ever—I thank you for making *2001*. I believe that art is a psychological necessity for man—a provider of emotional fuel and mental food. And *2001* has appeared at a time when most artists are poisoning their audiences with anti-art and anti-heroes.

I would not be at all afraid to state that with *2001* you may have quite possibly saved any number of spiritual and physical lives. For it is within the power of a film such as yours to give people a reason to go on living—to give them the courage to go on living. For *2001* implies much more than just an artistic revelation. On a philosophical level, it implies that if man is capable of this, he is capable of anything—anything rational and heroic and glorious and good. Think of how many men and women might very possibly thrust off the shackles of the monotonous stagnation of their day-to-day existence—how many might strive to reach goals they thought impossible before—how many might find elation and pleasure hitherto denied them by their own lack of courage. How can man now be content to consider the trivial and mundane, when you have shown them a world full of stars, a world beyond the infinite?

Stephen Grosscup
Santa Monica, California

Mr. Kubrick responded:
Your letter of 4th May was overwhelming. What can I say in reply?

"Perhaps I'm just projecting my own concern about it."

For eighteen months, Frederick I. Ordway served as scientific and technical consultant on 2001. Ordway was educated in astronomy and the geosciences at Harvard University. Performed two years' graduate work at the Upper Atmosphere Physics Laboratory, Faculty of Sciences, University of Paris. Performed additional graduate work at the universities of Barcelona, Algiers, Innsbruck, and U.S. Air University. He is senior research scientist at the University of Alabama Research Institute, adjacent to NASA's George C. Marshall Space Flight Center, Huntsville. He is president of General Astronautics Research Corp. and vice president of International Space Museum and Gallery. He is the author or co-author of many books, including Intelligence in the Universe, Life in Other Solar Systems, Careers in Rocketry and Astronautics, *and* L'Histoire Mondiale d'Astronautique.

Frederick I. Ordway

MY ASSOCIATION with the film and with Stanley Kubrick was perhaps the most unplanned major project in my life. It all began in January, 1965, on an extended trip to the Northeast from Huntsville. On the 20th, I attended the Inaugural Ball of President Lyndon B. Johnson, and on the 21st was in Philadelphia attending meetings at the Franklin Institute. The next day I reached New York and lunched with Paul Mathias, New York bureau chief of *Paris Match*; Leland Hayward, the Broadway producer; and Maria Cooper, daughter of Gary Cooper, who is married to pianist Byron Janis. In the afternoon, I rang Arthur C. Clarke, an old friend of mine, and asked him to join Harry Lange and me for drinks at the Harvard Club on 44th Street. During the course of conversations, Clarke related to us that he had been approached by Stanley Kubrick with the view of coming up with a screenplay dealing with the general theme of extra-solar (beyond the solar system) intelligence. I had never heard of Stanley Kubrick and was unaware of his stature as a film-

Frederick I. Ordway, Kubrick aide, in cockpit of simulated spacecraft.

maker, and therefore, my first reaction was that Arthur's ideas would not come across well on the screen. I recall saying to Arthur that "You have your extrasolar project, and we have ours," and then telling him about the MacGowan-Ordway book, *Intelligence in the Universe*, then in an advanced state of preparation; Harry Lange had done all the artwork for it, and the manuscript, or at least most of it, was already in the hands of Prentice-Hall, the publisher.

About 8 P.M. we bade good-bye to Arthur and went upstairs to get our topcoats to go out to a dinner party on Park Avenue. It was snowing hard, and we had a bit of trouble getting a cab. While we were waiting in front of the club, the doorman called me and said there was a telephone call. I went in, and discovered to my great surprise that Stanley Kubrick was calling. Arthur had rung him and spoken to him of Harry and me, and obviously raised his interest. We discussed a whole gamut of problems of relating to intelligence beyond our solar system, my experience with NASA on advanced Mars exploration craft, and so on. He asked if Harry Lange and I could meet him at his penthouse the next day with Arthur, which we subsequently did.

I soon discovered that Kubrick had read voraciously on the subjects of science fiction and space science and technology, and had developed quite a lingo—he would often surprise me with a new acquisition. He would often suggest a "systems" approach to this or that problem, ask for parameters, and state that he had just "locked on" to an idea. He was particularly fascinated with computers of the voice input-output type, and would talk about logic elements, neural nets, central processors, integrated computer networks, heuristic systems, etc.

On the 5th of August, 1965, shortly after making a whirlwind trip to Minneapolis, Chicago, and Philadelphia on behalf of the film, my family and I departed with dozens of trunks full of drawings and technical data for England and production of *2001*.

Ordway advice to Kubrick after the film was released:

1. The "Dawn of Man" scene should be shortened, and above all *narrated*. The importance of this cannot be overemphasized. No one with whom I talked understood the real meaning of this visually beautiful and deeply significant sequence. Its intended impact was lost. Certainly, some reviewers, aided by press releases and Arthur Clarke's lucid comments, knew what it was all about, but the audience doesn't. And the audience not only has a right but a need to know, if the sequence is to have relevance.

Go back to the splendid words of narration:

> The remorseless drought had lasted now for ten
> million years, and would not end for another million.
> The reign of the terrible lizards had long since
> passed, but here on the continent which would one
> day be known as Africa, the battle for survival had
> reached a new climax of ferocity, and the victor was
> not yet in sight. In this dry and barren land, only the
> small or the swift or the fierce could flourish, or even
> hope to exist. The man-apes of the field had none of
> these attributes, and they were on the long, pathetic
> road to racial extinction.

The sequence now has real meaning. We are concerned with nothing less than racial extinction, the end of a line that eventually evolved into man. The audience cannot help but identify itself with this struggle for survival, and feel haunting rapport with these primitive creatures across the awesome chasm of time.

Narration is also essential to cast Moon-Watcher into a mold of reality.

> As he looks out now upon the hostile world, there is
> already something in his gaze beyond the capacity
> of any ape. In those dark, deep-set eyes is a dawning
> awareness—the first intimations of an intelligence
> that would not fulfill itself for another four million years.

Narration can also reveal that the man-apes were starving in the midst of plenty because they had not yet learned to consume meat. After the artifact appears, they mysteriously learn—or rather, are taught—to use bone weapons and to eat the animals they soon will slaughter. The narrator's words softly tell us:

> They have no conscious memory of what they had seen; but that night, as he sits brooding at the entrance of his lair, his ears attuned to the noises of the world around him, Moon-Watcher feels the first twinges of a new and potent emotion—the urge to kill. He has taken his first step toward humanity.

The terminal narration of the "Dawn of Man" sequence leads to anticipation. As he throws the bone, his new weapon, up and down, Moon-Watcher thinks:

> Now he was the master of the world, and he was not sure what to do next. But he would think of something.

2. Without warning, we cut to the orbiting bombs. And to a short, introductory narration, missing in the present version.

3. The Orion III sequences are satisfactory and the Space Station-V portion came through well, though I was disappointed that the picturephone automated information request scene was deleted. The Aries-IB scenes were good as far as they went, but their effectiveness was lost by the deletion of (1) narration at the beginning (only a few lines are necessary), (2) the delightful dialogue between the stewardess, captain, and copilot, (3) the brief dialogue between the captain and Floyd, and (4) the following narration for the landing sequence:

> The laws of Earthly aesthetics did not apply here; this world had been shaped and molded by other than terrestrial forces, operating over eons of time unknown to the young, verdant Earth, with its fleeting ice-ages, its swiftly rising and falling seas, its mountain ranges dissolving like mists before dawn. Here was age inconceivable—but not death, for the Moon had never lived until now.

4. Consider what was lost after the TMA-1 artifact emitted its burst of electromagnetic energy:

> Radiation detectors analyzed incoming cosmic rays from the galaxy and points beyond . . . gusts and hurricanes of the solar winds, as the sun breathed

million-mile-an-hour blasts of plasma into the faces
of its circling children . . . but now a deep-space
monitoring probe had noted something strange . . .
the faint yet unmistakable disturbance rippling
across the solar system, and quite unlike any
natural phenomena it had ever observed in the past.

With these missing, but available, pieces, the great symphony becomes coherent. In an age of super science, of incredible information-processing and display devices, of computer-assisted thinking and delicately tuned responses, nothing less than total understanding can be tolerated. We are now on the Discovery midway between Earth and Jupiter. And the audience must know why. Fuzzy thinking, incomplete explanations, lost coupling scenes, missing bits of essential information have no place in *2001*.

5. I was fairly content with the Discovery portion of the film, but only fairly. Impressive though it was, there is too much exercising around the centrifuge for Poole, and the pod EVA sequences could be shortened—particularly since there are two of them. Indispensable dialogue regarding the three hibernating astronauts was lacking; see particularly C12, where Bowman and Poole first become aware that "there is something about the mission the sleeping beauties know and that we don't know. . . ." These few words are probably the most critical to the logic structure of the entire film, and lead to a valid reason why HAL breaks down. Yet they were inexplicably cut out. Poole tells HAL that there is

something about this mission that we weren't told.
Something the rest of the crew know and that you
know. We would like to know whether this is true.

HAL enigmatically answers:

I'm sorry, Frank, but I don't think I can answer that
question without knowing everything that all of you
know.

Several pages of superb and absolutely required dialogue follow, without which nothing that happens later can make much sense.

From the moment HAL reports the failure of the antenna's azimuth control unit, the film progresses well, but because of unfortunate cutting of key preceding material, much is lost to even the most perceptive members of the audience. It's like a marvelously complicated and beautiful puzzle that has taken years to prepare. Yet, when one sits down to put it together, one finds that many of the pieces are missing. There is nothing striking, intellectually or visually, about gaping empty spaces where gaping empty spaces don't belong.

6. Another point. The dialogue by Simonson, over the mission control circuit in C148, and that of Floyd in C150, must be reinserted as applicable to the revised script. And the narration in D1. With it, the interstellar sequence can proceed without change, but will mean so much more to the viewers when they see the mysterious artifact once again:

> For four million years, it had circled Jupiter,
> awaiting a moment of destiny that might never
> come. Now, the long wait was ending. On yet
> another world intelligence had been born and was
> escaping from its planetary cradle. An ancient
> experiment was about to reach its climax.

Alex North
FILM COMPOSER

I was living in the Chelsea Hotel in New York (where Arthur Clarke was living) and got a phone call from Kubrick from London asking me of my availability to come over and do a score for *2001*. He told me that I was the film composer he most respected, and he looked forward to working together. I was ecstatic at the idea of working with Kubrick again (*Spartacus* was an extremely exciting experience for me), as I regard Kubrick as the most gifted of the younger-generation directors, and that goes for the older as well. And to do a film score where there were about twenty-five minutes of dialogue and no sound effects! What a dreamy assignment, after *Who's Afraid of Virginia Woolf?*, loaded with dialogue.

I flew over to London for two days in early December to discuss music with Kubrick. He was direct and honest with me concerning his desire to retain some of the "temporary" music tracks which he had been using for the past years. I realized that he liked these tracks, but I couldn't accept the idea of composing part of the score interpolated with other composers. I felt I could compose music that had the ingredients and essence of what Kubrick wanted and give it a consistency and homogeneity and contemporary feel. In any case, I returned to London December 24th [1967] to start work for recording on January 1, after having seen and discussed the first hour of film for scoring.

Kubrick arranged a magnificent apartment for me on the Chelsea Embankment, and furnished me with all the things to make me happy: record player, tape machine, good records, etc. I worked day and night to meet the first recording date, but with the stress and strain, I came down with muscle spasms and back trouble. I had to go to the recording in an ambulance, and the man who helped me with the orchestration, Henry Brant, conducted while I was in the control room. Kubrick was present, in and out; he was pressured for time as well. He made very good suggestions, musically. I had written two sequences for the opening, and he was definitely favorable to one, which was my favorite as well. So I assumed all was going well, what with his participation and interest in the recording. But somehow I had the hunch that whatever I wrote to supplant Strauss' *Zarathustra* would not satisfy Kubrick, even though I used the same structure but brought it up to date in idiom and dramatic punch. Also, how could I compete with Mendelssohn's Scherzo from *Midsummer Night's Dream*? Well, I thought I did pretty damned well in that respect.

In any case, after having composed and recorded over forty minutes of music in those two weeks, I waited around for the opportunity to look at the balance of the film, spot the music, etc. During that period I was rewriting some of the stuff that I was not completely satisfied with, and Kubrick even suggested over the phone certain changes that I could make in the subsequent recording. After eleven tense days of waiting to see more film in order to record in early February, I received word from Kubrick that no more score was necessary, that he was going to use breathing effects for the remainder of the film. It was all very strange, and I thought perhaps I would still be called upon to compose more music; I even suggested to Kubrick that I could do whatever necessary back in L.A. at the M-G-M studios. Nothing happened. I went to a screening in New York, and there were most of the "temporary" tracks.

Well, what can I say? It was a great, frustrating experience, and despite the mixed reaction to the music, I think the Victorian approach with mid-European overtones was just not in keeping with the brilliant concept of Clarke and Kubrick.

Con Pederson
SPECIAL PHOTOGRAPHIC EFFECTS SUPERVISOR

I'll always feel we might have done one more major thing. A lot of time went into a section of the book that would have explained a good deal of the film—the history of the extraterres-

trials and their blocks, their wonderful machines. I spent several
months designing some possible visual material for this; Stanley
was keen for portraying their story, and he talked about what
magical things may lie beyond our ken. It was not to be; it could
have been too much. We did do a few of the things, and they
filtered into the collection of "trip" scenes, but as a cohesive
sequence, again relying on narration, it was too much to cope
with. Well, it would have added about ten minutes — one reel —
but the work to make it credible . . . who knows? If you read the
novel, you'll sense the obstacles of just making the scenes more
than *Star Trek*. It is almost as hard to portray the alien world
as the alien himself, because the audience is less prepared to
accept it in a highly literal but non-story-oriented (a contradiction, really) form. If the styles were more impressionistic, one
might get away with it. Nothing — but nothing — has ever been
produced in a science-fiction movie that is an artfully done,
beautifully alien world or alien being. Not even remotely. I
think they're trying to tell us something out there.

But what *has* been done, and has worked, and has really produced emotional responses is the clever use of the ordinary, the
commonplace. Even H.G. Wells, in *The Time Machine*, de-
scribes the most distant point in the future in terms that relate
to a very mundane situation — and one could visualize it working in a film as well as in words: the empty, desolate beach and
the gigantic crustaceans grubbing around. Our minds respond
to familiar events and use our own images to build on. I think,
to be successful, it is wise for a maker of this kind of picture to
be prudent in selecting imagery. Stanley certainly was.

"Affirmative, Dave. I read you."

KUBRICK: *"Margaret Stackhouse's speculations on the film are perhaps the most intelligent that I've read anywhere, and I am, of course, including all the reviews and the articles that have appeared on the film and the many hundreds of letters that I have received. What a first-rate intelligence!"*

Miss Stackhouse was a junior at North Plainfield (N. J.) High School and 17 years old when she wrote her reflections on *2001*. She is "primarily interested in science and mathematics. However, I don't wish to limit myself when there are so many other fascinating fields to explore: psychology, art, music, philosophy, history, anthropology, political science, literature, education, languages, etc. I may decide to go into nuclear physics or abstract (pure) math, or I may make a study of the mind. I would like to try to find the relationships, if any, in the physical, emotional, and spiritual levels of the mind. (For example, are there any biochemical bases for the 'soul'?) My major concern at this stage is to find a challenge — only then can I discover my intellectual, social, and spiritual identity. The most outstanding people I have ever known have a basic self-assurance that has enabled them to live life fully and zestfully. This type of living is my goal." Miss Stackhouse is in the Princeton University class of 1974.

Miss Stackhouse's reflections on *2001* were forwarded to Kubrick by David Alpert, of the science department, North Plainfield High School.

Margaret Stackhouse

I. *The monolith* — source of infinite knowledge and intelligence

  A. Perfection represented in its shape; its color — black — could symbolize:
    1. Evil and death, which result from man's misuse of knowledge;
    2. The *incomprehensible* — man, with his limited senses, cannot comprehend the absence (perfect black) of color or light.

  B. Its first appearance.
    1. Movie implies that life has reached the stage when it is ready for inspiration, a divine gift, perhaps. [It is interesting that the apes are expectant, waiting for something.]

2. Maybe apes become men when this inspiration is given. [Question: Is man really a separate entity, with something (soul?) that no other form of life possesses, or is the difference merely in quantity (rather than quality) of intelligence? Is the evolution gradual and continuous or in defined levels? Does the difference in quantity become in fact this difference in quality?]

3. Inspiration is given:
   a. When men (apes) need it; or,
   b. When they seek it; or,
   c. At the whim of the force giving the gift; or,
   d. In various combinations of these three.

4. The purpose of the gift may be to allow man to create life-sustaining forces. [In this "cycle," he creates only death; interesting — death from death (bones).]

5. Its disappearance (after weapon is made) — Reasons:
   a. It is taken away in punishment for misuse of knowledge; or,
   b. It is no longer sought — apes (men) consider themselves masters now and try to continue on their own energies after the initial impulse. Maybe the monolith is always present, but is invisible to those who don't wish to see it or to whom it does not wish to be visible; or,
   c. It is taken away by the force that gave it, to prevent mortal understanding of everything.

C. Its second appearance (on Moon).

1. Reasons for appearance:
   a. Man is subconsciously seeking it again; or,
   b. It is needed to remind him of his insignificance; or,
   c. It is given as a new opportunity to create a meaningful existence for humanity.

2. Men on Moon touch monolith in the same way that the apes did — this indicates no basic change in man's nature. Then, after touching it, they have the audacity to try to take photo — still conceited, still lacking in understanding of the gift.

3. From Moon, there is a strong magnetic field directed toward Jupiter (this is where man will go next). This indicates that man will still fail and will need monolith again when he reaches the next stage of exploration. Monolith is always beyond human scope — man is still reaching at death.

4. It is ironic that men on Moon believe that the monolith was made by a more advanced civilization. This to them is the ultimate — they can't comprehend that anything could be above the mortal level.

  D. The monolith and infinity.
   1. After HAL is made, man shows that once again he has refused, through ignorance and conceit, to take advantage of the chance to obtain superhuman intelligence. Maybe the system is slowing down and it is impossible for man to progress any further on his own energies.
   2. Now he is given another chance — the monolith shows him infinity, perfect knowledge, and the beginning of the universe, but he can't comprehend it. Reasons for his being shown all this:
     a. It may be truly another chance for man; or,
     b. It may already be determined that he must die [maybe all people are shown perfect knowledge at death]; or,
     c. Maybe perfect knowledge (represented by monolith) is always present, but our understanding of it will always be imperfect.

II. *HAL*

  A. He is evil, but only because he reflects human nature.

  B. His uneasiness about the mission implies that even the highest development of human intelligence is imperfect in ability to understand.

  C. Man, trying to progress independently of divine aid, attempts, either consciously or unconsciously, to create life, in the form of HAL. This is not allowed. Man is reaching, or is being forced to reach, a limit in his ability to progress further.

  D. Reasons for HAL's failure:
   1. Eternal human error once again in evidence; or,
   2. This may be a divine punishment; or,
   3. God will not allow man to become subordinate to his own foolish creations.

  E. The fact that man can overcome HAL's evil is optimistic; however, to do this he must destroy HAL, who is nearly a living being — again, the theme of death, futility. [This and triviality are shown in HAL's "song."]

III. *The room* (at end)

  A. It is elegant, maybe to show man's cultural achievements, but it is sterile and silent — nothing has meaning without the spirit of the monolith. This is man's universe, that with which he is supposedly familiar, but even this is hostile to him.

B. Room could represent:
1. All that man can comprehend (finite) of infinity. Even in this limited scope, he is confused; or,
2. Man's cultural history, as men remember their past before they die; or,
3. The trivia for which he relinquished the monolith (then at death he realizes his need for it); or,
4. A reminder of man's failure to draw on past—it could contain more wisdom than the present. [Monkeys responded to the monolith better than modern man—race is slowly degenerating.]

C. In this room, man must die, because:
1. He has reached his limit; or,
2. He has failed too much; or,
3. He has been shown infinity.

D. Question: Is his death (following degeneration) inevitable after being shown all knowledge, or is this experience still another chance to improve? Then, when man returns to trivia, perhaps this is the breaking point, the end of his opportunities.

E. Maybe he knows what is happening to him but is powerless to change it. The changes in the man may be a vision shown to him as punishment, or they may merely represent the various stages in the life of one man or of all men.

IV. *The themes*

A. Animalism and human failure
1. Throughout picture, there is constant eating, made to appear revolting; also, exercising, wrestling.
2. At end, goblet is broken. This may imply that man's failures will continue forever.
3. Animal nature and conceit remain the same throughout. Will there never be any true progress? The monolith is always shown with sunrise and crescent. When first seen, this is a sign of hope, of a beginning; but the sun is never any higher except when man is shown infinity. This last fact may symbolize hope that, despite all his past failures, man will ultimately rise above animalism; or it

may merely represent the perfect knowledge he cannot comprehend.
4. There is a delicate balance between the animal and divine nature in man. We will never be permitted to go beyond a certain point (as individuals and as a race).

B. Futility
  1. It is shown:
     a. In the rescue and subsequent release of Frank (after the struggle to catch him);
     b. In the meaningless talk—"People talking without speaking."
  2. Is all that we do in vain? Each person certainly dies without attaining all understanding. Will our race (history) also terminate and begin again, continually, with no progress ever made?

C. Whether the movie is terribly pessimistic or optimistic depends on the answer to the question, "Does the man at the end represent just our 'cycle' or all 'cycles' for eternity?"
  1. Pessimistic: Man may never become more "divine"—all chances for rebirth may be merely a mockery. Irony—no matter how much man ruins his life, chances for improvement are always given. Since he will probably continue ruining his life for eternity, this may be the cruel tantalizing by some capricious god.
  2. Optimistic: The preceding is impossible to believe if one assumes that there is some life-giving, life-sustaining force in the universe that is the source of absolute good. With this belief, one can hope that someday man will be able to use the divine inspiration offered him to propagate life-sustaining forces. Probably he will never be able to understand more, but he will use his understanding better. The sunrise, fetus, etc., seem to indicate this hope. Also, it seems that, despite human stupidity, new opportunities to become sublime are always given. Someday, perhaps, man will learn that he cannot truly "live" unless he accepts the gift, in the form of the monolith, that demands human subjugation to a divine force. Then he will not be required to create, and to experience, only death.

"Now I feel I've been in space twice."
— **Cosmonaut Alexei Leonov,**

after viewing *2001*

"It's the best testimonial to the film."
— **Arthur C. Clarke**

Arthur C. Clarke (right), with cosmonaut Alexei Leonov, reading *2001* zero gravity toilet instructions, at Conference on Peaceful Uses of Space, Vienna, August 1968.

"We'll get this info to you just as soon as we work it out."

From *The New York Times**

Renata Adler

EVEN THE M-G-M lion is stylized and abstracted in Stanley Kubrick's *2001: A Space Odyssey*, a film in which infinite care, intelligence, patience, imagination and Cinerama have been devoted to what looks like the apotheosis of the fantasy of a precocious, early nineteen-fifties city boy. The movie, on which Kubrick collaborated with the British science-fiction author Arthur C. Clarke, is nominally about the finding, in the year 2001, of a camera-shy sentient slab on the Moon and an expedition to the planet Jupiter to find whatever sentient being the slab is beaming its communications at.

There is evidence in the film of Clarke's belief that men's minds will ultimately develop to the point where they dissolve in a kind of world mind. There is a subplot in the old science-fiction nightmare of man at terminal odds with his computer. There is one ultimate science-fiction voyage of a man (Keir Dullea) through outer and inner space, through the phases of his own life in time thrown out of phase by some higher intelligence, to his death and rebirth in what looked like an inter-galactic embryo.

But all this is the weakest side of a very complicated, languid movie—in which almost a half-hour passes before the first man appears and the first word is spoken, and an entire hour goes by before the plot even begins to declare itself. Its real energy seems to derive from that bespectacled prodigy reading comic books around the block. The whole sensibility is intellectual

* © 1968 by The New York Times Company. Reprinted by permission.

fifties child: chess games, body-building exercises, beds on the spacecraft that look like camp bunks, other beds that look like Egyptian mummies, Richard Strauss music, time games, Strauss waltzes, Howard Johnson's birthday phone calls. In their space uniforms, the voyagers look like Jiminy Crickets. When they want to be let out of the craft, they say, "Pod bay doors open," as one might say "Bomb bay doors open" in every movie out of World War II.

When the voyagers go off to plot against HAL, the computer, it might be HAL, the camper, they are ganging up on. When HAL is expiring, he sings "Daisy." Even the problem posed when identical twin computers, previously infallible, disagree is the kind of sentence-that-says-of-itself-I-lie paradox, which—along with the song and the nightmare of ganging up—belongs to another age. When the final slab, a combination Prime Mover slab and coffin lid, closes in, it begins to resemble a fifties candy bar.

The movie is so completely absorbed in its own problems, its use of color and space, its fanatical devotion to science-fiction detail, that it is somewhere between hypnotic and immensely boring. (With intermission, it is three hours long.) Kubrick seems as occupied with the best use of the outer edge of the screen as any painter, and he is particularly fond of simultaneous rotations, revolving, and straight forward motions—the visual equivalent of rubbing the stomach and patting the head. All kinds of minor touches are perfectly done: there are carnivorous apes that look real; when they throw their first bone weapon into the air, Kubrick cuts to a spacecraft; the amiable HAL begins most of his sentences with "Well," and his answer to "How's everything?" is, naturally, "Everything's under control."

There is also a kind of fanaticism about other kinds of authenticity: space travelers look as sickly and exhausted as travelers usually do; they are exposed in space stations to depressing canned music; the viewer is often made to feel that the screen is the window of a spacecraft and as Kubrick introduces one piece of unfamiliar apparatus after another—a craft that looks, from one angle, like a plumber's helper with a fist on the end of it, a pod that resembles a limbed washing machine—the viewer is always made aware of exactly how it is used and where he is in it.

The special effects in the movie—particularly a voyage, either through Dullea's eye or through the slab and over the surface of Jupiter-Earth and into a period bedroom—are the best I have ever seen; and the number of ways in which the movie conveys visual information (there is very little dialogue) drives it to an outer limit of the visual.

And yet the uncompromising slowness of the movie makes it hard to sit through without talking — and people on all sides when I saw it were talking almost throughout the film. Very annoying. With all its attention to detail — a kind of reveling in its own I.Q. — the movie acknowledged no obligation to validate its conclusion for those, me for example, who are not science-fiction buffs. By the end, three unreconciled plot lines — the slabs, Dullea's aging, the period bedroom — are simply left there like a Rorschach, with murky implications of theology. This is a long step outside the convention, some extra scripts seem required, and the all-purpose answer, "relativity," does not really serve unless it can be verbalized.

From The New Yorker: After Man*

Penelope Gilliatt

I THINK Stanley Kubrick's *2001: A Space Odyssey* is some sort of great film, and an unforgettable endeavor. Technically and imaginatively, what he put into it is staggering: five years of his life; his novel and screenplay, with Arthur C. Clarke; his production, his direction, his special effects; his humor and stamina and particular disquiet. The film is not only hideously funny — like *Dr. Strangelove* — about human speech and response at a point where they have begun to seem computerized, and where more and more people sound like recordings left on while the soul is out. It is also a uniquely poetic piece of sci-fi, made by a man who truly possesses the drives of both science and fiction.

Kubrick's tale of quest in the year 2001, which eventually takes us to the Moon and Jupiter, begins on prehistoric Earth. Tapirs snuffle over the Valhalla landscape, and a leopard with broken-glass eyes guards the carcass of a zebra in the moonlight. Crowds of apes, scratching and ganging up, are disturbingly represented not by real animals, like the others, but by actors in costume. They are on the brink of evolving into men, and the overlap is horrible. Their stalking movements are already exactly ours: an old tramp's, drunk, at the end of his tether and

---

* Reprinted by permission; © 1968 The New Yorker Magazine, Inc.

fighting mad. Brute fear has been refined into the infinitely more painful human capacity for dread. The creatures are so nearly human that they have religious impulses. A slab that they suddenly come upon sends them into panicked reverence as they touch it, and the film emits a colossal sacred din of chanting. The shock of faith boots them forward a few thousand years, and one of the apes, squatting in front of a bed of bones, picks up his first weapon. In slow motion, the hairy arm swings up into an empty frame and then down again, and the smashed bones bounce into the air. What makes him do it? Curiosity? What makes people destroy anything, or throw away the known, or set off in spaceships? To see what Nothing feels like, driven by some bedrock instinct that it is time for something else? The last bone thrown in the air is matched, in the next cut, to a spaceship at the same angle. It is now 2001. The race has survived thirty-three years more without extinction, though not with any growth of spirit. There are no Negroes in this vision of America's space program; conversation with Russian scientists is brittle with mannerly terror, and the Chinese can still be dealt with only by pretending they're not there. But technological man has advanced no end. A space way station shaped like a Ferris wheel and housing a hotel called the Orbiter Hilton hangs off the pocked old cheek of Earth. The soundtrack, bless its sour heart, meanwhile thumps out *The Blue Danube*, to confer a little of the courtliness of bygone years on space. The civilization that Kubrick sees coming has the brains of a nuclear physicist and the sensibility of an airline hostess smiling through an oxygen-mask demonstration.

Kubrick is a clever man. The grim joke is that life in 2001 is only faintly more gruesome in its details of sophisticated affluence than it is now. When we first meet William Sylvester as a space scientist, for instance, he is in transit to the Moon, via the Orbiter Hilton, to investigate another of the mysterious slabs. The heroic man of intellect is given a nice meal on the way—a row of spacecraft foods to suck through straws out of little plastic cartons, each decorated with a picture of sweet corn, or whatever, to tell him that sweet corn is what he is sucking. He is really going through very much the same ersatz form of the experience of being well looked after as the foreigner who arrives at an airport now with a couple of babies, reads in five or six languages on luggage carts that he is welcome, and then finds that he has to manage his luggage and the babies without actual help from a porter. The scientist of 2001 is only more inured. He takes the inanities of space personnel on the chin. "Did you have a pleasant flight?" Smile, smile. Another smile, possibly pre-filmed, from a girl on a television monitor handling voice-print identification at Immigration. The Orbiter Hilton is decorated in fresh plumbing-white, with magenta armchairs shaped like pelvic bones scattered through it. Artificial gravity is provided by centrifugal force; inside the rotating Ferris wheel people have weight. The architecture gives the white floor of the Orbiter Hilton's conversation area quite a gradient, but no one lets slip a sign of humor about the slant. The citizens of 2001 have forgotten how to joke and resist, just as they have forgotten how to chat, speculate, grow intimate, or interest one another. But otherwise everything is splendid. They lack the mind for acknowledging that they have managed to diminish outer space into the ultimate in humdrum, or for dealing with the fact that they are spent and insufficient, like the apes.

The film is hypnotically entertaining, and it is funny without once being gaggy, but it is also rather harrowing. It is as eloquent about what is missing from the people of 2001 as about what is there. The characters seem isolated almost beyond endurance. Even in the most absurd scenes, there is often a fugitive melancholy—as astronauts solemnly watch themselves on homey B.B.C. interviews seen millions of miles from Earth, for instance, or as they burn their fingers on their space meals, prepared with the utmost scientific care but a shade too hot to touch, or as they plod around a centrifuge to get some exercise, shadowboxing alone past white coffins where the rest of the crew hibernates in deep freeze. Separation from other people is total and unmentioned. Kubrick has no characters in the film who are sexually related, nor any close friends. Communication is stuffy and guarded, made at the level of men together on committees or of someone being interviewed. The space scientist telephones his daughter by television for her birthday, but he has nothing to say, and his wife is out; an astronaut on the nine-month mission to Jupiter gets a prerecorded TV birthday message from his parents. That's the sum of intimacy. No enjoyment—only the mechanical celebration of the anniversaries of days when the race perpetuated itself. Again, another astronaut, played by Keir Dullea, takes a considerable risk to try to save a fellow-spaceman, but you feel it hasn't anything to do with affection or with courage. He has simply been trained to save an expensive colleague by a society that has slaughtered instinct. Fortitude is a matter of programming, and companionship seems lost. There remains only longing, and this is buried under banality, for English has finally been booted to death. Even informally, people say "Will that suffice?" for "Will that do?" The computer on the Jupiter spaceship—a chatty, fussy genius called HAL, which has nice manners and a rather querulous need for reassurance about being wanted—talks more like a human being than any human being does in the picture. HAL runs the craft, watches over the rotating quota of men in deep freeze, and plays chess. He gives a lot of thought to how he strikes others, and sometimes carries on about himself like a mother fussing on the telephone to keep a bored grown child hanging on. At a low ebb and growing paranoid, he tells a hysterical lie about a faulty piece of equipment to recover the crew's respect, but a less emotional twin computer on Earth coolly picks him up on the judgment and degradingly defines it as a mistake. HAL, his mimic humanness perfected, detests the witnesses of his humiliation and restores his ego by vengeance. He manages to kill all the astronauts but Keir Dullea, including the hibernating crew members, who die in the most chillingly modern death scene imaginable: warning lights simply signal "Computer Malfunction," and sets of electrophysiological needles above the sleepers run amok on the graphs and then record the straight lines of extinction. The survivor of HAL's marauding self-justification, alone on the craft, has to battle his way into the computer's redflashing brain, which is the size of your living room, to unscrew the high cerebral functions. HAL's sophisticated voice gradually slows and he loses his grip. All he can remember in the end is how to sing "Daisy" — which he was taught at the start of his training long ago — grinding down like an old phonograph. It is an upsetting image of human decay from command into senility. Kubrick makes it seem a lot worse than a berserk computer being controlled with a screwdriver.

The startling metaphysics of the picture are symbolized in the slabs. It is curious that we should all still be so subconsciously trained in apparently distant imagery. Even to atheists, the slabs wouldn't look simply like girders. They immediately have to do with Mosaic tablets or druidical stones. Four million years ago, says the story, an extraterrestrial intelligence existed. The slabs are its manifest sentinels. The one we first saw on prehistoric Earth is like the one discovered in 2001 on the Moon. The lunar finding sends out an upper-harmonic shriek to Jupiter and puts the scientists on the trail of the forces of creation. The surviving astronaut goes on alone and Jupiter's influence pulls him into a world where time and space are relative in ways beyond Einstein. Physically almost pulped, seeing visions of the planet's surface that are like chloroform nightmares and that sometimes turn into closeups of his own agonized eyeball and eardrum, he then suddenly lands, and he is in a tranquilly furnished repro Louis XVI room. The shot of it through the window of his space pod is one of the most heavily charged things in the whole picture, though its effect and its logic are hard to explain.

In the strange, fake room, which is movingly conventional, as if the most that the ill man's imagination can manage in conceiving a better world beyond the infinite is to recollect something he has once been taught to see as beautiful in a grand decorating magazine, time jumps and things disappear. The barely surviving astronaut sees an old grandee from the back, dining on the one decent meal in the film; and when the man turns around it is the astronaut himself in old age. The noise of the chair moving on the white marble in the silence is typical of the brilliantly selective soundtrack. The old man drops his wineglass, and then sees himself bald and dying on the bed, twenty or thirty years older still, with his hand up to another of the slabs, which has appeared in the room and stands more clearly than ever for the forces of change. Destruction and creation coexist in them. They are like Siva. The last shot of the man is totally transcendental, but in spite of my resistance to mysticism I found it stirring. It shows an X-raylike image of the dead man's skull re-created as a baby, and approaching Earth. His eyes are enormous. He looks like a mutant. Perhaps he is the first of the needed new species.

It might seem a risky notion to drive sci-fi into magic. But, as with *Strangelove*, Kubrick has gone too far and made it the poetically just place to go. He and his collaborator have found a powerful idea to impel space conquerors whom puny times have robbed of much curiosity. The hunt for the remnant of a civilization that has been signaling the existence of its intelligence to the future for four million years, tirelessly stating the fact that it occurred, turns the shots of emptied, comic, ludicrously dehumanized men into something more poignant. There is a hidden parallel to the shot of the ape's arm swinging up into the empty frame with its first weapon, enthralled by the liberation of something new to do; I keep remembering the shot of the space scientist asleep in a craft with the "Weightless Conditions" sign turned on, his body fixed down by his safety belt while one arm floats free in the air.

From *The Los Angeles Times**

Charles Champlin

STANLEY KUBRICK'S *2001: A Space Odyssey* is the picture which science-fiction enthusiasts of every age and in every corner of the world have prayed (sometimes forlornly) that the industry might one day give them.

It is an ultimate statement of the science-fiction film, an awesome realization of the spatial future. As a technical achievement—a graduation exercise in ingenuity and the making of film magic—it surpasses anything I've ever seen. In that sense, it is a milestone, a landmark for a spacemark, in the art of film.

A spacecraft resembling a vast Cubist centipede glides noiseless through deep space toward Jupiter. Men walk in space, and tumble in death toward an eternal orbit. Weightlessness is shown to be an accustomed state.

The Pan American commuter craft makes its ordinary way to the busy Moon, in this day only 33 years from now. So ordinary is the experience that the soundtrack is the old-fashioned "Blue Danube" waltz (which is only one of Kubrick's inventive strokes).

Daddy makes a visionphone call from the Moon station to chat with a daughter whose Earthly birthday party he's missing. The waiting lounge looks even more like a plastic vision of limbo than those already in existence, and indeed Kubrick and co-author Arthur C. Clarke are at frequent pains to contrast these lofty experiences with the rather mundane words and worries of those involved in them.

How it is all done I don't begin to know, but it's done in part with mirrors; that I do know. No matter; the effects are stunning. Keeping fit on the Jupiter voyage, Gary Lockwood runs in the vast centrifuge, which is rather like an enclosed Ferris wheel. He runs 360 degrees, 720 degrees: no cuts, no sign of a camera, no problems of gravity. Fantastic.

I spent the first half of the film nudging my wife black and blue and saying again and again, "I don't believe it."

The detail—down to the operating plaque for the Zero Gravity Toilet—is immense and unimpeachable, I'm sure. This must be the best-informed dream ever.

There is a plot, of course, and for my money it is right here that the pocketa-pocketa-queeps of malfunction become audible. (Let me be clear: I don't think the sci-fi-faithful will even hear the queeps of plotting, but the nonaddict with a more literal turn of mind may be in greater or lesser degree exasperated.)

The film begins with a fairly pretentious title: "The Dawn of Man," introducing a long—interminable—sequence (like everything else, beautifully photographed) in which our grandfathers, the apes, achieve the beginnings of humanity. They divide into warring camps and discover that an old bone makes a killing cudgel. In the desert the apes ponder a curious tall, black monolith, not natural, not theirs, not Earthly.

In 2001, a similar black monolith has been found buried beneath the Moon's surface. It's hushed up, for it can only mean the existence of other intelligent life in space, maybe unfriendly.

Clues point to Jupiter (I guess; things begin to get very elliptical and obscure). A spacecraft manned by Keir Dullea and Gary Lockwood, three hibernating scientists (to economize on life-support commodities) and a rather epicene talking computer named HAL ("Open the door, please, HAL") takes off for Jupiter.

Whether they make it, I honestly don't know. The computer turns villain (confirming a widely held suspicion) and at last Dullea enters into a very psychedelic-looking trip, the aurora borealis viewed from within, and absolutely dazzling, whatever it is meant to mean.

Ultimately the monolith reappears in a Regency drawing room; Dullea confronts himself in various stages of antiquity and our last view is of a thoughtful green embryo with huge haunting eyes. Like *Blow-Up,* this ending may be a kind of Cinerama inkblot test, in which there are no right answers to be deciphered but only ourselves to be revealed by our speculations. It is a kind of metaphysics that seems deeply a part of science-fiction's attraction.

One can read anything or nothing into the wordless last half-hour of *Space Odyssey.* Dullea, still in spacesuit, is a withered old man exploring an Earthlike house, his space pod parked in the bedroom. A mirror civilization, a periodicity of the whole human experience?

I don't know, and I confess to finding this evasion of a statement, this deliberate obscurantism, just that. There're certainly not any answers, but there is reasonable question whether the questions themselves must be murky.

However, any annoyance over the ending—if indeed it is widely felt—cannot really compromise Kubrick's epic achievement, his mastery of the techniques of screen sight and screen sound to create impact and illusion.

Some of next year's Academy Awards are already bespoken.

From *The Harvard Crimson*

Tim Hunter, with Stephen Kaplan and Peter Jaszi

> *This review of* 2001: A Space Odyssey *is said to be the longest film review ever published in* The Harvard Crimson.

AS A FILM about progress — physical, social, and technological — Stanley Kubrick's huge and provocative *2001: A Space Odyssey* remains essentially linear until its extraordinary ending. In the final transfiguration, director Kubrick and co-author Arthur Clarke (*Childhood's End*) suggest that evolutionary progress may in fact be cyclical, perhaps in the shape of a helix formation. Man progresses to a certain point in evolution, then begins again from scratch on a higher level. Much of *2001*'s conceptual originality derives from its being both anti-Christian *and* anti-evolutionary in its theme of man's progress controlled by an ambiguous extraterrestrial force, possibly both capricious and destructive.

If the above seems a roundabout way to open a discussion of an eleven-million-dollar Cinerama spectacular, it can only be said that Kubrick's film is as personal as it is expensive, and as ambitious an attempt at metaphysical philosophy as it is at creating a superb science-fiction *genre* film. Consequently, *2001* is probable commercial poison. A sure-fire audience baffler guaranteed to empty any theater of ten percent of its audience, *2001* is even now being reedited by Kubrick to shorten the 165-minute length by 15-odd minutes. *2001*, as it is being shown in Boston now, is in a transitional stage, the theater currently exhibiting a splice-ridden rough-cut while awaiting new prints from the M-G-M labs.

Although some sequences are gone, most of the cutting consists of shortening lengthy shots that dwelled on the slow and difficult operation of space-age machinery. Kubrick probably regrets his current job of attempting to satisfy future audiences: the trimming of two sequences involving the mechanics of entering and controlling "space pods," one-man spaceships launched from the larger craft, may emphasize plot action but only at the expense of the eerie and important continuity of technology that dominates most of the film. *2001* is, among other things, a slow-paced intricate stab at creating an aesthetic from natural and material things we have never seen before: the film's opening, "The Dawn of Man," takes place four million years ago (with a cast composed solely of australopithecines, tapirs, and a prehistoric leopard), and a quick cut takes us past the history of man into the future.

Kubrick's dilemma in terms of satisfying an audience is that his best work in *2001* is plotless slow-paced material, an always successful creation of often ritualistic behavior of apes, men, and machines with whom we are totally unfamiliar. In the longer version, the opening of Astronaut Poole's (Gary Lockwood) pod scene is shot identically to the preceding pod scene with astronaut Bowman (Keir Dullea), stressing standardized operational method by duplicating camera setups. This laborious preparation may appear initially repetitive until Poole's com-

puter-controlled pod turns on him and murders him in space,
thus justifying the prior duplication by undercutting it with a
terrifyingly different conclusion. Throughout *2001*, Kubrick
suggests a constantly shifting balance between man and his
tools, a dimension that largely vanishes from this particular
scene in cutting the first half and making the murder more abrupt
dramatically than any other single action in the film.

Even compromised in order to placate audiences, Kubrick's
handling of the visual relationship between time and space is
more than impressive. He has discovered that slow movement
(of spacecraft, for example) is as impressive on a Cinerama
screen as fast movement (the famous Cinerama roller-coaster
approach), also that properly timed sequences of slow movement actually appear more real — sometimes even faster — than
equally long long sequences of fast motion shots. No film in
history achieves the degree of three-dimensional depth maintained consistently in *2001* (and climaxed rhapsodically in a
shot of a pulsating stellar galaxy); Kubrick frequently focuses
our attention to one side of the wide screen, then introduces an
element from the opposite corner, forcing a reorientation which
heightens our sense of personal observation of spontaneous
reality.

His triumph, both in terms of film technique and directorial
approach, is in the audience's almost immediate acceptance of
special effects as reality: after we have seen a stewardess walk
up a wall and across the ceiling early in the film, we no longer
question similar amazements and accept Kubrick's *new world*
without question. The credibility of the special effects established, we can suspend disbelief, to use a justifiable cliché, and
revel in the beauty and imagination of Kubrick/Clarke's space.
And turn to the challenging substance of the excellent screenplay.

2001 begins with a shot of an eclipse condition: the Earth,
Moon, and sun in orbital conjunction, shown on a single vertical
plane in center screen. The image is central and becomes one of
three prerequisites for each major progression made in the film.

The initial act of progress is evolutionary. A series of brief
scenes establishes the life cycle of the australopithecine before
its division into what became both ape and man — they eat grass,
are victimized by carnivores, huddle together defensively. One
morning they awake to find in their midst a tall, thin, black rectangular monolith, its base embedded in the ground, towering
monumentally above them, plainly not a natural formation.
They touch it, and we note at that moment that the Moon and
sun are in orbital conjunction.

In the following scene, an australopithecine discovers what

we will call the *tool*, a bone from a skeleton which, when used as an extension of the arm, adds considerably to the creature's strength. The discovery is executed in brilliant slow-motion montage of the pre-ape destroying the skeleton with the bone, establishing Kubrick and Clarke's subjective anthropological notion that the discovery of the tool was identical to that of the *weapon*. The "dawn of man," then, is represented by a coupling of progress and destruction; a theme of murder runs through *2001* simultaneously with that of progress. Ultimately, Kubrick shows an ambiguous spiritual growth *through* physical death.

The transition from prehistory to future becomes a simple cut from the bone descending in the air to a rocket preparing to land at a space station midway between Earth and Moon. A classic example of Bazin's "associative montage," the cut proves an effective, if simplistic, method of bypassing history and setting up the link between bone and rocket as the spectral tools of man, one primitive and one incredibly sophisticated.

On the Moon, American scientists discover an identical black monolith, apparently buried over four million years before, completely inert save for the constant emission of a powerful radio signal directed toward Jupiter. The scientists examine it (touching it tentatively as the apes did) at a moment when the Earth and sun are in conjunctive orbit. They conclude that some form of life on Jupiter may have placed the monolith there and, fourteen months later, an expedition is sent to Jupiter to investigate.

Two major progressions have been made: an evolutionary progression in the discovery of the tool, and a technological progression inherent in the trip to Jupiter. The discovery of the monolith has preceded each advance, and with it the conjunction of the sun and moons of a given planet, as well as the presence of ape or human at a stage of development where they are *ready* to make the significant progression. The monolith, then, begins to represent something of a deity; for our own purposes, we will assume that, given the three conditions, the inert monolith actually teaches or inspires ape and man to make the crucial advance. Therefore, it becomes a major force in man's evolution: man is *not* responsible for his own development, and perhaps the monolith even *brings* the men to it at the precise moment of the conjunctive orbits.

To Kubrick, this dehumanization is more than the result of the undefined force exerted by the monolith and proves a direct consequence of advanced technology. Kubrick is no stranger to the subject: *The Killing* and *Lolita* both involve man's self-expression through the automobile; Spartacus's defeat comes because he is not adequately prepared to meet the advanced military technology of the Roman army; *Dr. Strangelove,* of course, contains a running motif of machines assuming human characteristics (the machine sexuality of its opening titles) while humans become machinelike, a theme carried further in *2001.* The central portion of *2001,* the trip to Jupiter, can, as an odyssey *toward* a final progression of man, concern itself largely with Kubrick's persistent preoccupation of the relationship between man and his tools.

Kubrick prepares us for the ultimate emotional detachment of Bowman and Poole; his characterization of Dr. Floyd, the protagonist of the Moon sequence and the initiator of the Jupiter expedition, stresses his coldness, noticeably in a telephone conversation with his young daughter, a dialogue which suggests a reliance on manipulating her more than it demonstrates any love for her. These men, all professional, are no longer excited by space travel: they sleep during flights and pay no attention to the what-we-consider-extraordinary phenomenon occurring before their eyes (the rapid rotation of the Earth in the background during the telephone scene).

Bowman and Poole are inhuman. Their faces register no emotion and they show no tension; their few decisions are always logical and the two always agree; Poole greets a televised birthday message from his gauche middle-class parents on Earth with complete lack of interest—he is, for practical purposes, no longer their child. With subtle humor, Kubrick separates one from the other only in their choice of food from the dispensing machine: Poole chooses food with clashing colors and Bowman selects a meal composed entirely within the ochre-to-dark-brown range. In a fascinating selection of material, Kubrick omits the actual act of Poole's murder, cutting to his body in space directly after the mechanical pod-hands sever his air hose, thus taking emphasis off any identification we might suddenly feel and turning the murder into cold, further dehumanized abstraction.

The only human in the film is HAL 9000, the super-computer which runs the ship and exhibits all the emotional traits lacking in Bowman and Poole. The script development is, again, linear: the accepted relationship of man using machine is presented initially, then discarded in favor of an equal balance between the two (HAL, for example, asks Bowman to show him some sketches, then comments on them). This equilibrium where men and machine perversely share characteristics shatters only when HAL mistakenly detects a fault in the communications system. The HAL computers *cannot* make mistakes and a confirmation of the error would necessitate disconnection. At this point the balance shifts again: Bowman asks HAL to explain his mistake and HAL denies it, attributing it to "human error"; we are reminded of the maxim, "a bad workman blames his tools," and realize HAL is acting from a distinctly human point of view in trying to cover up his error.

As the only human in the film HAL proves a greater murderer than any of the men. Returning *2001* to the theme of inherent destruction in social and technological progress, Kubrick's chilling last-shot-before-the-intermission (a shot from HAL's point-of-view, lip-reading a conversation of Bowman and Poole deciding to dismantle him if the mistake is confirmed) suggests the potential of machine to control man, the ultimate reversal of roles in a situation where man makes machines in his own image. HAL's success is partial; he murders Poole, and the three doctors on the ship in a state of induced hibernation. The murder of the sleeping doctors is filmed almost entirely as close-ups of electronically controlled charts, a pulsating coordination of respiration regulators, cardiographs, and encephalographs. HAL shuts his power off gradually and we experience the ultimate dehumanization of watching men die not in their bed-coffins but in the diminished activity of the lines on the charts.

In attempting to reenter the ship from the pod he has used to retrieve Poole's corpse, Bowman must *improvise* — for the first time — ad-lib emergency procedures to break in against HAL's wishes. His determination is perhaps motivated by the first anger he has shown, and is certainly indicative of a crucial re-assertion of man over machine, again shifting the film's balance concerning the relationship between man and tool. In a brilliant and indescribable sequence, preceded by some stunning low-angle camera gyrations as Bowman makes his way toward HAL's controls, the man performs a lobotomy on the computer, dismantling all except its mechanical functions. Symbolically, it is the murder of an equal, and HAL's "death" becomes the only empathy-evoking scene in *2001*. Unlike any of the humans, HAL dies a natural human death at Bowman's hand, slowing down into senility and second childhood, until he remembers only his first programmed memory, the song "Daisy," which he sings until his final expiration.

Bowman's complex act parallels that of the australopithecus: his use of the pod ejector to reenter the craft was improvisational, the mechanism undoubtedly designed for a different purpose — this referring to the use of bone as weapon-tool. Finally in committing murder, Bowman has essentially lost his dehumanization and become an archetypal new being: one worthy of the transcendental experience that follows. For the last part of the film, we must assume Bowman an individual by virtue of his improvised triumph over the complex computer.

Left alone in the spaceship, Bowman sees the monolith slab floating in space in Jupiter's atmosphere and takes off in a pod to follow it; knowing by now the properties of the pod, we can conjure images of the mechanical arms controlled by Bowman reaching to touch the monolith as did the australopithecines and the humans. The nine moons of Jupiter are in orbital conjunction (a near-impossible astronomical occurrence) and the monolith floats into that orbit and disappears. Bowman follows it and enters what Clarke calls the *timespace warp*, a zone "beyond the infinite" conceived cinematically as a five-minute three-part light show, and intercut with frozen details of Bowman's reactions.

If the monolith has previously guided man to major evolutionary and technological progression, it leads Bowman now into a realm of perception man cannot conceive, an experience unbearable for him to endure while simultaneously marking a new level in his progress. The frozen shots intercut with the light sequences show, debatably, Bowman's horror in terms of perception and physical ordeal, and his physical death: the last of many multicolored solarized close-ups of his eye appears entirely flesh-colored, and, if we are justified in creating a color metaphor, the eye is totally wasted, almost subsumed into a pallid flesh. When man journeys far enough into time and space, Kubrick and Clarke are saying, man will find things he has no right to see.

But this is not, as Clarke suggests in *Life*, the end of an Ahab-like quest on the part of men driven to seek the outer reaches of the universe. Bowman is led into the time warp by the monolith. The Moon monolith's radio signals directed toward Jupiter were not indicative of life as we know it on Jupiter, but were a roadmap, in effect, to show Bowman how to find his way to the monolith that guides him toward transcendent experience.

At the end, Bowman, probably dead (if we are to interpret makeup in conventional terms), finds himself in a room decorated with Louis XVI period furniture with fluorescent-lighted floors. He sees himself at different stages of old age and physical decay. Perhaps he is seeing representative stages of what his life would have been had he not been drawn into the infinite. As a bed-ridden dying man, the monolith appears before him and he reaches out to it. He is replaced by a glowing embryo on the bed and, presumably, reborn or transfigured into an embryo-baby enclosed in a sphere in our own solar system, watching Earth. He has plainly become an integral part of the cosmos, perhaps as *Life* suggests, as a "star-child" or, as Penelope Gilliatt suggests, as the first of a species of mutant that will inhabit the Earth and begin to grow. What seemed a linear progression may ultimately be cyclical, in that the final effect of the monolith on man can be interpreted as a progress ending in the beginning of a new revolutionary cycle on a vastly higher plane. But the intrinsic suggestiveness of the final image is such that any consistent theory about the nature of *2001* can be extended to apply to the last shot: there are no clear answers.

Several less-than-affirmative ideas can be advanced. The monolith is a representation of an extraterrestrial force which keeps mankind (and finally Bowman) under observation, and manipulates it at will. Man's progress is not of his own making, but a function of the monolith—man cannot predict, therefore, the ensuing stages of his own evolution. That the initiation of man into higher stages of development involves murder casts ambiguity as to the nature of the monolith force. In its statement that man cannot control his destiny, *2001* is antihumanistic—this also in the concept that what we consider humanity is actually a finite set of traits reproducible by machines.

The final appearance of the Louis XVI room suggests that Bowman was, in fact, being observed as if he were a rat in a maze, perhaps to test his readiness for a further progression, this time a transcendence. The decor of the room is probably not significant, and is either an arbitrary choice made by the observers, or else a projection of Bowman's own personality (the floor and the food are specifically within Bowman's immediate frame of reference).

If Kubrick's superb film has a problem, it may simply be that great philosophical-metaphysical films about human progress and man's relationship to the cosmos have one strike against them when they attempt to be literally just that. Rossellini's radiant religious films or Bresson's meditative asceticism ultimately say far more, I think, than Kubrick's far-more-ambitious attempt at synthesizing genre and meaning.

Nevertheless, *2001: A Space Odyssey* cannot be easily judged if only because of its dazzling technical perfection. To be able to see beyond that may take a few years. When we have grown used to beautiful strange machines, and the wonder of Kubrick's special effects wears off by duplication in other Hollywood films, then we can probe confidently beyond *2001*'s initial fascination and decide what kind of a film it really is.

From *The New Republic:*
Lost in the Stars*

Stanley Kauffmann

STANLEY KUBRICK'S *2001: A Space Odyssey* took five years and $10 million to make, and it's easy to see where the time and the money have gone. It's less easy to understand how, for five years, Kubrick managed to concentrate on his ingenuity and ignore his talent. In the first 30 seconds, this film gets off on the wrong foot and, although there are plenty of clever effects and some amusing spots, it never recovers. Because this is a major effort by an important director, it is a major disappointment.

Part of the trouble is sheer distention. A short story by Arthur C. Clarke, "The Sentinel," has been amplified and padded to make it bear the weight of this three-hour film. (Including intermission.) It cannot. "The Sentinel," as I remember, tells of a group of astronauts who reach the Moon and discover a slab, clearly an artifact, that emits radio waves when they approach it. They assume it is a kind of DEW marker, set up by beings from a farther planet to signal them that men are at last able to travel this far from Earth; and the astronauts sit down to await the beings who will respond to the signal. A neat little open-ended thriller.

The screenplay by Kubrick and Clarke begins with a prologue four million years ago in which, among other things, one of those slabs is set up on Earth. Then, with another set of characters, of course, it jumps to the year 2001. Pan Am is running a regular service to the Moon with a way stop at an orbiting space station, and on the Moon a similar slab has been discovered, which the U.S. is keeping secret from the Russians. (We are never told why.) Then we get the third part, with still another set of characters: a huge spaceship is sent to Jupiter to find the source or target of the slab's radio waves.

On this Jupiter trip there are only two astronauts. Conscious ones, that is. Three others—as in *Planet of the Apes*—are in suspended animation under glass. Kubrick had to fill in this lengthy trip with some sort of action, so he devised a conflict between the two men and the giant computer on the ship. It is not exactly fresh science fiction to endow a machine with a personality and voice, but Kubrick wrings the last drop out of this conflict because *something* has to happen during the voy-

* Reprinted by permission of *The New Republic*; © 1968, Harrison Blaine of New Jersey, Inc.

age. None of this man-versus-machine rivalry has anything to do with the main story, but it goes on so long that by the time we return to the main story, the ending feels appended. It states one of Clarke's favorite themes — that, compared with life elsewhere, man is only a child; but this theme, presumably the point of the whole long picture, is sloughed off.

2001 tells us, perhaps, what space travel will be like, but it does so with almost none of the wit of *Dr. Strangelove* or *Lolita* and with little of the visual acuity of *Paths of Glory* or *Spartacus*. What is most shocking is that Kubrick's sense of narrative is so feeble. Take the very opening (embarrassingly labeled "The Dawn of Man"). Great Cinerama landscapes of desert are plunked down in front of us, each shot held too long, with no sense of rhythm or relation. Then we see an elaborate, extremely slow charade enacted by two groups of ape-men, fighting over a waterhole. Not interwoven with this but clumsily inserted is the discovery of one of those black slabs by some of the ape-men. Then one ape-man learns that he can use a bone as a weapon, pulverizes an enemy, tosses the weapon triumphantly in the air . . . and it dissolves into a spaceship 33 years from now. Already we are painfully aware that this is not the Kubrick we knew. The sharp edge, the selective intelligence, the personal mark of his best work seem swamped in a Superproduction aimed at hard-ticket theaters. This prologue is just a tedious basketful of mixed materials dumped in our laps for future reference. What's worse, we don't need it. Nothing in the rest of the film depends on it.

Without that heavy and homiletic prologue, we would at least open with the best moments of the film — real Kubrick. We are in space — immense blue and ghastly lunar light — and the first time we see it, it's exciting to think that men are there. A spaceship is about to dock in a spaceport that rotates as it orbits the Earth. All these vasty motions in space are accompanied by *The Blue Danube*, loud and stereophonic on the soundtrack. As the waltz continues, we go inside the spaceship. It is like a superjet cabin, with a discreet electric sign announcing Weightless Condition with the gentility of a seat belt sign. To prove the condition, a ballpoint pen floats in the air next to a dozing passenger, a U.S. envoy. In comes a hostess wearing Pan Am Grip Shoes to keep her from floating — and also wearing that same hostess smile that hasn't changed since 1968. When the ship docks and we enter the spaceport there is a Howard Johnson, a Hilton, and so on. For a minute our hopes are up. Kubrick has created the future with fantastic realism, we think, but he is not content with that, he is going to do something with it.

Not so. Very quickly we see that the gadgets are there for

themselves, not for use in an artwork. We sense this as the envoy makes an utterly inane phone call back to earth just to show off the mechanism. We sense it further through the poor dialogue and acting, which make the story only a trite setting for a series of exhibits from Expo '01. There is a scene between the envoy and some Russians that would disgrace late-night TV. There is a scene with the envoy and some U.S. officials in secret conference that is even worse. I kept hoping that the director of the War Room sequence in *Dr. Strangelove* was putting me on; but he wasn't. He was so in love with his gadgets and special effects, so impatient to get to them, that he seems to have cared very little about what his actors said and did. There are only 43 minutes of dialogue in this long film, which wouldn't matter in itself except that those 43 minutes are pretty thoroughly banal.

He contrives some startling effects. For instance, on the Jupiter trip, one of the astronauts (Keir Dullea) returns to the ship from a small auxiliary capsule used for making exterior repairs on the craft. He doesn't have his helmet with him and has to blow himself in through an airlock. (A scene suggested by another Clarke story, "Take A Deep Breath.") Kubrick doesn't cut away: he blows Dullea right at the camera. The detail work throughout is painstaking. For instance, we frequently see the astronauts at their controls reading an instrument panel that contains about a dozen small screens. On each of those screens flows a series of equations, diagrams, and signals. I suppose that each of those smaller screens needed a separate roll of film, projected from behind. Multiply the number of small instrument-panel screens by the number of scenes in which we see instrument panels, and you get the number of small films of mathematical symbols that had to be prepared. And that is only one incidental part of the mechanical fireworks.

But all for what? To make a film that is so dull, it even dulls our interest in the technical ingenuity for the sake of which Kubrick has allowed it to become dull. He is so infatuated with technology — of film and of the future — that it has numbed his formerly keen feeling for attention-span. The first few moments that we watch an astronaut jogging around the capsule for exercise — really *around* the tubular interior, up one side, across the top, and down the other side to the floor — it's amusing. An earlier Kubrick would have stopped while it was still amusing. The same is true of an episode with the repair capsule, which could easily have been condensed — and which is subsequently repeated without even much condensation of the first episode. High marks for Kubrick the special-effects man; but where was Kubrick the director?

His film has one special effect which certainly he did not intend. He has clarified for me why I dislike the idea of space ex-

ploration. A few weeks ago Louis J. Halle wrote in this journal
that he favors space exploration because

> Life, as we know it within the terms of our Earthly
> prison, makes no ultimate sense that we can dis-
> cover; but I cannot, myself, escape the conviction
> that, in terms of a larger knowledge than is accessi-
> ble to us today, it does make such sense.

I disbelieve in this sophomoric definition of "sense," but anyway Halle's argument disproves itself. Man's knowledge of his
world has been increasing, but life has, in Halle's terms, made
less and less sense. Why should further expansion of physical
knowledge make life more sensible? Still it is not on philosophic
ground that I dislike space exploration, nor even on the valid
practical ground that the money and the skills are more urgently
needed on Earth. (I was delighted to read recently that U.S.
space appropriations are diminishing and that there seems to
be no further space program after we land men on the Moon,
if we do, in a year or so.) Kubrick dramatizes a more physical
and personal objection for me.

Space, as he shows us, is thrillingly immense, but, as he also
shows us, men out there are imprisoned, have *less* space than
on Earth. The largest expanse in which men can look and live
like men is the spaceport, which is rather like spending many
billions and many years so that we can travel millions of miles
to a celestial Kennedy Airport. Everywhere outside the spaceport, men are constricted and dehumanized. They cannot move
without cumbersome suits and helmets. They have to hibernate
in glass coffins. The food they eat is processed into sanitized
swill. Admittedly, the interior of Kubrick's spaceship is not
greatly different from that of a jetliner, but at least planes go
from one human environment to another. No argument that I
have read for the existence of life elsewhere has maintained
that other planets would be suitable for men. Imagine zooming
millions of miles — all those tiresome enclosed days, even weeks
— in order to live inside a space suit.

Kubrick makes the paradox graphic. Space only *seems* large.
For human beings, it is confining. That is why, despite the size
of the starry firmament, the idea of space travel gives me claus-
trophobia.

Louise Sweeney, New York-based film critic for The Christian Science Monitor, *wrote a generally favorable review following the New York premiere. Boston staff critic John Allen's full-page review appeared in the* Monitor *a month later and M-G-M reprinted it as an ad in a Sunday edition of* The New York Times.

From *The Christian Science Monitor**

Louise Sweeney

STANLEY KUBRICK'S *2001: A Space Odyssey* is a brilliant inter-gallactic satire on modern technology.

It's also a dazzling 160-minute tour on the Kubrick filmship through the universe out there beyond our Earth. The awesome authenticity of Mr. Kubrick's visit to another small planet (Jupiter) makes most of the science-fiction films that have gone before it look like interstellar waxworks. His *2001* is the ultimate trip.

But this is a trip that can be taken on two levels. It can be taken as a joy ride into the 21st century. Or it can be taken as a rocketing satire of the society which makes technology its god. For the creator of *Dr. Strangelove* has come up with a film that could be subtitled *How I Learned to Stop Worrying and Love the HAL. 9000.* The HAL 9000 is that technological dream, a talking computer. It is the electronic brain of the Kubrick spaceship, programmed to make every decision in the journey from the Earth to Jupiter. It's affectionately known as HAL by the crew, who rely on it to wake them up, play chess, fix dinner, relay their satellite messages from home, mastermind the ship's technical data, and, of course, chat with them.

HAL appears to the audience as an electronic eye — a bright yellow pupil inside bands of red, garnet, and blue light. Unlike the gravel-voiced computer that runs Godard's *Alphaville*, HAL's voice is neuter, neutral, all the words carefully, slowly enunciated with mechanical politeness. But as one of the crew members asks, do you suppose HAL has emotions, too? It turns out that HAL does: pride and anger.

This supercomputer, which prides itself on never having made a mistake, is caught in a major electric gaffe. As the human crew members seal themselves off in a "pod" spacemobile to talk about disconnecting HAL, he reads their lips and plots their deaths with electronic efficiency. The lethal parallel between the "infallible" HAL and the "infallible" missile-warning system in *Dr. Strangelove* seems clear.

But that's not all. As the M-G-M space odyssey begins, we glide through navy-blue space and stars, past the most convincing Moon ever seen on a screen, to the rollicking schmaltz of *The Blue Danube*. Mr. Kubrick's waltzing us into the 21st Century is reminiscent of his ironic use of pop songs like "Try a Little Tenderness" in the thermonuclear black comedy, *Dr. Strangelove*.

For the first stage of this space odyssey we watch a giant bobbin-shaped "Space Station Five" orbiting around the equator. It all looks superscientific, and it is, but once inside Mr. Kubrick is still poking fun at the achievements of 2001: There's a Howard Johnson's "Earthlight" dining room, a space-station Hilton, the stewardesses wear Pan Am centrifugal-grip shoes, and there's a zero-gravity toilet with a deftly worded warning. And over the loudspeaker comes an announcement: "A lady's cashmere sweater has just been found in the lounge."

The machines seem to lead an exotic life, but civilians in Mr. Kubrick's 2001 dress pretty drably—the men in linsey-woolsey shirts to match their dark, shapeless suits, the women in dark textured stockings, and tacky black outfits with longish skirts. Passengers sip liquid fruit and vegetables through straws or mess around with paste foods that come in painter's-palette form.

But while Mr. Kubrick is having his laugh at interplanetary progress, he's also hurtling viewers along on an eyeball-glazing trip through space. To ensure its authenticity Mr. Kubrick ordered a $750,000 centrifuge for the necessary weightless atmosphere. It gives a whirling realism to the scenes which Keir Dullea and Gary Lockwood, as astronauts Bowman and Poole, play with such robotlike impassivity.

Mr. Kubrick and the gifted science writer Arthur C. Clarke reportedly spent 2,400 hours writing the script for *2001*. It shows. Not in the dialogue, which is minimal, but in the fantastic attention to scientific detail. There's a giant infrared spaceship hangar at Clavius base on the Moon, for instance, which opens like a hydraulically operated Venus flytrap.

Mr. Kubrick's *2001* does have its flaws, and, like the rest of the picture, they're monumental. The first half hour of the film, called "The Dawn of Man," is a wordless ode to evolution unpleasantly reminiscent of *Planet of the Apes*. It should have been cut. In this sequence the apes find a tall rectangular black slab (possibly onyx or slate) which emits signals symbolizing the first intelligent life.

The singing slab turns up later during the space odyssey and in the last section of the film, which also should have been cut. It's an allegorical scene, straight out of Fellini, in which Mr. Dullea confronts himself at various ages and finally makes his peace with the slab, after which he becomes a Steuben-glass embryo.

The slow-motion pace of some space scenes, the uncomfortable loudness of the soundtrack (the rasping breath of the astronauts which sometimes serves as the only sound, the ear-jangling pitch of the singing slab) also detract from the impact of the film.

But the superb photography alone, even without sound, makes *2001* worth seeing. Geoffrey Unsworth and John Alcott, under producer-director Kubrick, have created a visual odyssey without equal. Not to be missed: the rainbow explosion near the end, in which Mr. Dullea pilots the spaceship through canyons of light that make the psychedelic scene look pale.

From *The Christian Science Monitor**

John Allen

WHENEVER THE THUNDER of critical controversy rips through the air, one thing is certain: Lightning has struck. Stanley Kubrick's *2001: A Space Odyssey* is just such a bolt of brilliant, high-voltage cinema.

Like any sudden flash accompanied by a loud noise, the film is both startling and illuminating. If it has temporarily left viewers more dazed and curious than enlightened, this is perhaps intentional. The evocation of wonder and awe is perhaps the primary aim of the film.

Whether one wonders what the black metallic monoliths are or what the surrealistic end of the film is supposed to mean or what the opening prehistoric sequence signifies—or simply what the film world is coming to—is temporarily beside the point. What matters is that the imagination and the intellect are jolted out of complacency by the experience of seeing the film. Wonder, like laughter or tears, is a legitimate emotional response.

Such a response, however, cannot be evoked by a work of art that is too pat, too readily comprehended, too easily flattened by the onrush of tradition or sheer intellect. Since science and technology themselves have stunned our sense of wonder into numbness by the very habit of providing new mysteries daily, it is not only fair but essential that the arts (including film) take up arms against our indifference.

It must be remembered, however, that the mystery which surrounds *2001* is not the result of arbitrary obscurantism designed to confuse. It is the mystery of self-containment that makes certain works of art (and not a few human beings) fascinating and irritating in turn.

It is part of the genius of *2001* that it must be approached on several levels at once. There are, in a sense, at least four films on the screen at all times — three of them available to all viewers and a fourth one perhaps unique to each viewer. Ways of looking at the first three and hints about the latter follow.

The first three are comparable to the wrapping paper, box, and gift that mark some special occasion. What that occasion means depends on the one receiving the gift, however. That is at once the most important aspect of the experience and the least easily verbalized. If anything can be said about it at all, it is necessary to start with the simpler aspects.

Strangely enough, confusion sets in at the level of the wrapping paper — the outermost and least important of the four films that are simultaneously given to the viewer.

On its most superficial level *2001* is a science-fiction film full of gadgets and special effects — a film about space travel in the near future and man's encounter with a strange slab that seems to prove the existence of intelligent life elsewhere in the universe.

It is on this same superficial level that one gets disturbed about the lack of plot, dialogue, and character. It is as though wrapping a gift in newspaper, like a fish, would have been better than using a paper of bold new design and color.

It is on this level, too, that questions arise about the meaning of the slab, the point of the film's beginning and ending, and the general direction of cinema as it hurtles out of the 1960s into the 1970s.

We are in the habit of approaching film as though it were a book that needed only to be opened and read. Most films succeed at this level. Most of them must or there would not be such confusion over a film that treats such a level of comprehension as a mere covering that must be torn away.

If this film succeeds at this level, it is a tribute to Stanley Kubrick's courage as producer and director that he so flagrantly sets his film in opposition to tradition. But he assumes (quite rightly, one suspects) he is dealing with a generation that has been brought up on television as much as on the written word, a generation oriented to visual images and the grammar of the visual more than to the slow plodding of language.

For such viewers he has made a film that operates on a second level of comprehension. It corresponds to the box inside the wrapping paper. It is so beautifully wrought and so intricately carved and inlaid as to defy description. If it has a name, it is called the art of filmmaking.

It has little or nothing to do with the design of model spaceships, the gimmickry of showing weightlessness on the screen, or cataloguing the potential inventions or conditions of the year 2001. It is the use of these things to achieve a kinesthetic and psychological effect on the viewer. It is also film as poetry, film as painting and music, film as dance.

It is the result of using film for what it is: the motion picture. Attention must be paid, quite consciously, to both the motion and the picture — movement and the visual images. The resemblances between images as to form, outline, and color must be seen and felt just as their patterns of appearance and variation must be noted.

The movement of objects on the screen and especially the sense of movement experienced by the viewer as the result of the camera's mobility bring to the audience a sense of being in space. In some ways *2001* is not simply *about* space and time travel and the encounter with the unknown: watching it is *like* such travel and to some extent *like* such an encounter.

All these elements are so beyond the approach of words as to render criticism of the film at this level almost impossible. For one thing, *2001* is so full of such touches of cinematic artistry and sleight of hand as to require that a book, rather than an essay, be written to catalogue and describe them. But the catalogue already exists: The film is its own catalogue.

Hints can be given, however, through one example that strikes this viewer as both brilliant and significant: the music that was selected — rather than written — for the soundtrack. Specifically intriguing is the use of Richard Strauss's opening measures from the tone poem *Thus Spake Zarathustra*, which open the film.

On the first level of comprehension, it works well — almost too well. The grandiose swell of sound is almost a self-parody of grandiose-sounding music.

Yet on this second level — in which the fitness of the parts to the whole on an aesthetic level is paramount — it is magnificently appropriate. It is, first of all, a bit of music known as the World-riddle theme, introduced by an ascending line of three notes, C-G-C. When it is first heard, at the opening of the curtain, the camera, too, is rising, and three spheres appear in alignment: the Moon, the Earth, and the sun. As the theme reaches its climax, the image of the sun has risen above the curvature of the Earth.

Virtually every element of the film—from its sometimes ironical indebtedness to Nietzsche, to the emphasis on the appearance of things in threes (or three times), to the tension between straight lines and curves—can be traced outward from these three notes of music. In some ways the best program guide one could read in preparing for the images and ideas that flow across the screen during the film is the prologue to Nietzsche's *Thus Spake Zarathustra*.

The best clue to their artistic organization and development is contained in the number three—mother-father-child, the eternal triangle, two's company three's a crowd, the three primary colors, and the three dimensionality of the universe we normally think of as "real," perhaps even the Trinity and three as a magic number for infinity.

2001, of course, is not pictures meant to accompany one's reading of Nietzsche or one's hearing of Strauss. It is whole and complete in itself with its own ends and its own means of organizing time and space—through light, movement, and imagery—as a means of accomplishing those ends. Synthesis, rather than eclectic derivation, is the basis of its indebtedness to other cultural phenomena.

Once we begin to look at the film *as* a film in this way, the otherwise obscure relationship between the continuity, flow, and duration of images on the screen—their reappearances and significance—begins to come clear. We begin to comprehend what kind of cinematic thunderbolt has been hurled into our midst.

Out of this approach emerge some inklings about the third dimension of the film—its gift of a myth and a warning for contemporary man, a myth *about* man in the 1960s.

Mr. Kubrick's tracing of mankind's development from prehistoric past to post-fantastic future is the old theme of "ape-man-angel" (or ape-man-superman, to put it into Nietzsche's terms) translated somewhat literally yet strikingly into cinema. The unifying prop that becomes a terrifying protagonist is the machine—the weapon, or tool, that is the clever extension of man's arm, eye, or brain.

As Hitler was a false human version of the superman, so the HAL 9000 computer becomes an equally destructive mechanical version of the superman. The reason for this destructiveness is that the machine appears, in fact, altogether too human. It is presented as capable of pride, envy, rivalry, fear, murder, and the false notion that a scientific mission is more important than life. In short, it is insane, and its insanity threatens to destroy life.

Its insanity, of course, is no greater than that of any fallible mortal who assumes fallible mortals can create, out of their own cleverness, an infallible machine.

As the myth ends, the human hero undergoes a kind of death and transfiguration—after a Last Supper accompanied by bread and wine. His transformation is the result of his having been swept out of time and space altogether into some contact with intelligent beings of pure energy.

It is at this point that the film itself enters a kind of fourth dimension (the three primary colors are finally abandoned for a palette of greens), and further interpretation of the film becomes highly subjective.

On a fourth level of comprehension, however, it is precisely this level of subjective response—the film having virtually left the screen and entered into the experience of the viewer—that matters most.

Even if one assumes that intelligent beings of nonterrestrial origin are meant to be taken literally rather than allegorically in this film (or anywhere in science fiction, for that matter) there is still a basic problem:

If intelligent beings from elsewhere in time and space are needed to effect the regeneration of man, who effected the change for them? Where does the search for the ultimate cause of intelligence lead, inside or outside this film, inside or outside time and space?

Inside the film, the search involves a plot twist that sweeps a man outside time and space altogether into a fourth dimension. Between the film and the filmgoer, it involves a brushing aside, through effective cinematography, of traditional notions of filmic time and space—the establishment of a kinesthetic and emotional breakthrough into realms of imagery and experience not normally found in film.

Ultimately for the filmgoer, however, the search involves turning inward. If seeing the film once isn't enough, it may be because passive viewing of the film won't do. It is thinking about the film, approaching it intelligently, reaching toward it and beyond it that counts.

If the black rectangular slab—that calling card of the unknown and that doorway to the future—is like any signpost in one's present experience, it may very well resemble *2001* itself.

Neither the slab nor the film is the ultimate mystery, of course. Both are tokens that someone who cares has passed this way. One of the tokens, at least, is already a part of human history here in the 1960s.

There is no telling what will turn up by the time 2001 gets here, is there?

Is there?

From *Take One* magazine
(Canadian film periodical)

John Hofsess

DUE TO THE OOHING and ahhing that passes for criticism of "psychedelic" art, the true dimensions of *2001: A Space Odyssey* have rarely been suggested. John Allen's perceptive comments in *The Christian Science Monitor* and Clyde Gilmour's columns in *The Toronto Telegram* represent the best attempts to explore the film in depth. For the rest we've been told to groove or grok as best we can with wide eyes and dilated pupils, and to drop the names of Marcuse or McLuhan if anyone suspects we don't know much about Kubrick.

2001 no less than *Dr. Strangelove* is an apocalyptic vision: it is an *alternate* future but no less pessimistic. Beneath its austerely beautiful surface an alarm is sounded for us to examine a problem of which *Dr. Strangelove* was a pronounced symptom: the possibility that man is as much at the mercy of his own artifacts as ever he was of the forces of nature. The film depicts three leaps in evolution each time augured by the appearance of mysterious slabs. The apelike creatures discover the use of a weapon/tool based on recent findings of a carnivorous predator who used rudimentary weapons. Modern man, as depicted in the film, has built his entire civilization as an extension of this predatory beginning, and when he in turn encounters the slab, it signifies the obsolescence of man and the emergence of machine-intelligence such as H.A.L. 9000. But HAL too has pathological characteristics, and, for no more reason than that he is *capable* of killing, attempts to destroy the human crew and in all but one case succeeds. Finally, Kubrick envisions a complete breakthrough (not a further step in this progression of predators but a *break* in the chain), drawing upon the resources of a different type of human, the details of which are left to the imagination of each viewer to dream his own dream, to find out within himself what is salvageable and what requires change. Kubrick makes it clear, however, that astronaut Bowman alone displays any sign of non-cognitive skills; his sketches (of hibernating humans) are the only evidence of artistic wonder and curiosity, and represent one of the few activities and uses of the mind that HAL is not programmed to emulate. To Bowman is given the task of dismantling HAL.

Reviewers who pursue the "man's greatest adventure—man on the threshold of space—a roller-coaster experience" type of approach to the film must consistently be missing the irony. Kubrick is much more likely to regard man (as presently constituted and socially organized) as a superannuated form of life, rather than as a promoter for NASA would, mindlessly extolling the platitudes of "progress." That the music of Mr. Kubrick's spheres should be that of a German nationalist is one of his inspired jokes. (The main point of *Dr. Strangelove*, if we can narrow it down to one, isn't to illustrate the "fail-safe" crisis— but to point out to what extent Germany *won* the last world war.)

Dr. Strangelove dealt with savagely funny caricatures of various types of sexual pathology. From the mechanical copulation of two airplanes, to Slim Pickens disappearing from view astride a missile shouting "Ya! Hoo!," sexual hysteria and social catastrophe are inseparable in *Dr. Strangelove*.

2001 moves progressively away from the "animal warmth" of the apelike creatures huddling together, to the "*ballet mechanique*" of man's complex technology, suppressing every form of human relationship. When Dr. Heywood Floyd arrives at the Moon base, he meets a woman scientist who casually remarks that she doesn't see much of her husband any more due to his research in oceanography. When Dr. Floyd contacts his home on Earth (his wife is absent), he speaks to a pale color image (his daughter, about six years old, wearing lipstick) and promises to bring her a present as a substitute for not being able to attend her birthday. Astronaut Poole, receiving a taped transmission from Earth, stares at his mother and father congratulating him on *his* birthday, completely void of any response. The line between humans and machines is blurred in the film not only because HAL is semi-human but because the humans are semi-mechanical, and as long as superiority is measured by the ability to destroy, HAL with his instantaneous memory-banks and improved logistics *is* the logical successor to man. As Abraham Maslow writes in *The Psychology of Science* (1966) "prediction, control, orderliness, rationality, organization—are all capable of being pathologized when pushed to the extreme."

Frequently when critics discussed *Lolita*, both as a novel and film, they literally interpreted it as dealing with pedophilia. But Nabokov is a big-game hunter in everything but lepidoptera, and *Lolita* is nothing less than the definitive satire on romantic love—and the age-difference between Lolita and Humbert merely a distancing device to make the self-deception, pathos, desperation and possessiveness seem remote from the reader and his "mature" loves. But when the joke is unsprung, it makes the satire all the more biting. Looked at unsparingly, by a man of Olympian wit and disdain, western forms of love rarely rise above the level of *Lolita*. For Kubrick, *Lolita* is no more about pedophilia than *2001* is about space travel—he is drawn to psychological insights and satire, and his continuing exploration in *Lolita*, *Dr. Strangelove*, and *2001* is that of psychological space. Repeatedly in *2001* he nudges us with satirical jabs ("Are those sandwiches ham? Chicken? They *look* like ham." "Yes, well they're getting better at it all the time.") to make it clear that he does not regard change necessarily as progress. Indeed, he inverts the Nietzschian myth of ape-man-superman to show that each stage is progressively *worse* than the one preceding it, for each time the circumference of its predatory powers is enlarged and the creature becomes increasingly singleminded in its destructiveness.

Critics who have rhapsodized about the film (and falsified it) have overlooked the salient fact that it clearly depicts an early death for modern man. The assertion that man can only save himself through a thoroughgoing psychological reorientation or "resurrection" is irony of an Olympian order. Mr. Kubrick offers man two futures, and both of them are funerals. In *Dr. Strangelove* he dies in nuclear war, unconscious of what drives him or his war machine. In *2001* he gains sufficient self-awareness to unplug his machines and phase himself out of existence, which is like imagining a cancer considerate enough to destroy itself.

Literary critic Harry Levin is reported to have said of James Joyce's *Ulysses* that it set such a standard of excellence as to make the writing of novels thereafter much more difficult. Mr. Kubrick has presented a similar challenge to all filmmakers. An inarticulate rave is no substitute for understanding, and *2001* is about as well understood in its first year of release as *Ulysses* was in its first edition.

From *London Magazine:*
Plans That Go Wrong

Philip French

STANLEY KUBRICK'S *2001: A Space Odyssey* is remarkable on a number of counts. Firstly, it is perhaps the first multi-million-dollar supercolossal movie since D. W. Griffith's *Intolerance* fifty years ago which can genuinely be regarded as the work of one man. True, Kubrick acknowledges assistance on the screenplay from the science-fiction author Arthur Clarke, and he is immensely indebted to his director of photography (Geoffrey Unsworth), his production designers and special effects team; but he has supervised each phase of the film personally, and can be said to be wholly responsible for its every aspect. In doing so he has established that it is possible for such a picture to be as personal as any small budget *nouvelle vague* film. To do this a director needs the necessary talent, authority, time and stamina (five years of Kubrick's life are invested here): take away one of these elements and the result would be different. For instance, the other young American director with whom Kubrick might be compared, John Frankenheimer, embarked on an equally expensive (if less ambitious) undertaking with *Grand Prix*—concentrating on the action sequences Frankenheimer clearly lost control of the movie's personal side which turned out lifeless and cliché-ridden. Like most directors, Frankenheimer had a tight schedule both for shooting the picture and preparing it for exhibition. The more expensive a film the more necessary it becomes to get it shown rapidly, for every day more interest is accumulating on the bank loans. As a result spectacular movies are often more rushed—and, consequently, rougher round the edges—than much cheaper pictures. Moreover, Kubrick has made his picture without any established stars of the kind banks usually insist on as the only obvious guarantee of box-office success. He has used several moderately well-known actors, but their roles are small; Kubrick's name alone appears on most advertising. I would say, therefore, with regret, that Kubrick's film is likely to remain a rare exception within the prevailing commercial system.

A second point—*Space Odyssey* is important as the high-water mark of science-fiction movie making, or at least of the genre's futuristic branch. Oddly enough, SF was the first cinematic genre to be established—by the great pioneer Georges Méliès at the turn of the century, with films such as *Le voyage dans la lune* and *Le voyage à travers l'impossible*—and the last to become fully accepted both artistically and commercially. Before World War II there were few major SF films: only Fritz Lang's *Metropolis* (1926) and William Cameron Menzies' *Things to Come* (1936), both of which I imagine have influenced Kubrick, come readily to mind. For a variety of political and social reasons, SF movies began to flourish in the 1950s in the United States (mainly movies seizing on McCarthy era paranoia), followed by Europe in the 1960s. From Czechoslovakia we had the brilliant, if pretentious, *Ikaria XB1* (a film close in spirit to the Swedish space opera *Aniara*), and from Russia *First Cosmonauts on Venus*, a modest, charming movie that was apparently one of a number produced by a Russian company set up especially to make SF films. But, most significantly, the French directors Jean-Luc Godard (*Alphaville*), François Truffaut (*Fahrenheit 451*) and Chris Marker (*La Jettée*) found methods of making imaginative futuristic SF films without being drawn into the prohibitive expense, and consequent lack of artistic control, that these films usually entail.

Thirdly, *Space Odyssey* is of great interest as a further stage in the development of Stanley Kubrick, a fastidious director of small output. Varied as the subjects and settings of his films have been, he has consistently pursued personal themes and preoccupations to the extent that his first major film, *The Killing* (1956), and the five that have followed it constitute an *oeuvre*. Stylistically, Kubrick has few obvious distinguishing features. Critics have pointed out the expressionistic effects that dominated *Killer's Kiss* (1954) and still linger on in *The Killing*, the penchant for elaborate camera movements one finds occasionally in *Lolita*, that might be inspired by his favourite director Max Ophuls, and the frequent recourse to tracking shots. And there's no denying that his experience as a magazine photographer has given him an eye for composition. Nevertheless, it seems to me that Kubrick's camera style generally eschews elaborate fancy flourishes, idiosyncrasy, or hollow striking effects. Precision is the keynote. When he wants you to listen to what is being said he keeps his camera still; when in *Dr. Strangelove* he wishes the audience to take different attitudes to his four simultaneous centres of action—the airbase, the bomber, the war room, and the attacking land force—he devises a different but consistent form of lighting and camera movement for each. Yet, while the visual style sensibly varies according to the subject, Kubrick does usually have resort to some kind of opening commentary, either a first-person narrator, or as in the case of *The Killing* and *Spartacus* an impersonal voice establishing the scene. He also develops his plots in similar ways to bring out themes that especially interest him. As it took several movies to make this obvious, one used to think of Kubrick as a somewhat impersonal director.

Tom Milne (*Sight and Sound*, Spring 1964) has seen Kubrick's movies as traps for their heroes, and has compared them with classical tragedy. On similar lines I once suggested — and the idea has since been elaborated by David Sylvester and Paul Mayersberg — that all Kubrick's pictures are about plans that go wrong. Most obviously, in *The Killing* there is an immensely elaborate scheme to rob a race track that is ruined by an accidental betrayal of one participant. There's nothing wrong with the scheme itself, merely with the people who operate it. And the film develops on parallel lines — the careful plan going forward alongside the forces leading to its inevitable destruction. The same pattern underlies *Paths of Glory, Spartacus, Lolita* and *Dr. Strangelove*, and they all have the same wry, semi-tragic underplayed ending, part coda, part calculated anticlimax, that manages to be both surprising and inexorable. His characters are overreachers who have committed themselves to an unattainable perfection, a scheme to control the disorder of the universe, to impose form upon their lives, and instead of this liberating them they are damned by it. Each movie, of course, raises other issues in terms of its subject, yet each has this particular underlying movement. One comes across it again very precisely in *Space Odyssey.* . . .

•

Laurence M. Janifer, *Triumph* (Washington monthly)

Mr. Kubrick is perhaps the best camera director now working — it may be that Alfred Hitchcock is his only serious rival. Once again he has presented us with the gift of a picture in which dialogue does only dialogue's work, and has elected, wherever possible, to show us a scene, an emotion, a relationship, an idea, rather than tell us about it. This is, of course, what movies are for, and I wish someone else out there would provide even tentative evidence that he was familiar with the fact.

Roger Ebert, *Chicago Sun-Times*

It was e.e. cummings, the poet, who said he'd rather learn from one bird how to sing than teach 10,000 stars how not to dance. I imagine cummings would not have enjoyed Stanley Kubrick's *2001*, in which stars dance but birds do not sing.

Marjorie Adams, *Boston Globe*

The world's most extraordinary film. Nothing like it has ever been shown in Boston before, or, for that matter, anywhere. . . . This film is as exciting as the discovery of a new dimension in life.

Howard Junker, Channel 13, New York

2001 is a bad trip. But I loved it. It is as boring as only space travel will be. It is also pretentious and thoroughly old-fashioned, which is also why I loved it. . . . Kubrick is a sentimental pessimist appalled at his benighted vision of the world to come. Deep down, he is nostalgic for the kind of simple-minded fantasy-tomorrow that science fiction used to offer. But the future unfortunately is already here.

Variety

2001: A Space Odyssey
(CINERAMA — SUPER
PANAVISION — COLOR)

Big, beautiful but plodding sci-fi epic. Superb photography major asset to confusing, long-unfolding plot. But should do biz in initial release.

. . . *2001* is not a cinematic landmark. It compares with, but does not best, previous efforts at filmed science fiction; lacking the humanity of *Forbidden Planet*, the imagination of *Things to Come* and the simplicity of *Of Stars and Men*. It actually belongs to the technically slick group previously dominated by George Pal and the Japanese.

Variety follow-up (January 15, 1969)
2001: In 35m version

Even its enemies concede that not since the travelogs which introduced the process 15 years ago has there been a pic which so utilized the advantages of Cinerama projection as does Stanley Kubrick's *2001: A Space Odyssey*. But the M-G-M pic's fans — who tend to be youthful, fervent and legion — have overreacted to the current episode in its playoff history, which sees the scifi epic moving into grind engagements in 35m Panavision. One thinks here especially of the Gotham radio commentator who practically held a wake last month during pic's final day at the Cinerama Theatre.

2001 does prove somewhat different in 35m form—but, surprisingly, not necessarily worse. For what the "flatter" screen reveals is a whole new film—not the psychedelic "trip" so promoted by many, but a tight, closely-knit, rigorously-structured narrative that basically takes the form of an anecdote.

A cosmic anecdote to be sure. On the 35m screen *2001* reminds of nothing less than one of those chilling Robert Frost poems which start in everyday reality and 14 lines later are propounding a frightening universal absolute. ("Design" is probably the best example, but the more familiar "Stopping by Woods on a Snowy Evening" can also serve.) In Cinerama, the pic seemed cosmic from the beginning—more like (to continue the poetic analogy) Yeats' "Second Coming" or Frost's own "Once By the Pacific."

Those who see *2001* as "a film for groovin', not understandin'" (as one commentator put it) probably won't find the experience they seek in the 35m version, especially since, robbed of the Cinerama proportions for which they were designed, the special effects do look more "fake." But those of its admirers who always saw the psychedelia argument anent *2001* as a lot of hogwash will be reinforced by current prints. Cinerama emphasized pic's mind-bending complexity, 35m its fable-like simplicity. *2001* is a big enough film to accommodate both.

Byro

Del Carnes, *Denver Post*

I suspect that Kubrick confronted us with so many questions (which he doesn't answer) because he wants us to see the film again, and possibly again, so that we may find our own solutions.

Catholic Film Newsletter

In his celebrated book, *Theory of Film*, Siegfried Kracauer maintains that the proper object of the art of film is the recording of unrecognizable physical reality. Belief in an unrecognizable or unfamiliar physical reality depends upon a relentless faithfulness to details. If these are abundant and abiding, he argues, the film will convince. If Kracauer is right, then *2001* is perhaps the most credible alien world yet conceived for the film medium. Viewers who adhere to rigid categorical forms or who have never aspired to any unorthodox speculation had better stay away, as should small children, who would likely be more confused and frightened than entertained. The film is for youth and imaginative adults; the curious and the adventurous.

Andrew Sarris, who introduced the "auteur" theory in the United States ten years ago, was never a Kubrick advocate. In his volume on American directors (The American Cinema, Directors and Directions 1929-1968), he places Kubrick in the "Strained Seriousness" section, along with John Frankenheimer, Richard Lester, and John Schlesinger, among others. He writes: "Kubrick's tragedy may have been that he was hailed as a great artist before he had become a competent craftsman. However, it is more likely that he has chosen to exploit the giddiness of middlebrow audiences on the satiric level of Mad magazine. Ultimately, Stanley Kubrick shares with Claude Lelouch a naïve faith in the power of images to transcend fuzzy feelings and vague ideas."

To his less than favorable opinion of Kubrick, Sarris brought a further prejudice to the project of 2001: "I don't like science fiction by and large. I think the people who write science fiction, and a lot of people who read it, are a little crackers in some ways" (WBAI Radio, New York, April 3, 1968); "People who read and write science fiction have always struck me as a bit creepy for expending so much emotional and intellectual energy to cop out on the human condition" (The Village Voice, April 11, 1968).

While never vacillating from his negative verdict on 2001, Sarris gradually intimated his reaction might be the result of a generation gap:

Sarris, WBAI Radio, New York (April 3, 1968)

2001 is one of the grimmest films I have ever seen in my life. And I am struck by it because, as I understand it, Stanley Kubrick doesn't even fly a plane. He has to get everywhere by ship and train. He can't even make the Los Angeles premiere because he won't fly. And this, I find one of the most extraordinary aspects of the whole thing, that Kubrick quite obviously is cast in the mold, perhaps, in some ways, of the old-fashioned humanist who is against science, who is against the optimistic claims of science. At this point in his career, Kubrick has gone pretty much the way John Huston has gone. I think that Kubrick is someone who is too intelligent, too cynical, too pessimistic about man, or about men rather, and I think that as it turns out, *2001* is a disaster because it is much too abstract to make its abstract points.

Sarris, WBAI Radio, New York (April 24, 1968)

(Comparing *2001* and *Belle de Jour*): I find that most of the young people who see *Belle de Jour*, people in my [university] classes for example, don't like it as much as they liked *2001: A Space Odyssey*. . . . I think there's a separation there in sensibilities between the young and old, and I think *Belle de Jour* is a film that would appeal to those who grew up with a certain measure of frustration in their lives and not to the people who've grown up with so much erotic affluence that they're bored by it. . . . I think perhaps Stanley Kubrick belongs to this generation, to the new generation in a certain way. And therefore, I think it is almost impossible to reconcile these two positions, to reconcile these two reactions, reaction to *Belle de Jour*, which I think is the best film of the year by far, and my reaction to *2001*.

Sarris, WBAI Radio, New York (May 1, 1968)

The issue is simply that, on this occasion, Mr. Kubrick was unable to translate his ideas into adequate patterns of expression, and that's all there is to it. It doesn't mean that it would have been a better film if everybody on the Metro lot had been able to give his opinion of what was going on and suggest improvements and so forth. I think it would have been a much bigger mess than it turned out to be.

Sarris, *The Village Voice* (January 9, 1969)

Stanley Kubrick's *2001* seems more relevant since the curiously dispiriting Moon shot than it did before. Previous heroes suggested some sort of heroic pose either of flying or sailing, some intrepid image of personal defiance. The three astronauts, particularly Borman, seem to have been chosen in a computer by an organization that was careful also to screen their wives and children so that they would not misbehave in the crucial moments of television exposure.

> *In his review of Sarris'* American Cinema (The Village Voice, *April 27, 1969*), *Stuart Byron described the impact of Sarris' writings and his great influence over a whole generation of film enthusiasts. Byron's one reservation: "Of course, as Sarris himself enters middle age, major disagreements with his younger followers do occur — viz., his current lamentable misunderstanding of Stanley Kubrick's* 2001: A Space Odyssey."

Edwin Newman, NBC Television News

I do not put this one in the class with *Strangelove*, which was a brilliant satire and which moved along at a tremendous clip. *2001* is a leisurely film, much too slow-moving and deliberate, I thought, taking too long to make its point. But it does have effects as remarkable as anything I've seen on the screen.

John Simon, *The New Leader*

A regrettable failure, though not a total one. This long film is fascinating when it concentrates on apes or machines (though there is too much of this, too), and dreadful when dealing with the in-betweens: human beings. . . . The slab is never explained, leaving *2001*, for all its lively visual and mechanical spectacle, a kind of space-*Spartacus* and, more pretentious still, a shaggy God story.

Richard Roud (Director, Lincoln Center Film Festival), *London Guardian*

The idea would seem to be that for this other world, past, present and future are one. This, it would have seemed to me, is where the film might almost have begun. Instead, it ends there, an interstellar shaggy dog story. Now speculation and ambiguity are fine, but it does rather look as if Kubrick and Clarke just haven't thought it through.

Clifford Terry, *Chicago Tribune*

One suspects Kubrick has designed this bit of intellectual intrigue as a diversion from the previous famine of involvement. Still, it just might touch off the biggest cocktail controversy since someone suggested that J. D. Salinger's Franny was really pregnant.

Mary Knoblauch, *Chicago American*

2001 is going to start a lot of arguments at cocktail parties . . . a familiarly decorated apartment, complete with a fully equipped bathroom. . . . Just the sort of film you might expect from Kubrick, who could make a comedy about man destroying himself in an atomic war.

Sam Lesner, *Chicago Daily News*

I have seen Stanley Kubrick's mind-bending, maddening,

awesome, debilitating, demoniacal, dehumanizing, and miraculous extraterrestrial fantasy-drama twice. At first I thought Kubrick had flipped his lid. Now I believe he is a genius.

Jim Foertsch, *West Omaha Dundee-Sun*

2001 is the epic movie that proves that people have been fed so many Walt Disney marshmallows that this challenging two-and-one-half-hour strip of celluloid manages either to scare or confuse to the point of no return.

James Meade, *San Diego Union*

To orient the audience to the unfamiliar, Kubrick has used known trade names such as Hilton, Pan Am, and Bell Telephone. The film has little humor — its principal fault.

Newsweek

Somewhere between Earth and Jupiter, Kubrick gets confused about the proper scale of things himself. His potentially majestic myth about man's first encounter with a higher life form than his own dwindles into a whimsical space operetta, then frantically inflates itself again for a surreal climax in which the imagery is just obscure enough to be annoying, just precise enough to be banal.

David Goldman, CBS Radio, New York

Add to the problems of the plot the problems of the Cinerama screen, which makes people on the sides look hunchbacked and worse, and a stereo track that gives us pretentious music and weird effects, and you have, in summary, a most unsatisfying movie.

Logan Westover, *Films in Review*

[Kubrick's] post-hoc rationalization about "feeling" being more prescient than "words" is the stock eyewash with which poseurs in all the arts are now defrauding the public. . . . Kubrick deserves the ire of M-G-M stockholders.

Pauline Kael, *Harper's Magazine*

It's fun to think about Kubrick really doing every dumb thing he wanted to do, building enormous science-fiction sets and equipment, never even bothering to figure out what he was going to do with them. In some ways it's the biggest amateur movie of them all, complete even to the amateur-movie obligatory scene — the director's little daughter (in curls) telling daddy what kind of present she wants. It's a monumentally unimaginative movie.

Saturday Evening Post

2001 illustrates, above all else, the still unappreciated drama of our time, the triumphant revolution in technology. What other major movie has ever relied, for important twists of plot, on the electroencephalograph, the print-out, the explosive bolt, the magnetized shoe?

Donald Jonjack, *ChicagoLand and FM Guide*

A fresh set of inner eyes must be used to "watch" this movie. In seeing it, a person must certainly ask himself many universal questions, if he has any intelligence or sensitivity at all. Kubrick should win a Nobel prize for filmmaking.

Arthur Schlesinger, Jr., *Vogue*

It is morally pretentious, intellectually obscure, and inordinately long. The concluding statement is too private, too profound, or perhaps too shallow for immediate comprehension.

Peter Davis Dibble (film critic), *Women's Wear Daily* (April 3, 1968)

2001 is not the worst film I've ever seen. It's simply the dullest.

Martin Gottfried (film critic), *Women's Wear Daily* (September 5, 1968)

Perhaps more than any film I've ever seen, 2001 is a motion picture — before anything else, it is a sight to see. It is a brilliant, absolutely brilliant work. . . . If there was any doubt that Kubrick is America's finest film director, it could not possibly exist any longer.

Wilfred Sheed, *Esquire*

After the apes have departed, it settles into being the first s-f no-movie. . . . If your pants weren't securely fastened to your seat, mainly by the high price you paid for it, you would probably float to the top of the theater and fall asleep on the ceiling — *but I was haunted by the total experience.*

Larry Lee, *Rat*

Granted: *2001* is the head flick of all time. Note the faintly resinous spoor of the audience, the people fighting at intermission to get those 50-cent chocolate bars, the spaced-out few who contemplate the curtain for long minutes after the movie ends.

Lester del Rey, *Galaxy**

Nobody slept at the New York press preview, but only because the raucous and silly noise from the soundtrack screamed painfully into our ears. . . . The pictorial part was superb. The color photography was generally excellent and the special effects and technical tricks were the best ever done. [But Stanley Kubrick, Arthur C. Clarke] gave us dullness and confusion. The real message, of course, is one Kubrick has used before: Intelligence is perhaps evil and certainly useless. The humanoid reaction and pointless madness of the computer shows this. Men can only be saved by some vague and unshown mystic experience by aliens. This isn't a normal science-fiction movie at all, you see. It's the first of the New Wave-Thing movies, with the usual empty symbolism. The New Thing advocates were exulting over it as a mind-blowing experience. It takes very little to blow some minds. But for the rest of us, it's a disaster. It will be probably a box-office disaster, too, and thus set major science-fiction moviemaking back another ten years. It's a great pity.

Stanley Eichelbaum, *San Francisco Examiner*

I am one of the over-30s who found the film stupendous and absolutely enthralling. It takes a special attitude to enjoy it, like most any new art form.

Archer Winsten, *New York Post* (April 4, 1968)

Since this is the first time that director Stanley Kubrick has lost touch with any large part of his audience, one can only guess that the space-journey theme hypnotized him. And while under this mighty influence, he stubbed his toe.

Mr. Winsten again, *New York Post* (July 15, 1968)

Let me say that *The Odd Couple* leads every picture in town in the wide, consistent appeal of its humor. There are a dozen other pictures that get my vote but with qualifications indicating that not everyone would agree and I can understand why. . . . Among my special-specials is *2001: A Space Odyssey* for the travel and scenery.

Mr. Winsten, again, *New York Post*, Ten Best List:

1. *The Fifth Horseman Is Fear*
2. *Hour of the Wolf*
3. *The Sea Gull*
4. *Rachel, Rachel*
5. *The Odd Couple*
6. *The Subject Was Roses*
7. *2001: A Space Odyssey*
8. *Romeo and Juliet*
9. *War and Peace*
10. *The Lion in Winter*

Time

The ambiguous ending is at once appropriate and wrong. It guarantees that the film will arouse controversy, but it leaves doubt that the filmmakers themselves knew precisely what they were flying at. [See page 364 for further *Time* comments.]

John Huddy, *Columbus Dispatch*

2001 is technically the finest, and most beautiful, film ever made. It is almost the most intellectually stimulating and rewarding film I have ever seen. It is also quite true that many persons, through their own unwillingness to keep quiet during the film and think, will not understand and therefore fully appreciate the film.

Will Jones, *Minneapolis Tribune*

My wife went to the ladies' room in the middle of the overly long psychedelic sequence. While there, she met another truant. "Do you like it?" "Like it?" said the beautiful woman I have married. "After this I don't even like *Dr. Strangelove* any more." . . . What he has made in *2001* is not so much a movie as a stunt. It is one of the dullest movies of the year.

Giles M. Fowler, *Kansas City Star*

Kubrick is an incredible technician who can spread before us in breathtaking detail the shape of our future technology against a far more awesome unknown.

Ivor Rogers, *Bad Badger* (Green Bay, Wisconsin)

More than any other film that I have seen in the past dozen years, this film excites the "sense of wonder" that is at the heart of every bit of good storytelling — whether visual or verbal.

Morris Beja, *Extrapolation: a science-fiction newsletter*

The choice of the date 2001 strikes me as one of the most intriguing things about the movie. With its connotations of a new start (. . . 0001) built on past millennia (2000 . . .), it recalls many theories of the cyclical nature of universal history. For me, it has been illuminating in particular to consider this element of the film against the background of William Butler Yeats' stress on 2000-year cycles, at the end of which we have a birth and takeover by a new god. Any student of Yeats, certainly, is not going to pass lightly over the crucial significance of the year 2001, of all possible dates. It seems especially enlightening to compare what Kubrick and Clarke are attempting in *2001* with what Yeats is attempting in such a poem as "Sailing to Byzantium." In "Sailing to Byzantium," of course, Yeats is concerned with what faces each individual soul as it tries to turn from our sensual and physical world — "that country," as Yeats calls it — to the next world, the world of the spirit and eternity, symbolized by the holy city of Byzantium. In his quest, he beseeches the aid of the "sages" in "God's holy fire," asking them to "come from the holy fire, perne in a gyre" — that is, to leave their condition of eternity for the mid-realm of the gyre, so that they may teach *him* how to be gathered "into the artifice of eternity." [At the end, Bowman] has been gathered into eternity, and that is no country for old men. So his bodily form is changed into that of a child. But a god-child: the new god coming in the magnus annus, the Great Year 2001 — the beginning of the new 2000-year cycle. Or, at least, he is a supernatural antinatural child: what the sequel to Yeats' poem "Byzantium" will hail as "the superhuman."

Judith Crist, *New York* magazine

Were *2001* cut in half it would be a pithy and potent film, with an impact that might resolve the "enigma" of its point and preclude our wondering why exactly Mr. Kubrick has brought us to outer space in the year 2001. . . . We hope he just sticks to his cameras and stays down to earth — for that is where his triumph remains.

Robert W. Prehoda, *The Futurist*

Those of us long associated with space exploration have been amused, disappointed, or angered at almost all of the films which have attempted to project what space exploration will be and will mean in the 21st Century. *2001* dramatically demonstrates that space exploration is not just a weight-lifting contest between major powers, but a continuation of man's inborn drive to explore, discover and colonize, and that man is destined to go to the Moon, to Mars, and eventually to the stars. . . . The dialogue between man and machine excels even the classic 1940 Buck Rogers radio show, when its 25th-Century hero was on a planet populated by super-robots. HAL is a feasible machine, a logical extrapolation of current cybernetics research. Some contemporary computer programs already include the use of mild profanity to permit better man-machine rapport. . . . The color coordination in all sets was superb, but the drab costumes on both men and women lacked any future inspiration. One might expect that females in 2001 would wear a combination of body paint covered by ethereal minidresses, perhaps partly transparent. The best costume was HAL's command panel.

John Keasler, *Miami News*

Entranced by a bemusing movie called *2001* — the photography is so beautiful I almost wish I knew what they were taking pictures of.

Sheldon Landwehr, WNCN Radio, New York

The sad news this week is that *2001* has been made into an incredible and tedious three-hour motion picture. It's a matter of regret. Being an intellectual dropout, I shamefully confess that if Kubrick had something to say in this towering film . . . whatever it was, was lost on this critic. . . . Use of color was employed far more dramatically than perhaps ever before. Astronauts Lockwood and Dullea tie the drama together, and spark what little excitement prevails . . . but let's not hold anything against them . . . for they were helpless against producer Stanley Kubrick's direction and screenplay. Thank you, and good night.

"This sort of thing has cropped up before, and it has always been due to human error."

John Coleman, *New Statesman*, London
   The guesses of Messrs. Kubrick and Clarke must be as good as ours.

Yasushi Kawarabata, *Eiga Hyoron*, Tokyo
   This is a kind of religious film, because the producer brings forth a concept of God to differentiate between the small efforts of mankind and the unfathomable vastness of the universe. And he shows all this in a very stately fashion on the big Cinerama screen. He is a far greater person than I had imagined.

Donald Richie, *The Japan Times*, Tokyo
   On the trip out, the music of the spheres turns out to be Muzak—lush and mindless reiterations of "Blue Danube Waltz." . . . The theme of the film: man's vaulting ambition is matched by nothing approaching the necessary qualifications and man's outreaching himself is, at once, noble, funny, stupid, and sad.

Il Messaggero, Rome
   . . . speculates about the more or less imminent destiny of the human race.

Corriere della Sera, Milan
   . . . without doubt an epoch-making film, with great merits and some large defects. Preoccupied with making good images, Kubrick as commentator makes a ludicrous blunder: the warning given against a mechanized civilization about to be consumed by the most perfect gadgets it has constructed belongs to a polemic a bit old. It is a film of terror, in this case the terror of the infinite, in which cosmic stations with lugubrious metal reflexes, pulsating clicks, the continual humming of

valves, the shrieking of spheres, and images of men sent smile-
less toward the unknown, replace the dusty castles inhabited
by phantoms, the creaking doors and somber butlers. There is
also much that is nightmarish in the film, but the tumultuous
frame of Cinerama and the realization of missiles, capsules, and
airbuses that pass between the stars combine to produce a degree of cinematic fantasy that hitherto films of the future have
not had. A film to see and, always keep in mind, perhaps without the children.

Il Giorno, Milan

Kubrick wanted to define the actual limits of our scientific
knowledge and logic, suggesting that . . . some metaphysical
essences, superior to us in every way, are watching over the
universe in the expectation that we will reach their level in the
next series of years. Einstein united with surrealism; there must
be a point where all contradictions cease between life and death,
reality and imagination, past and present.

Pierre Billard, *L'Express*, Paris

A film full of mystery uniting, in original form, science and
true art, and marking an epoch — Year One in the cinema of the
future.

> *The following review was in part of a series, "The
> U.S.A. on the Threshold of the 70's," under the head-
> ing, "Little Man, What Next?"*

Pravda, Moscow (translated by George Malko)

In America, the car lives best, with all the conveniences designed for it: broad streets, good parking lots, etc. Man, on the
contrary, is pressed close to his fellow man, tense, unhappy.
These two examples symbolize modern America, where scientific and technological progress are not concerned with the
general good, but with the interests of a small group of people
who earn millions. The average citizen lives with polluted air,
has more and more nightmares, etc., etc. The talented film director Stanley Kubrick has created, based on the scenario of
the well-known writer-scientist Arthur C. Clarke, a film parable, in which is reflected the dark philosophy of this nightmare
existence: Cosmonauts of the Twenty-First Century are flying
toward distant stars under the command of an automat named
HAL 9000; an accident occurs, the cosmonauts emerge into

space to make the necessary repairs, but the automat won't let them back in—he already does not trust people and decides to do without them, having taken everything into his own hands. One cosmonaut manages just the same to get back into the cosmic ship and he, in a frantic rage, destroys the automat. But for this he pays dearly: He brings the ship to Jupiter, but to return he will be unable—the automat, wiser than man, is dead. Thus the artist demonstrates the conflict between soulless technology and man's quivering thought.

Pravda, Moscow

Washington, June 3, 1969—The American entry in next month's Moscow Film Festival will be Metro-Goldwyn-Mayer's *2001: A Space Odyssey*. The film was selected by a State Department-appointed panel consisting of Frank Capra, the director, Walter Mirisch, the producer, and Michael Straight, the author.

George Durner, *Australian Science Fiction Review*

This is in every sense an experimental film, but artistically it breaks no new ground. Its ancestors are such works as *Last Year in Marienbad*, $8\frac{1}{2}$, and *The Trial*, but it is not as difficult as any of these and does not require a previous indoctrination in the techniques of symbolism or avant-garde pretensions. But—it would be unwise to approach it with anything in mind but a willingness to observe and absorb, to be carried with it, and to accept what it gives.

Colin Graham, *Supernatural,* London

2001 is destined to be for the second half of the 20th Century what *Things To Come* was for the first half. With its flashing lights, segmented story, and lack of hero, it creates a picture that breaks all the traditional rules, for only in this way can Kubrick get through to the cliché-ridden mass of humanity; only in this fashion can his film leap out from the cinematic debris of the 1960s.

Dilys Powell, *Sunday Times,* London

I wish he had cut down the human evolution stuff and concentrated on the problem, only too imminent, of man versus the machines of the future.

Philip Strick, *Sight and Sound,* London
   Kubrick has always pushed men to extremes in his films, finding them in the last resort incapable, and with the immense canvas of *Space Odyssey* he again appears to be expressing that vote of no confidence, which has been, after all, the constant theme of most written science-fiction. . . . His film is beautiful to watch . . . the definitive affirmation that every last coin spent on the space race will be worth it.

Rob Fleming, *Canadian High News,* Toronto
   . . . you could see it a dozen times and still not understand it. But then, you didn't really expect to understand a movie that took $10.5 million and four years to make, did you?

•

"Deliberately buried, huh?"

Arthur Clarke remembers that the novel was written simultaneously with the script, "with feedback in both directions." Dell Publishing Company offered $160,000 for publication rights, but, Clarke says, "Stanley would not sign the contract. I once asked him if he were deliberately delaying publication of the book until the film was out, so that it would not appear that the film was based on the book. He made a genuine protestation that he was not up to that. He said that he believed that the book needed further work and that he did not then have the time to read it. It was a very sad period for me. When Stanley approved the book for publication, not a word had been changed. There seems to be a right way to do things, a wrong way, and Stanley's way."

Ten months after publication of the book, by The New American Library, Clarke was considering a slight change in the book's ending. There had been some confusion, he said, that the star-child destroys the Earth with nuclear bombs. Clarke decided later not to change the ending. "It seems clear to me that he only destroys a ring of bombs surrounding the Earth."

Eliot Fremont-Smith, *The New York Times*
    . . . all of it becomes clear and convincing in the novel. It is indeed an odyssey. . . .

Herbert A. Kenny, *Boston Globe*
    Since the motion picture has its baffling moments, a perusal of the book will help, and indeed, the motion picture helps elucidate the book.

Don Thompson, *Cleveland Press*
    Novels made from movies are seldom, if ever, good novels, even when the novelist wrote the movie. Such novels tend to be synopses. Alas, Arthur Clarke's *2001* is a synopsis.

The Washington Post

The book does something that the Stanley Kubrick movie cannot: It leaves the vision to your imagination — and an awesome vision it is. However majestic the film visions, they are finite, immense, and breathtaking but inevitably anchored, nailed down, where Clarke's conception soars and takes you along, stretching your imagination as only good fiction can do.

Phil Thomas, *Santa Ana California Register*

An interesting thing accompanying the book and which the general public won't see is the press release announcing its publication. The publisher says the release is the first produced for it by a computer. The computer makes some wonderful goofs. Such as setting publication for the book for "June 34" and then announcing "The year 1002 is only a short time away." It also says the publisher has received advance orders for 23 billion copies of the book and refers to the "infallyble computer."

> *Interest in* 2001 *was reflected in the enormous sales of Clarke's book. Over one million copies of the paperback edition were in print by The New American Library within one year of publication. Interest in Clarke was also reflected in accelerated sales of his many other books. In 1969, there were three printings of* Childhood's End *and a movie based on the book went into production. Clarke also appeared in CBS Television's coverage of the first two Moon walks.*

"Yes. I'd like to hear it, HAL. Sing it for me."

M-G-M's *record division released a long-playing record of* 2001's *music.*

From *The Chicago Tribune**

Thomas Willis

THE SWEDISH COMPOSER Karl-Birger Blomdahl, who died seven weeks ago tomorrow, will be remembered primarily for *Aniara*, the "space opera" introduced at the Stockholm Opera in 1959. Its setting is a space ship, rocketing thru the void toward Mars in the year 2038 A.D. Some 8,000 people are aboard the colossus, the final remnant of life on Earth. They are fleeing the holocaust. Contact with the outside is only by means of Mima, the giant computer which serves both as guide and interpreter. On the recording the most interesting sections are those which the Swedish Radio blended from electronic and concrete sources for the dooming voice of the god-guide which ultimately fails, leaving the man-made planetoid to wander forever with its skeleton cargo.

It does not take a genius to realize the science-fiction parallel shared by this pioneer opera and Stanley Kubrick's motion picture, *2001: A Space Odyssey*. Although the opera is a flight and the movie is a quest, the point of view remains the same. The Kubrick computer is far more human than godlike, and it does not sing *musique concrète*. But both advancing technology and the receding space frontier are primary ingredients in both works.

The Blomdahl is, however, an opera, designed to be heard live in a theater and composed in one piece. In some places, the author is not up to his task, and a derivative homogeneity reminiscent of William Walton's mid-range works is the result. And for all the variety of effects employed, there is a sameness in the patterns which clearly belongs to the recent past and not the distant future.

As a motion-picture creator, Mr. Kubrick has no reason to fear a plagiarism suit. Today, film scores run the gamut from the improvised — and intentional — crudity of *Bonnie and Clyde*'s banjo to the most complicated stereophonic collages of voices, sound effects, and more conventional music patterns. Before long, every studio will have an electronic synthesizer and one or two tape specialists, for the attitudes shared by the advanced experimental composers and the super-professional film technicians are closer than one might believe.

Considering all this, it might seem unnecessary to point out that neither *Aniara* nor *2001* contains any music of the future. The new, cyclic, and serial time controls may still sound unfamiliar. The shifting clusters of voices and instruments which György Ligeti uses in the three works employed in *2001* — "Atmospheres," "Requiem," and "Lux Aeterna" — are up-to-date examples of the undulant, uncompromising new romanticism which has forsaken chords and metric organization for more subtle and sophisticated programming. But this is the "now" scene, not tomorrow's.

And before you scoff at *The Blue Danube*, that exercise adagio from Khatchaturian's *Gayne*, or the fragment of the Superman Strauss' *Thus Spake Zarathustra*, stop and take stock for a bit. With records so plentiful and so faithful to their sound subjects, people by and large can hear what they wish. All that is really necessary is a little effort. It is possible that they may be tranquilized by the Muzak-minded media into considering any music as background and all talk as small. But it somehow seems unlikely. As long as people make music, they will listen, and more people are making music than ever before.

The results of their activity are often naïve, simple constructions which turn away those of us with low tolerance for monotony. The chordal base is simple — as simple as, say, "The Blue Danube." The better singers spin out an introspective line, a little lonely, a little over-sad, rather like "Gayne." And the ones who like to turn the volume up enjoy reveling in sheer sound — a good sample being the opening bars of *Thus Spake*.

So if you are really interested in what the music of the future will be, take note of the evergreens of the past. For the technology which is producing the brilliant and effective experiments also is insuring the survival of the fittest.

The *2001* music is released as M-G-M's SIE-13 ST, which contains the Deutsche Grammophon original sources: Herbert Von Karajan's Strauss, the Leningrad Philharmonic's "Gayne" and the Ligeti excerpts as recorded by Stuttgart and Bavarian ensembles.

For the same price, you can have a less flossy Columbia package [MS 7176] which assembles most of the same music from records by Leonard Bernstein and the New York Philharmonic, Eugene Ormandy and the Philadelphia Orchestra, and the Gregg Smith Singers. All this is on one side, tied together by Morton Subotnick's viscous splashes of synthetic sound. On the other is the Werner Janssen-Vienna Volksoper recording of — you guessed — the orchestral suite from *Aniara*.

Greer Johnson, *Cue*

Kubrick's great, inspiritingly original film is less of an obfuscation than is the year we fancy we're living in. M-G-M has put together a most effective album of the picture's haunting aural envelope . . . *Blue Danube* too redolent of old Vienna and inconceivably so of a spaceport.

Roger Beck, *TV and Movie Screen*

Music from the soundtrack is not original. It's mostly classical stuff already recorded in Germany and pieced together to provide a mood for the space adventure epic. Not much market for the young set here.

Time

As the ship arcs through the planetary void, it is an object of remarkable beauty — but in an effort to convey the idea of careening motion, the soundtrack accompanying the trek plays *The Blue Danube* until the banality undoes the stunning photography.

"I've still got the greatest enthusiasm and confidence in the mission and I want to help you."

From *The Minneapolis Tribune*: *Involvement is the message*

Mike Steele

THIS IS the electronic age of the arts, the age of television, sensory involvement and Marshall McLuhan. And though our schools haven't recognized it yet, the age of literature has diminished.

The specific event that has caused this outflow of thought is the movie *2001: A Space Odyssey*, by Stanley Kubrick. Kubrick has done what so far has been the bailiwick of the avant-garde. He's made story line incidental. He's put his images on the screen out of sequence and moved closer to the purity of the film. In *2001* the medium is indeed the message. The end result isn't literature, it's cinema, essential cinema.

Listening to audiences after the movie and reading most of the reviews only verify the opinion that we're still hung up on literary interpretation, even though we've been surrounded by various forms of this nonlinear, nonsequential attitude.

Most of the problem comes from our schooling when we were led to believe every art form had a "meaning." We reduced an author's prose to simplicity to find the message. We were even told that music had a meaning outside itself, that it was supposed to represent a spring night or a waterfall or a feeling. We, from then on, were a bit terrified to talk about music, since we could never agree on what that meaning was.

It really isn't a new idea to present images out of sequence. Beckett and Ionesco led the theater away from the belief that a play had to "tell a story." They made *Marat/Sade* possible and the Firehouse's *Jack-Jack*.

We could groove on the individual actions for their own sakes, try to let the images hit us as entities in themselves, and not worry over a story, over continuity, transitions, characterizations or plot.

Marat/Sade had little meaning to most audiences, yet they walked away excited, gripped, startled, shaken. The Broadway musical *Hair* dropped all semblance of story line to present simple images. If the audience could groove with an image of ecstasy or love, that was the meaning.

Television commercials have led the field in many ways. I have no doubts that persons under 25 who grew up on television images will understand 2001. *They've seen commercials dealing with nothing but stomachs.*

Kubrick simply recognized his medium. Given the huge Cinerama screen and the technological knowhow of the '60s, he wisely decided to have a go at the intrinsic capabilities of the screen. The result is what underground artists have taken to calling the "feelie."

As Kubrick himself has said, "The truth of a thing is in the feel of it, not the think of it." What he's speaking of is an off-shoot of the happenings of the '50s and the underground theater and movies of the '60s. Don't try to understand the event, try to experience it.

Thus, when Kubrick allows his camera to linger on the space-ship, go completely around it, caress it, he's doing much more than saying that the ship is simply a vehicle to move the plot along. The important thing isn't whether the spacecraft will reach the Moon and more action, the important thing is the spacecraft. Once we begin to get with his images we see the spaceship as beauty, as sculpture, as power and as sex.

His sudden transition from the primitive prehumanoids to a spacecraft flying through space isn't clumsy moviemaking, it's a calculated juxtaposition. Two powerful images back to back, one preman, one at the dawn of the space age.

The artist has a long history of instructing his viewer to look around him, open his eyes to his world, groove with his environment. Kubrick goes farther. He forces it on us. If we aren't hung up on trying to trace the story, trying to find a literary interpretation, we soon have no choice but to study the spacecraft and we are dragged, kicking and scratching, into Kubrick's images.

This isn't to say there's no meaning in the picture. That would be like saying there's no meaning to a mountain. But like a mountain, the meaning isn't literary. Kubrick is a bit more specific, and his experimental images are more directed.

We do learn something about man's relation to his universe, to his cosmos, to space and time. The dawning of man was a dawning of his perceptions. The history of man is a history of broadening his perceptions.

But the beauty and the meaning is in the total picture. In the past, a movie or play depended on specific plot points with extraneous action used to carry these along. Just as in the past airlines advertised how fast you could get somewhere and how nice it was to get there. Now they advertise the fun of going.

Those who saw Guthrie's The House of Atreus *last year and didn't catch the meaning—and there were many who didn't—still felt involvement in Guthrie's awesome images.*

There are many who don't understand modern art yet continue to become involved with it and see beauty in it.

But we've never asked much of our art forms beyond an easy, predigested quality. Let the artist tell us something, but don't involve us. Now Kubrick has involved us—at least he has if we let him. He's let us demand a great deal from him, an experience, and he's come through.

From *Newsday* (April 4, 1968):
'Space Odyssey' fails most gloriously
Joseph Gelmis

FILMMAKER STANLEY KUBRICK'S brilliance and egotism have goaded him into trying to surpass the originality, audacity and prophecies of his *Dr. Strangelove*. His immense talent and vaulting conceit have produced in *2001: A Space Odyssey* one of the most bizarre movies ever made.

The preparations for this ambitious evolutionary allegory about the origins and destinations of mankind began shortly after the opening four years ago of *Dr. Strangelove*, Kubrick's black comedy about the end of the world. By conventional standards of drama, this new film is, I suppose, a spectacular, glorious failure.

But I'm not completely sure that ordinary standards may fairly be applied to *2001: A Space Odyssey*. Although it is dramatically disjointed and pretentious, its special effects create its own other-worldly reality and put it in a class of its own where there are no standards against which it can properly be judged. It exists on its own terms as a unique experience.

The Stanley Kubrick-Arthur Clarke screenplay is an expansion of a Clarke short story, "The Sentinel," about the discovery on the moon of a signal beacon left by a superior alien race as an alarm to alert them when humans evolved enough to leave earth and grope toward space.

In the film, the alien (which looks, through man's limited senses, like a black tabletop on end) acts like a midwife in the evolution of man. Running three hours, with an intermission, the film is a saga of evolution, from Leakey's man-apes to modern man in the 21st century and, finally, to a new (unspecified) stage of development. The alien is there to inspire each change.

This mysterious slab appears on Earth among the apes at the dawn of man, on the Moon when modern man is on the threshold of discovering how he fits into the universe, in orbit around Jupiter, and at the foot of the symbolic deathbed, where the contemporary race of men is to pass on into the next evolutionary stage. The slab seems to represent for Kubrick the Life Force, or an Evolutionary Principle, or God, or an Alien Superthing weaning humanity in various rebirths.

In its space-travel special effects, *2001: A Space Odyssey* is an unparalleled movie spectacle. Every minute detail of the operation routine of the Earth-shuttle, the Hilton Space Station, the moon ferry, the moon base and the interplanetary spaceship is shown matter-of-factly. The sets, constructed with the technical assistance of major corporations, are the most realistic and functional ever seen in science-fiction films.

In scenes like the one in which the camera follows Gary Lockwood around and around in a continuous circle as he does his daily exercises by jogging along the floor and up the ceiling with his magnetic shoes, Kubrick stunningly establishes a way and rhythm of life that seem commonplace in the context of his remarkable film but that in fact will not exist anywhere outside the film for decades.

There are convincingly real sequences with Keir Dullea and Gary Lockwood floating outside the spaceship doing repair work. If the rest of the film were as good as the special effects, *2001: A Space Odyssey* would be a masterpiece, a classic. Instead, it is, as a whole, disappointingly confusing, disjointed and unsatisfying.

Because its characters are standardized, bland, depersonalized near-automatons who have surrendered their humanity to the computers, the film is antidramatic and thus self-defeating. It moves at a slow, smug pace. It is patronizingly pedantic in some of its earnest history lessons. And while it dazzles the eye, it offends the ear with one of the worst soundtracks ever made.

Kubrick uses *The Blue Danube* to emphasize how men have turned the awesomeness of space travel to a banal commuting chore where the passengers nap or eat or read. The waltz, used to indicate mankind's going around in circles, is also an ironic counterpoint to the sexual imagery of the shuttle-rocket coupling with the space-station (as Kubrick used a romantic song as the background for the air-to-air refueling in *Dr. Strangelove*). But the whole thing is overdone and tiresome, as are all the other sound effects.

The film jarringly mixes clinical realism with metaphysical allegory. It abandons plot for symbol.

The ultrarealistic trip from the moon to Jupiter in search of aliens turns out to be an allegorical evolutionary trip. Dullea, as Everyman, wars with his computer to regain control of his destiny. In his ship, Discovery, Dullea seems ready to land on Jupiter but on his way he encounters the black slab and passes through a mind-expanding psychedelic experience, with kaleidoscopic arrangements of lights and colors. Then his ship, which is shaped like a spermatozoon, is symbolically united with the planet (i.e., his destination, mankind's goal).

And suddenly he has landed not on the planet but in the future, in an eerie room, where, as the symbol of all mankind, he grows old and, on his deathbed, reaches out to the Evolutionary Principle, which assists him to evolve into the next higher stage of development, an infant. The evolution appears to be a biblical allusion about how one must be reborn as a child before being allowed to enter the kingdom of heaven.

The film jumps erratically. The episodes aren't structured logically until the very last moments of the film. It is a mistake. Instead of suspense, there is surprise and confusion, and, for many, resentment.

> *His second time around,* Newsday *critic Joseph Gelmis called* 2001 *a masterwork. He became one of the film's leading proponents in New York.*

From *Newsday* (April 20, 1968):
Another Look at 'Space Odyssey'

Joseph Gelmis

ABOUT 100 YEARS AGO *Moby Dick* was eloquently damned and devastatingly dismissed by one of Britain's most influential and erudite literary critics. He argued persuasively that the book was a preposterous grab-bag. He ridiculed its self-indulgent lyricism and poetic mysticism. He said it was an unconditional failure because it didn't follow the accepted canons of how a 19th-century novel should be written. He was impeccably correct. Yet today there are perhaps a half-dozen scholars who can recall the critic's name, while every college freshman knows the name of the maligned novelist.

A professional critic is sometimes trapped by his own need for convenient categories, canons and conventions. He can't operate from day to day in a vacuum. So he builds an aesthetic frame of reference, a value system, to give him standards by which he can judge each new film. He approaches a film with preconceptions about what form it should have. He is the up-holder of the familiar, the promoter of the status quo.

When a film of such extraordinary originality as Stanley Kubrick's *2001: A Space Odyssey* comes along it upsets the members of the critical establishment because it exists outside their framework of apprehending and describing movies. They are threatened. Their most polished puns and witticisms are useless, because the conventional standards don't apply. They need an innocent eye, an unconditioned reflex and a flexible vocabulary. With one exception (*The New Yorker's* Penelope Gilliatt), the daily and weekly reviewers offhandedly dismissed the film as a disappointment or found it an ambitious failure.

In my own review, I wrote: "By conventional standards of drama, this new film is, I suppose, a spectacular, glorious failure. But I'm not completely sure that ordinary standards may fairly be applied to *2001: A Space Odyssey*. Although it is dramatically disjointed and pretentious, its special effects create its own otherworldly reality and put it in a class of its own where there are no standards against which it can properly be judged. It exists on its own terms as a unique experience."

I had struggled, on deadline, with the initial review, writing and rewriting it three times. It never said quite what I had hoped to say. Basically, I wanted to call it a fascinating film that didn't work. Then I read the other reviews and they were almost all guilty, as the villains in Kubrick's own *Dr. Strangelove* were, of a hysterical overkill.

One of the axioms of the movie-reviewing dodge is that if you don't flip over a film the first time, forget it, because neither will the audience. An audience gets just one chance to see a film, so it has to make its points as clearly and as quickly as possible. For purely economic reasons, this is especially true when the film is a $12,000,000 Cinerama adventure epic which must appeal to a mass audience to recoup its investment.

I went back to see the film again, anyway. I suspected that the critical overkill was a symptom of a nervous reaction not unlike the 19th-century literary critic's hostility to a new form that threatened the assumptions of his expertise.

After seeing *2001: A Space Odyssey* a second time, I'm convinced it is a masterwork. Take it from one who mistrusts superlatives and who suspects that most critics who second-guess themselves are grandstanding: this awesome film is light-years ahead of any science fiction you have ever seen and owes more to the mystical visions of Jung and William Blake than to H. G. Wells or Jules Verne.

The problem in recommending *2001: A Space Odyssey* is simply that it may not fall into place for you until the second viewing. And that's asking, perhaps, too much stamina and cash outlay in the case of a three-hour (with intermission) reserved-seat film with admission costing more than $3 a person. The alternative may be to find out in detail what is going to happen, so you will be less concerned with the apparent adventure and more aware of the nitty-gritty details.

Kubrick's depersonalized human beings are antidramatic and that is cinematically self-defeating. The pace is so leisurely and the characters so uninteresting that you may become impatient to get on with the plot. You may, as I did, want to sacrifice the minute details of the operation of the spaceship. But it is precisely this cumulative weight of having experienced a kind of living hell with Keir Dullea that makes the symbolic rebirth of this automaton Everyman of the 21st Century so profoundly stirring and such a joyous reaffirmation of life.

The film failed as drama the first viewing because it did not keep me spellbound. The tedium was the message. But the vision of space-age humanity being just a bone's throw away from prehistoric man didn't seem structurally related to the rest of the film until the final scenes. It was unemotionally realistic, and then suddenly Kubrick sprung his allegorical surprises on us.

Because Kubrick uses surprise, rather than suspense, the film is full of sequences that seem too long or confusing, until they are seen in context a second time. Alfred Hitchcock, the master of the milieu, says that for suspense the public has to "be made perfectly aware of all the facts involved." In a mystery, or whodunit, he says, "there is no suspense, but a sort of intellectual puzzle. The whodunit generates the kind of curiosity that is void of emotion, and emotion is an essential ingredient of suspense."

The prologue with the man-apes and the epilogue with the evolution of the star-baby are two of the most riveting and exhilarating emotional moments in *2001: A Space Odyssey*. The special effects, particularly Dullea floating in midair while performing a lobotomy on the computer HAL after its nervous breakdown, are remarkable. Since the film opened at New York's Capitol Theater, Kubrick has trimmed about 19 minutes to speed the action and he has reduced the piercing soundtrack level and added two titles to set the place of the action more clearly. They are the only concessions he has made in a film which uncompromisingly demands acceptance on its own unique terms.

From *Newsday* (April 5, 1969): *Understanding the Message of* 2001

Joseph Gelmis

STANLEY KUBRICK'S *2001: A Space Odyssey* is such an extraordinary film that often now when I read a piece of cultural criticism there are passages which seem to have almost been written in direct response to the film.

In *Understanding Media*, Marshall McLuhan says, "The artist picks up the message of cultural and technological challenge decades before its transforming impact occurs. He then builds models or Noah's Arks for facing the change that is at hand." The odd spermatozoon-shaped spaceship, The Discovery, in *2001* is a kind of ark.

"The artist," says McLuhan, "is the man in any field, scientific or humanistic, who grasps the implications of his actions and of new knowledge in his own time. He is the man of integral awareness."

McLuhan speaks of art as "precise advance knowledge of how to cope with the psychic and social consequences of annexed technology" and of the need to "begin a translation of new art forms into social navigation charts." McLuhan adds, "I am curious to know what would happen if art were suddenly seen for what it is, namely, exact information of how to rearrange one's psyche in order to anticipate the next blow from our own extended faculties."

The relevance of *2001* in light of McLuhan's theories is staggering. But no more so than the insight into the film one gets from reading *The Savage and Beautiful Country* by the British Jungian psychiatrist Alan McGlashan. *The Savage and Beautiful Country* (Houghton Mifflin: $4) has had a profound influence on my own life and is one of the most significant prophetic works of the decade. Both McLuhan's and McGlashan's books appeared before *2001* was released in 1968.

In his foreword, McGlashan says that the purpose of his

book is to indicate a new direction of perception: "An almost imperceptive inner change—a willed suspension of conventional judgments, a poised still awareness, a *stillness* in which long-smothered voices that speak the language of the soul can be heard again.

"To suggest that mankind is on the verge of a crucial psychic mutation, a breakthrough to an enhanced personality that can grasp without flinching the formidable values of an inner world, while retaining its intellectual grip on externalities—is to sail extremely close to the wind."

He suggests that Nietzsche glimpsed the truth, which hadn't been forcefully promoted since Pythagoras, that what was needed was not another new philosophy, but that "man should surpass himself." And in *2001* the evolutionary stepups move on up from Leakey's man-ape to the current species of *homo sapiens* to the newborn star-baby in a cocoon—an infant angel, or superman.

Says McGlashan, "The brain, Bergson believes, limits man's conscious awareness of the exterior world to what is practically useful. . . . Yet one may not reproach the human brain for its ruthless censorship of (other) perceptions. Consciousness has quite enough of a job mediating, like a harassed traffic policeman, between the hostile environment and the precarious spark of individual life which it guards—without being simultaneously distracted by data arriving from beyond space and time.

"This may, in fact, be the secret of the incalculable strength of the 'common-sense' attitude. . . . Busy life simply cannot afford the time to listen too raptly to the faint voices hailing him from far beyond the boundaries of his own demanding world."

From *The East Village Other: Thilm*

Lita Eliscu

A short scenario: 2001-The Morning After.

Starring: An avant-garde film buff and a Hollywood treadmill artist.

AG: Gahhh! it's all been done before! and better! (gets reverent look on face, chants:) Belson/ Brakhage/Jordan/Breer.

Not to mention DW Griffith and Charlie Chaplin.

Hollywd: Gahhh. Waddit all mean, hunh. No sense. Dumb.

THE END

SOMEWHERE, lost in the delicate web of obscurities conversation is, is *2001: A Space Odyssey*, trying to simply emerge. For some it was a trip already taken too many times for their pleasure; for others, a trip always to be taken blindfolded because seeing requires too much effort expended. 'Strue, nobody told you the plot in the first five minutes.

Instead, there was a series of puns, all contained within the structured intergalactic framework of just that — the universe — surely the biggest pun of them all. Puns here being defined as one verbalized/visualized difference between reality and appearance and involving a sense of humor, or perspective. *2001* stands as one of the more profound puns for the age, maybe even as an epitomization. It looks for the boundary between life and art . . . theater and cinema . . . seeing and just seeing. Life is the continuous process, a somehow interrelated, continual series of information-filled experiences; art is the culmination, the knowledge gained from the information, turned into a summary of the cause/effect. Cinema, or film, or flicks, or moovees — or theater: they all have scripts, directors, producers, money, sets, actors. Movies have a movie camera, however, a third eye which may not see as much as a pineal gland but certainly alters the kind of suspension of disbelief necessary. There is no stage to create the metaphorical framework, and a screen is somehow not the same. The screen's existential framework is and has always been that world out there — it was born as godchild to all the other accepted art forms, a child of this age, into a world nearly capable of sending men to the Moon and yet still blithely allowing thousands to starve. What do you use to convey the mystery? People wink as easily from a screen as they ever did from the street, thanks to Godard, Tony Richardson, et al.

In a year which starred LBJ, Hong Kong flu, and Community Night at the Fillmore it isn't really a surprise that *The Lion in Winter* was voted best picture by the N.Y. Film Critics. Bless their acumen, they all righteously mentioned *2001* quite honorably; what else to do with a film so obviously — ah, different? — from the rest. Big studio, big name, big money, big slick write-ups. Obviously (not to be confused with the Warhol flick — or is it?) *Lion in Winter* was about a normal 20th-Century family set in merrie oldengland, of course — for that historical touch. One fag, one schmuck, one faceless, greasy throwback — My Three Sons; one daddy who would put it to anything including sheep, and etc: one big family. Identifiable, sort of a pre-neorealist Faces. Primitivo and the Titsqueezers revitalized.

What do you do when the first title is "The Dawn of Man," and some apes suddenly realize that the source of life — a waterhole—is not big enough for everyone; that a bone held at right-angles in the hand becomes a weapon; that a bone thrown up, up in the air can metamorphose into yet another "primitive" weapon (or tool) a spaceship; and that almost before the camera eye blinks again to the inside of the ship, one realizes there have been no jump-cuts, we're still there, in the dawn of man's history.

(Everybody tells a story, even if the details are left for each person to fill in, in good old advante-garde, do-it yourself fashion.)

This isn't meant to be a total recount of My Explanation of *2001*—there's no excuse for ruining the film for anyone else by overriding in the saddle and trying to legally define the movie in this column. Everyone has favorite moments, and mine was the opening sequence. Kubrick goes on, however, to play with more and more devastating puns, and maybe it is fair to wonder if the real stars of the movie aren't the stars themselves (yeah, yeah, stars of stage and screen, playing Themselves). As far as the too-much-expounded light trip: it stands there, and nobody else has done it, not *Relativity*, nor *LSD* (by Belson) nor your best friend who is an avant-garde filmmaker. The trip isn't meant to be taken twice; if you ever remember trying to recapture certain early memories in your head, you know that the initial freshness is never there again (vid. Intimations of Immortality) because you've been there before.

And this isn't the column to go into any depth of the whys, of why a particular scene's film technique seemed impressive, or fantastic or just worked, visually; there are just flashes: the spacepod hanging off the nose of the large spaceship: A silver minnow flashing in front of Moby Dick. The opening sequence where slide after slide of that first Great Desert come clicking by, and you just know Who is holding the camera. . . .

Other movies try to tell the story of a family, or of a people, or of a sensation; this movie tried to understand a whole mechanical age, the final pun being that it took so many machines to create the film.

From *The London Times:*
On *Seeing* 2001 *A Second Time*

John Russell Taylor

THERE ARE TIMES in the cinema these days when I begin to feel that perhaps I have a faint inkling of how the mammoth felt when the ice began to melt. It struck me with peculiar force this week when I took a friend to see *2001: A Space Odyssey*.

On second viewing, my pleasures, and my reservations, came in precisely the same places. I enjoyed, and was held by, the plotty bits, particularly the whole middle section in which the human inhabitants of the spaceship find themselves locked in deathly combat with a rogue robot which has gone mad and is bent on destroying them. I found the beginning as long drawn out, and the end as willfully obscure, as before. (I notice, by the way, that in the recently published novel-of-the-film both of these sections are much clarified: it is made explicit, for instance, that the black basalt slab the apes encounter is a teaching machine from outer space, and that the rococo room at the end is a tool of the astronaut's imagination, abandoned when he has no further use for it.)

I admired the elaboration of the technical scenes showing the arrival of the spaceship at the space station and so on, but still tended to feel that they were overlong in reaction to the film as a whole, as though Stanley Kubrick had had so much fun devising them that he failed, when editing the film, to appreciate that they would be considerably less interesting to an audience than they were to him.

Ah, but that was where I was wrong. In the audience when I saw the film again, there were lots of children, especially boys, under 15, generally with fathers and sometimes with mothers in tow. A characteristic group sat just behind me: father and mother in their mid-thirties, boy of about 11. And their reactions were fascinating. The mother was clearly a trifle restive. Like me, she was mostly held by the plot; otherwise, she kept asking her husband, *sotto voce*, what this meant, what was happening there, did he think a spacecraft would really be like that, and so on. To which he gave answers more hopeful than confident, I thought. But, evidently, what interested him above all was the purely mechanical side, the sort of thing which should appeal at

once to Meccano addicts; the plot for him seemed to be pretty
incidental, like the plot in a musical, something which was there
as the bread in the sandwich of really attractive items.

The boy, on the other hand, obviously loved it all. He shushed
his parents whenever their dialogue became too insistent, and
at intermission kept bubbling, "Isn't it good? Do you like it?
Don't you understand it? What's there difficult to understand?"
Maybe, of course, he was just an infant genius, but I doubt it.
He seemed an ordinary enough child. But clearly his attention
was not functioning in the same sort of way that his parents' was,
and that mine was. He was, that is to say, not in the slightest
worried by a nagging need to make connections, or to understand how one moment, one spectacular effort, fitted in with, led
up to or led on from another. He was accepting it like, dare one
say, an LSD trip, in which a succession of thrilling impressions
are flashed on to a brain free of the trammels of rational thought.
Nor can one put this down to his age and education: it is not,
after all, a particularly childish way of seeing things. As any
teacher will tell you, children tend on the whole, especially at
that age, to be the most stuffily rationalistic of all, constantly
demanding believable hows and whys.

No. It seems to me that what we have here, in a rather extreme
form, is a whole new way of assimilating narrative. It is not
only children who exemplify it: many young and some not-so-
young adults seem to accept things in the same way. What they
want, or at least what they accept without demur, is not an artic-
ulated plot, but a succession of vivid moments. They are, one
might say, the audience envisaged by Artaud in his proposed
Theater of Cruelty, ready-conditioned, perfectly prepared to
abandon ratiocination and take drama straight in the solar
plexus. Naturally, I have a theory to account for this, and it is
hardly a new one. But it seems to me that, despite Marshall
McLuhan and the sense he occasionally talks among a lot of
provocative nonsense, very little practical attention has yet
been paid to the way that a life with television is affecting our
mode of perception. In television, for all sorts of reasons — not
least the manifold distractions of life at home as against the
narrowly directed attention to stage or screen required of us in
a darkened theater — attention is always liable to drift away, and
in a matter of seconds rather than minutes. What is needed,
therefore, is not so much something which will keep one glued
to the small screen every instant of a program — that would be
too exhausting — but something which will keep bringing back
the wandering attention with a new tidbit at regular intervals.
How the transition from one tidbit to another is achieved remains fairly immaterial.

Hence, plot in particular does not matter greatly, and neither does an overall sense of form. Provided the attention-grabbers are spectacular enough in themselves, no one is going to question the rationale behind them too closely. And once this habit of mind is established, it is bound to affect other fields of activity, notably the screen and the stage. I find myself worried quite frequently by evident weak points in plot—there are, for example, quite blatant inconsistencies and violent ruptures of tone in both the new films about police methods and ethics, the British *The Strange Affair* and the American *The Detective*—but they seem, I find, to bother ordinary paying members of the audience not at all. To me, it would seem a mark against the possible popularity of the Beatles' movie *Yellow Submarine* that it has no coherent plot at all, but simply makes up its feature length out of varied bits and pieces. Not at all, though: where it has been shown it seems to have gone down very well with audiences, and not necessarily highbrow audiences either, on its power to excite and enliven, moment by moment.

I have, little by little, acclimatized myself to the Jerry Lewis–Frank Tashlin type of comedy, careless as it is of overall form, and dedicated to the elaboration of a succession of isolated gags. But evidently audiences habituated to television and the strip cartoon were there way ahead of me. I suppose I shall adjust eventually to incoherent plotting in drama, to films that are all flash and outbreak, with little sense beyond the sound and the fury. But meanwhile, it really is rather worrying to think of current cinema as an unknown territory into which, perhaps, only a little child can confidently lead me.

From *The Chicago Daily News Panorama* 2001: *Where Did It Go Right?*

Michaela Williams

STANLEY KUBRICK's *2001: A Space Odyssey* has inspired some of the most derisive (and funniest) writing in recent film criticism. After its first screening in April, East Coast critics came down on the picture almost with a single mind: Renata Adler in *The New York Times* found it intensely boring, "like three hours of Tolkien without the ring"; in *The Village Voice*, Andrew Sarris called it "merely a pretext for a pictorial spread in *Life* magazine"; John Simon in *The New Leader* attacked its metaphysical pretensions, dubbing it "a shaggy God story"; Judith Crist queried, "Stanley, why have you brought me here?" . . . the cosmos remained silent.

Not just the preview audience squirmed through the three-hour space adventure. M-G-M sucked in its corporate breath ($10,000,000, several reputations and perhaps the future of the company rode on *Space Odyssey*); Kubrick retired instantaneously to the cutting room and made some 30 delicate excisions amounting to about 20 minutes ("He could take out another hour and it wouldn't hurt," jeered the opposition). The scars are visible in the present two-hour-21-minute version only, as they say in the cosmetic surgery business, if you know the operation was made.

That there are probably a hundred people out there who could tell you precisely where the cuts come and feel hysterical about the loss of each snippet is an indication of the kind of mass worship the film has attracted outside of "influential" critical channels. As somebody is always around to say, nobody liked *2001* but people.

Now in its 14th week, the film is listed in *Variety* as fourth top box-office draw (after *The Odd Couple, Green Berets*, and *Rosemary's Baby*). It has kept ahead of M-G-M's *Dr. Zhivago*, which earned $76,000,000, and it is breaking house attendance records in Sydney, Tokyo and London.

An actual "2001 Fan Club" has developed, with Mike Nichols, Mick Jagger, John Lennon ("I see it every week"), Franco Zeffirelli, Roman Polanski, Richard Lester, et cetera, represented. Several critics have recanted their original reviews — every man should have his *Bonnie and Clyde* — and a lot of people are seeing it more than once.

Maurice Rapf, a lecturer on film at Dartmouth College, theorized in *Life* magazine that only Kubrick's 13th-hour cuts saved "an unconventional masterpiece from old-fashioned disaster." It is an interesting speculation, particularly in that it is untestable, but Rapf seems to be overstating the case. For one thing, the long version was screened simultaneously in New York, Washington, D.C., and Los Angeles and reviewers in the other two cities received it enthusiastically, if not without bewilderment.

Not having seen the original, but having viewed the cut version with three different audiences, it seems apparent that many of those who dig it would dig it for five hours if it happened to run that long. Even after $2\frac{1}{2}$ hours, people stay in their seats to watch the giant credits slide up the screen.

Many of those who don't admire it are probably bored with it before they get into the theater; they will suffer science-fiction only because Stanley Kubrick spent five years and a lot of money on it.

The amounts of time and money put out for *Space Odyssey* are repeated everywhere like a litany, as if vast investment of either were insurance against failure. On the contrary, says Henry Herx of the National Catholic Office for Motion Pictures. "It took two years from the time they finished shooting the film until it was released, and that means to me they had a great deal of trouble putting it together. And it shows; it has, basically, a narrative structure that doesn't go anyplace. I had chalked it up to a bad experience in Kubrick's life."

Herx, who has thought of Kubrick as "*the* American director," was sorely disappointed in the film. "Grooving and introspecting are not what I'm interested in film about."

The only defense against coming a-cropper is a consistent history of mediocrity, and with *Paths of Glory, Lolita,* and *Dr. Strangelove* behind him, Kubrick does not qualify.

One of the beautiful assessments of *Space Odyssey*, as well as one of the few positive ones to come from New York, was Penelope Gilliatt's. "I think it is some sort of great film," she said in her superb review in *The New Yorker*. Just what sort of "great" will probably be a topic for discussion until 2001 and beyond.

Ultimately (by 1970, say), the film will probably look more significant historically than aesthetically. What it does is launch the major elements of an extremely vital underground (in film, music, art, and combinations thereof) in the mainstream of commercial cultural activity.

It does what the Fillmore Auditoriums and Electric Theaters of this world would do, differently no doubt, if they only had the $10,000,000. It does what *Hair* did when it introduced sex, dirt, and pot uptown, and found them "commercially viable." *2001* puts mindlessness ("The truth of a thing is in the feel of it, not the think of it," says Kubrick), freaking out, and chromosome mutation in posh uptown movie houses with reserved seats and 50-cent popcorn.

It joins the current cultural revolution by destroying an institution — the anti-art, Hollywood formula picture. It dares to be longer than 90 minutes, obscure, boring, plotless and unique. It is untheatrical in ways that movies have traditionally not been, with little dialog, no character development and no acting in sight. Douglas Rain is present only as the (gay?) voice of HAL the computer.

In fact Keir Dullea, who must have been selected for his role as one of the astronauts on the basis of his limited range of expressions, has said of Kubrick, "Ideally, I think Stanley would like to have mechanical actors, but since they don't exist, he works with actors and appreciates their talent." Which is pretty decent, under the circumstances.

Shrewdly, there is something for nearly everyone in *2001* — sci-fi buff, post-print visualite, music lover, scientist, intellectual, formalist — but for all of its pleasure points it is not an integrated whole.

The first "Dawn of Man" segment can only be taken seriously as camp, or, as someone said, "an illustrated manual for fourth graders." (And how is it actors in ape suits are parents of real ape babies? Some evolution!)

There are abortive starts at character development which prove decoys; the battle between man and computer is a much overused story device; the suspense about what really is happening on Clavius is phony; the philosophy is about as profound as Kahlil Gibran's poetry; the end is needlessly ambiguous. (Parents report that even their children, who are supposed to have ideal responses to visual material, are quite dissatisfied with the end and the film's lack of resolution.) All of these flaws are completely unimportant to the film's fans.

It combines under one roof, so to speak, a whole panoply of underground innovations, without being better at them than individual underground practitioners (e.g.: Vanderbeek, for technical ingenuity and content; Warhol, for length and boredom; the non-underground films at Expo). Those who want to abandon themselves in the film's visual beauty wince at the story; and those interested in plot are bored by stars.

Brother Benjamin Colimore, a young ("Oh, I'm 30, isn't that terrible. But *I feel* 21") film student at Columbia who reviewed *Space Odyssey* for the Catholic Film Newsletter, made a fairly representative comment about this discrepancy: "I can see some objections, I suppose, but it didn't bother me a bit. I could accept anything because the environment was so extraordinary; I just went along with the whole thing."

(He did not, however, advise his readers to go along with the whole thing. In classifying it A II, morally unobjectionable for adults and adolescents, rather than for general patronage, he cautioned, "Viewers who adhere to rigid categorical forms or who have never aspired to any unorthodox speculation had better stay away. . . .")

Nonetheless, Brother Benjamin feels "there's a real philosophical, poetic strain running through the film that I find very optimistic. That life, knowledge, information, can't be destroyed; life keeps regenerating itself. The slab seems to represent some kind of life force or principle, a consciousness perpetuating itself in a higher form. As a visual symbol, I thought it worked; it was very concrete yet abstract at the same time. And did you notice it was the same shape as the elements of the computer's brain!"

Conversely, many people see Kubrick's message as extremely cautionary and pessimistic vis a vis the new human being, "the technitronic man," as Jerry Blumenthal, a former film instructor, now film editor for *Kartemquin,* says. "That's the new man, the kind of person Antonioni was talking about in *Red Desert.* They don't seem to feel, they communicate on a different level, a robot level. The two astronauts discussing what they should do to HAL, without a trace of human emotion, was great. Especially in contrast to both communications home—the little girl's (Kubrick's daughter) humanity, scratching her back. Those men would never scratch their backs; they wouldn't itch."

In summing up the film's appeal, perhaps Mama Cass put it best: "*2001* shows what the medium is all about. I've never had my chemistry changed by a movie before."

In Chicago, there is a group of young people who dress like hippies and go regularly to the Cinestage where they pay $2.90 for seats in the front rows. After the intermission, just before Dullea begins his spectacular trip toward infinity, across the landscape of his solarized cornea, the hippies relocate on the carpet in front of the screen, rest their heads on pillows or a friend's stomach, and silently, privately, groove. Berlitz has a crash program for learning a new language called "total immersion" that might be a useful term here.

There has been a tremendous amount of (rather specious) sorting and classifying about *2001* in the over-30 age bracket, that poor doomed group that is told by someone every hour its "relevance" is slipping.

Self-congratulation on the prized openness of mind that can tune into the nonlinear, discontiguous wave lengths of the TV-oriented young (reflecting the power of McLuhan suggestion?) tends to accompany the suspicion that any adult who does not like *2001* is personally threatened by change.

Contemporary trends in the arts, with which Kubrick is in tune, insist on the development and refinement of the senses over the intellect.

The specificity, the concreteness, of movies, however, presents special problems when dealing with an abstraction as *Space Odyssey* does. The eye insists on the reality of the image on the screen. Thus, when Kubrick, with thrilling gall, fills that

23-by-55-foot screen with meaningless formuli, vast geometric symbols and directional diagrams, it looks more like a primer on the landing of spacecraft than a fantasy thereon.

(At least the scientists I have spoken to did not recognize the flashing panels in the film as having any significance, unlike Godard's *Alphaville*, which incorporated Einstein's relativity theory — $E=MC^2$ — and the formula for nuclear fission into the winking neon cityscape.)

A far less successful solution to the problem presented by cinema reality is the black slab that represents an omniscient power from another system. The object looks more like a minimal sculpture by Tony Smith or an I-beam by Mies van der Rohe than a force beyond comprehension that seems to be programming human life and development. (Renata Adler, hopelessly locked into her theory that the film looks like the dreamworld of a precocious 1950s reader of comic books, described it as a combination "Prime Mover Slab and coffin lid," that came to resemble "a fifties candy bar.")

The Rolling Stone, a West Coast folk-rock paper, reports, however, an incident which would indicate that not all viewers interpret the black slab as an item that comes either plain or with almonds. As the monolith beckoned the astronaut into infinity, a young man in the audience succumbed to some kind of mystical trance, rose to his feet, ran down the aisle and crashed through the screen, shouting, "It's God! It's God!"

Dr. E. N. Parker, an astrophysicist at the University of Chicago, effectively put his finger on the most impressive aspect of the film — that is, Kubrick's genius for the orchestration of image and sound. Parker, and most of the science department, thought the whole was an imaginative tour de force, and that the usual scientific blunders had been avoided, "things like zero-G in orbit, and the fact that meteors don't come by red hot and roaring.

"From a purely fiction point of view, the story was pretty unimaginative," he said, "but it's really like going to an opera; if you stop to think about it, the plot of an opera is absurd. So you just sit back and listen to the music and enjoy every minute of it."

The space waltzes, in which the machines come into orbit for landings on the space station and on the Moon (to Strauss' *The Blue Danube*), are perhaps more lush and stunning than anything Visconti has conjured with people in baroque ballrooms.

Kubrick is said to have listened to over 400 tapes in selecting his music. It is somewhat astonishing that the pieces already existed, as they relate so perfectly to the visual material, particularly the works of the Hungarian avant-garde composer, György Ligeti.

His *Atmospheres*, which makes the awesome howl that accompanies the astronaut as he breaks through the "star gate" to his death and regeneration, was written in 1961. Leonard Bernstein and the New York Philharmonic presented it in concert in 1964 and it sank back into the sea of new works which are rarely tolerated in the concert hall.

What Kubrick demonstrates is that a whole new environment, outside of the concert hall where listening modes are fixed in past traditions, is more receptive to advanced music.

Ligeti's churchly, wordless hymns, *Requiem* and *Lux Aeterna*, are stunningly appropriate in introducing the Ur slab. As Leonard Meyer, head of the U. of C. music department, says, "It is purposeless, goalless music, that represents Kubrick's conception of a goalless, purposeless future." Meyer says further that the film shows "the time lag between high culture and popular culture is diminishing; there is growing feedback between art and advertising art, serious music and jazz, for instance. Eclecticism is really the art form of the times."

Print people, the dying species, will be pleased to know that Arthur C. Clarke's novel, *2001: A Space Odyssey*, has been published — without a single picture — and it is dramatically clear, where the film is most obscure, in the final bedroom scene.

The room, it seems, is a mock-up designed by the previous inhabitants of Jupiter as a congenial cage in which to study their captured Earth specimen. It has been modeled after a room in a movie picked up from Earth on Jupiter TV and is fitted, not only with a stage telephone and (empty) telephone book, but also with copies of hackneyed wall paintings (by Andrew Wyeth and Van Gogh). It is from this controlled environment that the earthling is conditioned for his next life among the mega-smart stars.

It may be, however, with apologies to Susan Sontag (*Against Interpretation*), that independent speculation as to what it all means has been more interesting than having it settled by its creators.

One last twilight-zone thought on the matter was contributed by an electronic engineer, who seems to play a major role in the film. His name is Shasti Chandra.

In both the movie and the book, when HAL is having his brain unscrewed, he poignantly digresses to his infant days "at the HAL Plant in Urbana, Ill." He repeats the tricks he was first programmed to perform: "Did you know the square root of 10 is 3 point 1622776601683879?" He sings :"Daisy, Daisy" and explains it was taught him by his first instructor, "Dr. Chandra."

Fearless reporter calls the University of Illinois to ask if there is such a person (well, everything else in the film is supposed to be authentic) and learns there is but that he, Shasti Chandra, is in Rochester, N. Y., with General Dynamics for the summer.

From Rochester, Mr. Chandra, bewildered, in polite Indian accents, confesses, "To the very best of my knowledge, I had nothing whatever to do with this 'Space Odyssey' you speak of."

Not only has he not seen it, he has never heard of it. He says, yes, he is interested in space, he is in fact writing his thesis on the attitude control of spacecraft. He became interested in the subject after reading books by Arthur C. Clarke; and he is the only Chandra at Urbana because he looked in the directory. But he truly knows nothing of this space odyssey.

How does he explain the extraordinary coincidences? "The only possibility that seems valid to me is that there is a world apart from what we see, that there is ESP, you know, and stuff like that, and that the person who wrote the screenplay was in contact with me in another world."

•

Stuart Byron of Variety over WBAI, New York

The main interest to us at *Variety* has been the unique way in which 2001 played off. 2001 is now pegged by M-G-M to take in domestically in rentals, which means not what comes to the box office, but that percentage of what comes to the box office which comes to M-G-M is now pegged to take in $25,000,000. Which would make it one of the top dozen grossers in U.S. film history. But it performed in a very special way.

Unlike most road shows, it did not depend very much on advance sales. Its fans would plunk their money down at the box office a half hour or fifteen minutes before the film was scheduled to begin as they would for a film that's on what's called continuous performances. Demographically, it did not attract what's normally thought of as a road-show audience. The theater party, the group sales, which normally include older, affluent couples, were not a very great market for the film. It in general has done best in those areas of the country which are fabled for having the greatest concentration of film enthusiasts, hippies, wild, young, McLuhan-ite people, which generally means almost any large city on the West Coast from Seattle down to Los Angeles and also those cities with great concentrations of colleges.

To us it made a very interesting comparison with *Gone With the Wind,* which probably in its current reissue will do even better than *2001* because, although each film was a smash success, they were so in exact opposite ways. Finally, there were ways in which the film was exhibited that were interesting. The seating in the front of houses, especially in so-called road-show houses, where there are 70-millimeter screens normally goes unsold when such a theater is doing capacity business. It's not counting the first ten rows of the orchestra, even a big road-show hit, a current one like *Funny Girl*. If you went to the Criterion Theater in New York, the first ten rows would be empty.

But that was where many of *2001*'s greatest fans wanted to sit. This gave the houses a greater capacity. And finally, and most reluctantly to us because we had feelings about besmirching the great film business, there was the phenomenon of this being a film which many youth elements liked to see when they were high on marijuana. Managers have been at their wits' end in its various locations in controlling this aspect."

•

From *The Washington Star:*
Exclusively Yours

Betty Beale

WASHINGTON HAD a taste of space in the year 2001 last evening and decided that 1968, with its wars, its crime and its sounds of mentally dulling decibles, was not so bad after all.

When the new M-G-M film, *2001: A Space Odyssey*, opened on a bunch of snarling, scrapping man-apes of four million years ago, everybody in the audience felt pretty much at home in this spring of a presidential campaign.

When it switched to the apparent peacefulness of immense infinity, it began to seem rather strange — especially when it did it all to the waltzing melodies of Strauss' music.

M-G-M gave Washington the kind of expensive premiere it usually reserves for Los Angeles and New York only. After the invitational opening at the Uptown Theater, there was a fancy buffet in the Shoreham's Regency Ballroom and dancing to Lester Lanin's orchestra.

Lynda Robb, accompanied by a friend and two Secret Servicemen, skipped the latter, but she stayed through the whole movie. In a long white dress with her black hair piled in a postiche of curls, she looked pretty but behind her smiling greetings there was not the radiant joy so apparent ever since she and Chuck became engaged.

Before the movie started she was telling someone she had not read the papers last Sunday. "I slept all morning; then, when I woke up — well," she said.

Obviously that was when her father's bombshell fell.

Was she pleased or sad?

"Well — you know — I can't run his life," replied Lynda, who did not mingle during intermission. Seeing Chuck off to war and hearing her father renounce his political career all in the space of a few hours must have been a real emotional strain.

Warrie Lynn Smith, extremely pretty in a ruffled-front, long white dress, was there with her frequent beau, goodlooking, bright Irvin Duggan of the White House staff, and they went on to the dance afterwards.

Jim Rowe, the President's campaign manager, and his wife were at the film and so were the Leonard Markses, the Dale Millers, Jane Langley with Gerson Nordlinger, the Brazilian ambassador, the Portuguese ambassador, the Hugh D. Auchinclosses, the Jack Valentis, the Herman Wouks, the George Stevenses Jr., the Ed Welches of NASA and Baron and Baroness Franco Fiorio.

Rowe said he, Marvin Watson and Larry O'Brien had spent Sunday afternoon on campaign plans, and he wasn't reached by phone until a few minutes after the President began his telecast.

There was a lot of sentiment for Hubert Humphrey expressed privately, but no one knew if there was time to build up his candidacy.

Humphrey, himself, probably has a better idea this morning. Last night he sat next to noted financier and "kingmaker" Sidney Weinberg at the annual dinner given in New York by Mike Cowles for the vice president, and Weinberg may have discussed it all with him.

Former Ambassador and Mrs. Bill Blair were at the movie premiere. When they were welcomed to Washington, Bill said, "I have been trying for years to come here to live. I love this city. I tried in '52 and '56, remember?"

Those were the times when he tried to get Adlai Stevenson elected president. Now he comes as director of the Kennedy Center.

Arthur Clarke, the space genius, author of science fiction and co-author of *2001,* was explaining to people during intermission that everything about the future in the movie up to that point would definitely take place by 2001.

The design of the spacecrafts was logical, the conversations with the brain computer were already an actuality, and the radio beacons received on Earth recently are exciting evidence of possible life on other planets.

Clarke is the man who back in 1945 originated the concept of the communications satellite, said Joseph Charyk, president of COMSAT, last night.

The movie is too slow-moving and too long, however, and it lost a lot of its audience at intermission. Despite its marvelous and elaborate sets and the perfection of its technique, it has a plot aimed at 7-year-olds.

Cracked a man in the movie business: "I have never seen such a piece of junk in my life." Said another observer: "It took three hours to find out that God is a monolith."

If Robert O'Brien, president of M-G-M, and Keir Dullea, the star, felt this way, they weren't showing it. Dullea brought to the party afterwards a beautiful young brunette from New York who is in the fashion business.

During the weeks after 2001 premiered, and contro-versy raged as to what he had had in mind, Stanley Kubrick gave only a couple of interviews. He agreed to be interviewed by the newspaper BOOKS — "news, not reviews" — on the condition that he could review and edit the transcript. The interview lasted for eight hours, but Kubrick approved only four comments for publication the next day. To fill the half of the front page that had been set aside for publication of tran-script highlights, BOOKS published its Kubrick in-terview as follows under the full-paper-width head-line "The Territorial Imperative of Stanley Kubrick":

We've just spent eight hours interviewing Stanley Kubrick.
We've just spent eight hours interviewing Stanley Kubrick.
"I'd rather not discuss the film."
We've just spent eight hours interviewing Stanley Kubrick.
We've just spent eight hours interviewing Stanley Kubrick.
"It takes about a year to let an idea reach an obsessional state so I know what I really want to do with it."
We've just spent eight hours interviewing Stanley Kubrick.
We've just spent eight hours interviewing Stanley Kubrick.
We've just spent eight hours interviewing Stanley Kubrick.
We've just spent eight hours interviewing Stanley Kubrick.
We've just spent eight hours interviewing Stanley Kubrick.
We've just spent eight hours interviewing Stanley Kubrick.
We've just spent eight hours interviewing Stanley Kubrick.
We've just spent eight hours interviewing Stanley Kubrick.
"The feel of the experience is the important thing, not the ability to verbalize or analyze it."
We've just spent eight hours interviewing Stanley Kubrick.
We've just spent eight hours interviewing Stanley Kubrick.
We've just spent eight hours interviewing Stanley Kubrick.
We've just spent eight hours interviewing Stanley Kubrick.
We've just spent eight hours interviewing Stanley Kubrick.
We've just spent eight hours interviewing Stanley Kubrick.
We've just spent eight hours interviewing Stanley Kubrick.
We've just spent eight hours interviewing Stanley Kubrick.
We've just spent eight hours interviewing Stanley Kubrick.
We've just spent eight hours interviewing Stanley Kubrick.
We've just spent eight hours interviewing Stanley Kubrick.
"You have to be prepared to make adjustments."
We've just spent eight hours interviewing Stanley Kubrick.
We've just spent eight hours interviewing Stanley Kubrick.

"Did the crew get back all right?"

Ted Mahar, drama editor of The Oregonian *(Portland, Oregon), and film instructor at the University of Portland, has a sharp eye and a good memory. In an unpublished critique of* 2001, *he zoomed in on many points that other critics missed completely. By comparing* 2001 *with Kubrick's other films, he places the futuristic beauty squarely in the present — Kubrick's present.*

MAHAR notes: For a man who has just spent in excess of $10,000,000 of M-G-M's money in three years on a motion picture that breaks every conventional bond, Kubrick is nevertheless a babe in the woods. "Kubrick has made only six major films. John Huston, John Ford, Henry Hathaway, Akira Kurosawa, Ingmar Bergman, Howard Hawks, Alfred Hitchcock — all have made more than a score of features, Ford well over a hundred." Yet, says Mahar, Kubrick already has a style as distinctive as any of them.

Mahar examines these films by Kubrick: *Paths of Glory, Spartacus* (to which Kubrick came as director after the script was finished and the production already underway, thus leaving him less than his usual total freedom of control), *Lolita, Dr. Strangelove,* and *2001.* In them, he finds several common themes: the fallibility of persons charged with management of a system, attempted communication with a person who cannot or will not understand, obedience unto death, no central normal love relationship.

Mahar also detects infatuation for machinery and for unconventional, often shocking material. Mahar cites Kubrick's sympathy with a moment in a Cocteau film ". . . in which a young poet asked an older man what he should do, what his aims should be. The answer was 'Astonish me.'" Kubrick, he says, astonishes us wherever possible. (Kubrick himself cited the Cocteau reference in answering correspondence from Mahar.)

That these themes are all present in *2001* is immediately clear: HAL, charged with the success of the mission, breaks down. Bowman cannot communicate with him at the pivotal moment when his life seems to depend on it — when he returns with Poole's body and demands to be permitted into the spaceship. (HAL, for his part, then is forced to plead vainly to deaf ears when, after gaining reentry, Bowman methodically disconnects him.) Bowman's obedience to the mission — whose goal he does not know—and disregard for his personal safety is nothing less than superhuman (and with superhuman results). That there is no love and no sex in *2001* has irritated many critics, who then clutch at straws by trying to find significance in HAL's asexual voice ("androgynous," says Mahar, who goes on to remind us that Kubrick actually emphasizes the lack of human sexual contact in many details: Floyd cannot even speak to his wife, the female Russian scientist admits that her husband is always away somewhere exploring the ocean floor, etc., and, as if that were not enough, it is only the apes who are seen in family groups). *2001* abounds in machinery of all kinds, machinery which "smothers" the human beings ("machines are kind of sexy," Mahar quotes Kubrick as saying), and as for unconventional themes—*2001* sets a new landmark.

Mahar's development of these themes in other Kubrick films is revealing. The failure of the man in control is illustrated by Kirk Douglas in both *Spartacus* and *Paths of Glory* (noble failings, says Mahar). Indeed, *Paths of Glory* is a study of failures of men in control, ending with the failure of the last instrument of justice, the court-martial. Humbert Humbert (James Mason) in *Lolita* became unable to control his love affair with a teenage girl, and ends up a pathetic figure. *Dr. Strangelove* is about little else *but* the failure of men charged with maintaining a failsafe system.

The uselessness of words when one party to a dialogue is beyond reach shows up throughout Kubrick films. In *Paths of Glory,* Mahar points out, not all the words in the world could "carry the simple message: the men on trial are innocent . . . because the court's mind had been made up for it before it had even been convened."

In *Lolita,* Quilty (Peter Sellers) argues for his life with Humbert, "but Humbert had gone beyond words, and he shot Quilty down as calmly as if he were turning off the cold water." In *Dr. Strangelove,* Peter Sellers as the U.S. President tries desperately to talk to the Russian premier, but the premier is drunk.

The call of duty calls many Kubrick characters beyond the point at which most men would follow. (Mahar also says that, with the exception of *Lolita*, Kubrick favors quasi-military situations where duty is of central importance.) *Paths of Glory* and *Spartacus* focus on this kind of obedience to a higher valor; in *Lolita* Humbert remains "loyal to his obsession," and Sterling Hayden as General Ripper in *Dr. Strangelove* "was being loyal to a personal obsession and felt that he was pushing the system to its logical end anyway." (Slim Pickens as Major

Kong in *Strangelove* crowns the black humor of that film with a loyalty that results in the world being blown up, and Mahar points out that Kubrick manages to trick the audience into actually rooting for the success of that loyalty.)

The only conventional love interest of importance in a Kubrick film, says Mahar, is that between Jean Simmons and Kirk Douglas in *Spartacus,* "but even there it was unconventional, having started when she was forced into his cage to satisfy his sexual appetites." Until the end of *Paths of Glory* there are no women. Homosexuality and bizarre sex are hinted at darkly in *Spartacus; Lolita* focuses on an outrageous alliance (made even more outrageous by the marriage of Humbert to Lolita's mother and, in the book at any rate, by Lolita's pre-pubescent wiles). In *Strangelove* mistresses abound, General Ripper suffers from premature ejaculation, Colonel "Bat" Guano (Keenan Wynn) hates and fears "preverts," and at the film's end Dr. Strangelove "led the war room inhabitants on a flight of fancy about surviving in deep mines where the monogamous way of life would have to be abandoned and where women would have to be chosen for their sexual attractiveness, since men would be called upon to render heroic sexual service, all in the interest of survival."

"A certain ambivalent relationship between man and machine," says Mahar, can be seen shaping up as early as *Paths of Glory.* In that film George Macready refuses to shell his own men because the order to do so reached him by telephone — thus leaving him without witnesses to the fact that he would be acting under orders. In *Lolita* the telephone again frustrates, because Humbert cannot reach Quilty or Lolita by phone, but Quilty can use it to harass Humbert. The telephone plays several important roles in *Strangelove,* too, as heads of state attempt to communicate over it; toward the end of the film the order that would save the world from destruction cannot be delivered because the plane carrying the crucial bomb load has had its radio damaged. "A most telling machinery scene occurs in *Strangelove* when Wynn has to rob one machine — the Coca-Cola dispenser — to make another one — a pay phone — work." And, of course, the whole plot of that film turns on the existence of the Russians' doomsday machine.

2001 has precedents in Kubrick films for many of its most important aspects, as Ted Mahar shows — which gives perspective to the widely held opinion that "because of its dazzling special effects, futuristic subject matter and unique stylistic 'feel,' nothing like *2001* has ever been seen before."

"I enjoy working with people."

A rosebud by any other name!
Here's what the artifact's been called:

Artifact
Metal prism
Pentalogue
Mies van der Rohe version of one-half
    the Tablets of the Law
Black basalt column
Black steel door
Long cement board
Pillar
The block
Monolith
That damn two-by-four
Teaching machine
Candy bar
Calling card
Transistor radio
Handball court wall
Cracker Jacks box
Vibrating Metallic Bar
God

•

William Blake: "If the doors of perception were cleansed, everything would appear to man as it is, infinite."

Confucius: "The way out is through the door."

John Cage: "Complaint: you open doors; what we want to know is which ones you close. (Doors I open close automatically after I go through.)"

Carl Jung: "Proceed from the dream outward."

In 1960, the Austrian Ernst Fuchs painted "The Unhinged Doors of Gaza." Aldous Huxley's *The Doors of Perception.* Jim Morrison's [LS]Doors.

Arthur C. Clarke: "We recently discovered there is actually a Buddhist sect that worships a large, black rectangular slab. The analogy of the Kaaba has also been mentioned. Though I certainly did not have it in mind at the time, the fact that the Black Stone sacred to Moslems is reputed to be a meteorite is more than quaint coincidence."

Erich von Daniken: In *Chariots of the Gods* he writes that the seventh of twelve tablets found in the hill of Kiyundjik at the turn of the century, and belonging originally to the library of the Assyrian King Assurbanipal, reports that a door arrived on Earth from another planet and spoke like a living person.

•

Four times a black monolith is seen in perfect conjunction with heavenly bodies. Each time represents a major change in man's fate:

— *When the ape-man suddenly learns to use a bone as a tool.*
— *When the scientists on the Moon examine the monolith and it sends its piercing signal toward Jupiter.*
— *When Bowman approaches Jupiter.*
— *When Bowman is reborn.*

•

Ed Rosenfeld discovered that the *Encyclopaedia Britannica* and the Smithsonian Institution say that the eighth satellite from Saturn is Iapetus. The Hayden Planetarium in New York says that it is Iapetus. *The Oxford Dictionary of the English Language* says it is Iapetus. *The Columbia Encyclopedia* says it is Iapetus. Arthur C. Clarke, the perfectionist, in his book, *2001,* has Dave Bowman land on the eighth satellite from Saturn: *Japetus.* Page 763, *Random House Unabridged Dictionary: Jape — to jest, joke; to mock or make fun of; a joke, jest, or quip.* Is Clarke trying to tell us something?

•

From *A to Z Horoscope Maker and Delineator:* When planets, or the cusp of a house and a planet, occupy the same degree of longitude, they are in conjunction. Some planets are good, some adverse, and some others are doubtful as to any influence at all. Some examples: When the Sun is in conjunction with Jupiter or Venus it is a favorable aspect; when the Sun is in conjunction with Uranus, Saturn, or Mars, it is an unfavorable aspect. It is doubtful that there is any influence when the Sun is in conjunct aspect to Neptune or Pluto. From *How To Judge a Nativity*: Conjunctions stand symbolically for union and synthesis. What effect the union will have depends on the nature of the combined planets. . . . When two notes are sounded together on a musical instrument, the resulting sound depends upon whether the two sets of vibrations harmonize or not. And so with planetary conjunctions. Planets considered good are Jupiter and Venus; bad, Pluto, Neptune, Uranus, Saturn, and Mars; and neutral or variable, the Sun, Moon, and Mercury. Margaret Hone, in *The Modern Text Book of Astrology,* defines conjunction as a strong focal point. The principles of the two planets will not be fused but will react on each other or modify each other. (Kubrick's Sun/Venus conjunction is an aspect that indicates ease in relations of love and with the opposite sex, plus ability with the fine arts. Grant Lewi, in *Heaven Knows What*, suggests that this aspect brings an idealistic sex appeal.) (Kubrick's astrological Sun sign is Leo—the same as Napoleon's.)

•

A brief interview with Robert H. O'Brien, on his last day as chairman of M-G-M:

"*2001* is a profitable picture. It will make M-G-M a profit. It is one of the greatest motion pictures of all times. Kubrick was consulted on all advertising and we listened to his ideas. He had good ideas, too. *2001* is a great picture. Kubrick made one of the greatest movies of all time. He did things no one has ever done before. No one knew how to do them. A great motion picture, one of the greatest."

What are your plans, Mr. O'Brien?
[Surprised] "Oh, just to clean things up here. No specific plans."

Stanley Kubrick comments on Robert O'Brien:

"My relations with Mr. O'Brien were very good. The cost of the film was ten and one-half million dollars, and Mr. O'Brien, being the president of the company at the time, was the one who authorized the money. Although he was bothered constantly by the problem of maintaining control of the company, warding off various attempts at usurpation of his authority, and having to win the affection of the stockholders, he never burdened me with any of these problems; he was very strong in not passing on his problems to me. He realized that it was necessary for us, somehow, to overcome the previously unsolved problem of making special effects in the film look completely realistic, and he understood that new techniques were being devised, engineered, and so forth, and that somebody *had* to get these right, otherwise the film would be expensive at any price. O'Brien had seen a lot of the film in sort of isolated form, but once the film was being cut—well, first of all, the film never *was* cut much before I left for California, and because of the slowness in getting the special effects completed there were huge sections of the film missing, and I didn't want to show it to anyone in that form. O'Brien had enough confidence that he would get what he was hoping for that he never insisted on seeing anything except whatever I wanted to show him. Nobody saw the cut film until it was finished, because there really wasn't any time for anyone to see it."

Were the stockholders growing restive and applying pressure to Mr. O'Brien because of the time it took you to complete 2001?

Kubrick: "Well, I don't know of any specific cases, and he never said there were, but I wouldn't be surprised if the film was an embarrassment to him during the making of it. It certainly hasn't been an embarrassment *since* then, but before anybody saw it I'm sure that they wondered what was going on."

•

Nearly thirty minutes pass before the first words are spoken in *2001*. Kubrick: "I tried to work things out so that nothing important was said in the dialogue, and that anything important in the film be translated in terms of action."

The first speech:
Orion hostess (to Dr. Floyd): Here you are, sir. Main level, please.
Floyd: See you on the way back.

Space station hostess: Did you have a pleasant flight?
Floyd: Yes, very nice, thanks.

Miller (of space-station security): Sorry I'm late [as though he had had far to go].

Floyd: That's quite all right.
Miller: Gee, you're looking great.
Floyd: Thank you.

Miller: Did you have a good flight?
Floyd: Very nice, indeed.

Public address system speaker: A woman's cashmere sweater has been found. . . .

> [And on it goes on the space station, ironyzing Floyd's comment to the Russian scientists, "I'm not at liberty to discuss this."]

Daughter: Are you coming to my party tomorrow?
Floyd: Well . . . [pause] . . . you know, Daddy's traveling. Very sorry about it, but I can't. . . . Tell Mommy that I telephoned and that I'll try to telephone again tomorrow . . . [raising voice, as in an Earthian long-distance call] Happy Birthday.

Floyd: Elena, you're looking wonderful.
Elena: Thank you. You're looking well, too.

Floyd: Did the crew get back all right?
Smyslov: Yes, yes. Fortunately they did.
Floyd: I'm glad about that.

Conference leader: Well, I know you will all want to join with me in welcoming our distinguished friend and colleague, Dr. Heywood Floyd. [Clapping]
Floyd: Hi, everybody. Nice to be back with you. [Chuckle in voice]

Moon bus companions: Well, anybody hungry? . . . You know that was an excellent speech you gave us, Heywood. . . . It certainly was. . . . I'm sure it beefed up morale a helluva lot.
Floyd: Thanks, Ralph. Oh, by the way, I want to say to both of you I think you've done a wonderful job. . . .

Floyd: Deliberately buried? [Chuckle]

Moon bus companion: Well, how about a little coffee.

Floyd: I don't suppose you have any idea what the damned thing is?
Companion: Wish the hell we did.

Floyd: I must say you guys have come up with something.

BBC announcer: How's everything going?
Bowman and Poole: Marvelous. We have no complaints.
BBC announcer: I'm very glad to hear that.

BBC announcer: Good afternoon, HAL. How's everything going?
HAL: Everything is going extremely well.

Father and Mother: Well, Frank, I can't think of anything else to say. . . . We wish you the very happiest of birthdays. . . . Happy birthday, Frank. . . . Mother and I are both feeling wonderful, too. . . . How do you like your cake, dear? . . . See you next Wednesday.

HAL: Good evening, Dave.
Bowman: How're you doin', HAL?

HAL: Thank you for a very enjoyable game.
Poole: Thank you.

HAL: May I see them . . . do you mind if I ask you a personal question? . . . Forgive me for being so inquisitive. . . .

Mission Control: Sorry you fellows are having a bit of trouble. . . . Sorry about this little snag, fellows.

Poole: Well, what do you think?
Bowman: I'm not sure. What do you think?
Poole: I've got a bad feeling about him.
Bowman: You do?
Poole: Yes. Definitely. Don't you?
Bowman: I can't put my finger on it, but I sense something strange about him.

Bowman: Where'd the hell you'd get that idea, HAL?

HAL: This conversation can serve no purpose any more. Goodbye.

Only one speech in the entire motion picture lets the audience in audibly on what it's been all about for two hours. It's the last speech from Mission Control, triggered on the television set when HAL is lobotomized; the secret springs out:

DR. FLOYD: Good day, gentlemen. This is a pre-recorded

briefing made prior to your departure at which for security reasons of the highest importance that've been known on board during the mission only by your HAL 9000 computer. Now that you are in Jupiter space, and the entire crew is revived, it can be told to you. Eighteen months ago, the first evidence of intelligent life off the Earth was discovered. It was buried forty feet below the lunar surface, near the crater Tycho. Except for a single, very powerful radio emission aimed at Jupiter, the four-million-year-old black monolith has remained completely inert, its origin and purpose still a total mystery.

•

Stanley Kubrick's interest in having one's just desserts, so to eat, continues. On every leg of the odyssey at hand, a little something is served. Dinners of tapir-meat and a leopard's portion of zebra, meals for everyone aboard the Aries, drinks on the space station, sandwiches on the Moon bus, Bowman and Poole's TV dinner. Dr. Floyd's daughter is about to have a birthday party—one can imagine the cake! Poole's parents show his birthday cake on screen: "How do you like your cake, dear?" When we last see Bowman, he is eating what appears to be the ultimate joke: himself. When he knocks the wine glass to the floor, well, who's perfect?

•

Stanley Kubrick's interest in the bathroom continues. There were the famous bathroom scenes in *Lolita* and *Spartacus*. Jack D. Ripper kills himself in a bathroom in *Dr. Strangelove*, and George C. Scott's entrance is preceded by the sound of a flushed toilet. In *2001*, Dr. Floyd always gets a big audience laugh when he reads, or tries to read, the zero gravity toilet instructions. Rachel, the baby-sitter, is in the bathroom. At film's "end," Bowman walks into a bathroom. (At the end of Homer's *Odyssey*: "Then the old woman bathed Laertes and rubbed him down with soft oil, and wrapped a fine robe about him: Athena stood by his side and put fullness into his limbs, so that he seemed stronger and bigger than before. When he came out of the bathroom, his son was astonished to see him like one come down from heaven. . . .")

Lots of killings:

2 apes
1 zebra
Miscellaneous tapirs
3 hibernating astronauts
1 H. A. L. 9000
Poole
Bowman (reborn)
Kubrick? ("I never discuss money,
but I own a good piece of it.")

Lots of little films:

Computer readouts
Welcome of the Voiceprint girl
Japanese wrestling
Aries landing at Clavius
Love scene in automobile
BBC "World Tonight"
Conferences with mission control
Dr. Floyd's final report detailing truth
about the mission
Dr. Floyd's daughter on Picturephone
Birthday greeting to Poole

Lots of snapshots:

I.D. badges
News photographer in the Moon conference room
Group picture in the TMA-1 pit.

•

Error in 2001:

Heywood Floyd's lunch is sipped; what he doesn't
sip then slides down his straw. It should have
stayed in the straw in the zero gravity of space.

•

Mission Commander Dave Bowman makes it to a room best described as:

"Louis Quinze"—Peter Dibble, *Women's Wear Daily*

"Brilliantly-lit Louis Seize"—Bruce Gillespie, *Australian Science Fiction Review*

"Louis XVI hotel suite"—Joseph Morgenstern, *Newsweek*

"Period French bedroom"—B. L. Drew, *Camden* (N. J.) *Courier Post*

"Strange Colonial room"—G. Youngblood, *Los Angeles Free Press*

"Room decorated in a modified Empire style"—G. Curner, *Australian Science Fiction Review*

"18th century hotel-room-like"—Judith Crist, *New York* magazine

"Magnificent marble palazzo"—S. Johnson, *Montreal Star*

"Startlingly conventional room, which seems to exist independently of time and space"—*T&D*, San Diego, Calif.

"Miami Beach hotel elegance"—G. Bourke, *Miami Herald*

Headlines over *2001* reviews and articles read like found poetry!

It may sound like Vienna, but it's outer space

A machine for all seasons

A superb wreck

Lost in the stars

Space for the tyro

Future tense, present tensions

Escaping into orbit

Stanley Kubrick, please come down

Kubrick, farther out

Up, up and away

After man

Is Stanley Kubrick Dr. Strange?

Kubrick's Cosmos

Space Odyssey May Curl Mind

Renaissance man in sci-fi

What eternity looks like

When technology displaces drama

Space, Spice and Speciousness

Waltzing through space, time and the unknown

Not quite as far as thought can reach

.

Look magazine decided that it would publish a special section of editorial and advertising matter plugged into *2001*. A twenty-minute color film was produced for promoting advertisers. Vernon Myers, *Look* publisher, made the pitch himself, mentioning von Braun, Saturn V rockets, Apollo astronauts, pay-loads, quarter-million miles. "The American people are not well prepared to comprehend the social impact of it all . . . they need movies like *2001* . . . *Look* stands ready as an educational back-drop. *Look* aims at nothing less than the indoctrination of our public with the consequences of cosmic communication."

Scenes of *2001* in production: Heywood Floyd opens a suitcase containing a telephone, television screen, tabulator, computer print-out. There's a "memory space help," to be "worn in the film by the six astronauts . . . these are memory packages that can be inserted . . . they will supply the astronauts with additional information."

2001, we are assured by the narrator, will begin on the Moon. It will "explore man's place in the universe and his position in the order of cosmic intelligence." Kubrick's "bizarre and incisive imagination" is running things. Arthur Clarke: "Space explora-tion is really the next step in the evolution of mankind, you can not live in the cradle forever." Keir Dullea: "Stanley Kubrick is surely one of the giants of our industry . . . as far as direction is concerned . . . Ulysses, by the way, would be the greatest analogy I could think of for this character . . . the part of Cap-tain David Bowman."

.

Michelangelo Antonioni: *"I don't like· 2001 completely. It* *very beautiful visually and technically as a film. But I don* *agree with Kubrick. I don't understand exactly what he's saying about technology. I think he's confused."*

•

Castle of Frankenstein: "Were you thrown any by the wildly abstract ending?"
Ray Bradbury: "I wasn't thrown off. I just didn't understand it."
Castle of Frankenstein: "Many fans were surprised when you panned *2001* in *Psychology Today*." [As follows]:

> Clarke, a voyager to the stars, is forced to carry the now inexplicably dull director Kubrick the albatross on his shoulders through an interminable journey of almost three hours. The idea, as conceived by Clarke, is immense and moving. Clarke should have done the screenplay totally on his own and not allowed Kubrick to lay hands on it. Technically and photographically, it is probably the most stunning film ever put on the screen. Surely all the people connected with the blueprinting of the look and feel of the picture should take all of the awards next year. . . . The test of the film is whether or not we care when one of the astronauts dies. We do not. . . . The freezing touch of Antonioni, whose ghost haunts Kubrick, has turned everything here to ice.

Bradbury: "I panned part of it. Only part of it. I think it's a gorgeous film. One of the most beautifully photographed pictures in the history of motion pictures. Unfortunately, there are no well-directed scenes, and the dialogue is banal to the point of extinction."
Castle of Frankenstein: "I read somewhere that was part of Kubrick's intention."
Bradbury: "I hope not. I'd like to believe Kubrick is more in-telligent than that. I just think he's a bad writer who got in the way of Arthur C. Clarke, who is a wonderful writer. . . ."

Clarke: "*I don't worry about Ray. He'll come around. They all do. Ray also claimed that I had been raped by Kubrick. I assure you, it was mutual.*"

•

Marshall McLuhan, *The Dew-Line*:
"A movie like *2001* belongs to 1901, or even to the world of Jules Verne. It is filled with Nineteenth-Century hardware and

Newtonian imagery. It has few, if any, twentieth-century qualities. This is natural. The public is not capable of being entertained by awareness of its own condition. Fish do not care to think about water, or men about air pollution."

•

Kubrick: "I have always thought that James Agee made one of the kindest remarks anyone has ever made to me. After seeing my first film, *Fear and Desire*, which was really a very inept and pretentious effort, Agee and I had a drink at a bar on Sixth Avenue in New York, a couple of blocks below West 4th Street, and he said to me, with a very pained and strained expression on his face, 'There are too many good things in the film to call it arty.'"

Fred Ordway: "The only time in all those years that I didn't hear Kubrick talk about *2001* was during the Israel-Arab War in 1967, when he kept saying, 'Where are the Russian advisers? Where are the Russian advisers?' Stanley, always the general. You can criticize old Kubrick, but it took a genius to put *2001* all together."

Clarke: "One of the biggest roles of science fiction is to prepare people to accept the future without pain and to encourage a flexibility of mind. Politicians should read science fiction, not Westerns and detective stories. Two-thirds of *2001* is realistic—hardware and technology—to establish a background for the metaphysical, philosophical, and religious meanings later."

•

What was it like on the set, Con Pederson, special effects man?

"It was mind-boggling. The amount of equipment, the extent of jury-rigged scaffolding, carpentry, camera boxes, lighting, wiring, motors, tracks, accessory furnishings, work tables, black velvet drapes, hardboard partitions sectioning things up, people pushing brooms and barrows, riggers shouting (they never just talk), sparks arguing (electricians), chippies hammering (carpenters). Before a shot was ready to go there was absolute chaos.

"Then, suddenly, a two- or three-hour take would begin, and the contrast was unbelievable. You would feel your way by faith and luck through the same labyrinth in total darkness, occasionally encountering a human head, which, somehow, could recognize you in the dark and direct your feet around the junction boxes; the silence was stifling, except for the patient whirring of the Panavision camera motors and track gears (cameras were sometimes louder than the massive drive mechanisms, when those motors were well away and muffled). Then a focus puller would yell a track reading, and the operator would sometimes repeat it when checking a corresponding reading, perhaps a footage count.

"The only thing that really revealed the true population would be finally at the cut, when the doorman would call out 'trolley,' for the tea trolley was the most vital aspect of all stage existence. And if they were shooting a 'seven o'clocker'—which was often, overtime being the normal procedure—there would be a dinner of ham rolls, 'bangers' on white bread laden with butter, or pork pies that would best be described in military slang.

"The only thing is that the days were long, ten to twelve hours, the weeks were long (six to seven days), the months were long—on and on, no respite. The routine was intense. In an airport terminal the routine lacks intensity except in a crisis. Our situation was always generating a crisis in order to function at maximum effort.

"It was like driving a tank. You'd like to turn off the motor once in a while, but you can't stop because your road is moving almost as fast. You'd like to race ahead, but your best gear is low—the others get you in other troubles, if you dig tanks."

•

Kubrick aide: *"The most incredible thing about Stanley's office was that he could never find a unit list (with everyone's phone number), even though there were dozens of office people to keep such a list up-to-date. He found it quickest to phone anyone whose number he could remember, and ask them if they knew where so-and-so was, and, by the way, how were things going. Kind of a random cascade reference program."*

•

The sketches shown to HAL by Bowman were made by Tony Masters, an art director on *2001*.

•

Fred Hoyle was asked to advise the production. He declined:
"I'm sorry, but I don't have the time." . . . Mel Maron, road-
show sales manager for M-G-M, quoted in *Variety*: "This
wasn't a picture for the Hadassah girls." . . . Clive Barnes, *The
New York Times* drama and ballet critic: "*2001* is woefully
underrated." . . . William Kloman, in *The Times*: "I suspect
that much of the critical hostility to *Space Odyssey* originated
in the theater lobby during intermission. Critics (some of whom
seemed to dislike movies and wish they were more like books)
met their friends and found that nobody was able to verbalize
what the film, so far, had 'meant.' They were back in high school
in the fifties, trying vainly to equate daffodils with yellow hair.
But Kubrick had denied them any translatable daffodils. The
damned spaceship just *sat* there, like a McCarthy button, asking
to be dug." . . . Leonard Bernstein got a big laugh from a children's audience at a New York Philharmonic Concert when he
greeted an electronic synthesizer that had been rolled onto the
stage, "Hello, HAL." . . . One of the expert interviewees was
B.F. Skinner, the celebrated Harvard psychologist. Skinner mis-
spelled "psychology" on a card he gave to a Kubrick aide; "I've
never known how to spell it," Skinner said. . . . A Seattle orchestra greeted U.S. astronauts with selections from *2001*.

•

Nahpets Vorodoch: "*Odyssey* = the journey of Odysseus
(Ulysses) who in the Joyce version at least meets his 'true' son
(Stephen) whose name is Dedalus (and Icarus, flying beyond
man's limits, etc.). Also, meeting one's self = transport of self
back to childhood (end of film). Mabbott Street = atmosphere of
Jupiter (with all those silly blinking oil-slicks)?? (Well, the chaos
before realization works in both anyway.) Wild drinking at end
of Mabbott Street—and glasses break! One of Joyce's fun words
is metempsychosis (Molly pronounces it met-him-pike-hosses?)
= 'rebirth of souls,' certainly descriptive of end of film."

•

Seventh Avenue executive, leaving 2001: "*Well,* that's *one
man's opinion.*" . . . *Full-page advertisement, for Macy's:*
"2001: A Space Odyssey *reveals its astonishing glimpse of the
future. . . . It's fun to speculate about the future, but it's even
more satisfying to have what you want when you want it. That's
why over a million people are enjoying Macy accounts . . . and
charging what they buy.*"

•

Milton Berliner, *Washington Daily News*: "Discovery of strange radio signals from outer space couldn't have come at a better time for M-G-M. It ties in beautifully with the company's current campaign directing attention to the opening of *2001*."

•

NEWS REPORT, CHICAGO, APRIL, 1969 — Man-like teeth and jaws have been found in southern Ethiopia that would nearly double the history of man's ancestors in East Africa from two million to four million years. "What we have found demonstrates a substantially longer evolutionary history for the Australopith man-ape than was suspected before."

•

Scenes cut before the premiere included: the showing of the purchase in Macy's of a bushbaby — "Macy's wasn't very happy that it was cut," said Clarke; on the Moon, youngsters playing, swans floating, men painting; what the astronauts' families were like; and, says Kubrick, "other minor documentary shots. We had a Ping-Pong table and a piano and a shower in the Discovery, but in the end they didn't seem worth putting into the film; one tries to tighten up a film wherever possible."

•

In the book, the monolith discovered on the Moon has dimensions in the ratio $1 \times 4 \times 9$, the squares of 1, 2, 3, which serve to emphasize the idea of mathematics as a truly universal language. Different-sized monoliths were used in the film. "The $1 \times 2^2 \times 3^2$ was my gimmick later," says Clarke.

•

Emerson Beauchamp, *Washington Evening Star:* "Arthur Clarke told a press preview audience that 'if you understand *2001* the first time, we would have failed completely.' Consider it a success, Mr. Clarke." ... Stan VanDerBeek, multi-mediast: "*2001* is a remarkable, a fascinating idea, but the film is too long. Kubrick's uneconomical in making his point. The ending bothered me a little bit, this sudden realistic flip-flop into surrealism, which is a good idea, great idea, but a little too suspended. He's provoking you to make you fill in the ending, although I'm in sympathy with the idea." •

•

Roger Ebert, *Chicago Sun-Times*: "After the film was over, someone suggested that maybe M-G-M should require an I.Q. test before allowing people into the theater. I can understand that point of view. If people do not have the courtesy to shut up during a film, they should at least be segregated into special Saturday kiddie matinees, no matter how advanced their years."

•

From Arthur Clarke's *Childhood's End:*

"It was lifeless, of course—not, as he had thought in that first moment of panic, consciously staring up at him. It filled almost all that great circular space, and the ruby light gleamed and shifted in its crystal depths.

"It was a single giant eye.

". . . His heart was still pounding violently as he stared down once more at that monstrous eye. Of course, it might have been a model, enormously enlarged as were microbes and insects in terrestrial museums. Yet even as he asked the question, Jan knew, with a sickening certainty, that it was no larger than life.

"Vindarten could tell him little: this was not his field of knowledge, and he was not particularly curious. From the Overlord's description, Jan built up a picture of a cyclopean beast living among the asteroidal rubble of some distant sun, its growth uninhibited by gravity, depending for food and life upon the range and resolving power of its single eye."

•

On the lecture circuit, Patrick R. Brostowin, English Department, Nassau Community College: "2001 is a significant literary attempt to forge a new epic in modern scientific terms, just as the Homeric and Miltonic epics were welded on mythical and theological frameworks."

•

A. Guichard, edita S. A., Lausanne, Switzerland: "My intention was to publish an illustrated book on 2001, and I met Mr. Kubrick. As a matter of fact, we never made precise plans about this book, and I decided to drop the project when I realized how complicated it would be to deal with M-G-M, Stanley Kubrick, and Arthur Clarke, as well as with many other people involved."

•

"Tonight, let's all make love in London as if it were 2001, the years of thrilling God." — Allen Ginsberg, June 8, 1965.

•

New York's Daily News *gave* 2001 *the lowest ranking it had given a reserved-seat film to date: two and one-half stars. In her pan, critic Kathleen Carroll thought the film muddled, puzzling, and confused. But more than the other two New York daily critics, and perhaps subconsciously, she seemed to recognize milestone possibilities. Her lead:* "2001: A Space Odyssey *is not a movie; it's an experience."*

Subsequently, the Daily News *devoted three editorials to* 2001, *unprecedented in film history. While reiterating Miss Carroll's reservations, the editorials urged* News *readers not to miss it:* "If you want an appetizing preview of what wonders man may achieve in space, see 2001: A Space Odyssey . . . the bulk of the picture has to do with the most fascinating space gadgets and stunts imaginable, plus marvelous color photography and near-miraculous camera trickery. Don't miss it." *(April 17, 1968)*

The publication of Arthur C. Clarke's novel spurred the second editorial. On the movie: "A must for any science-fiction fan." *On the novel:* "It is all written in beautiful style by a master of the English language — and is hereby recommended whether you're a science-fiction buff or not." *(September 9, 1968)*

And again, thirteen months after the film's New York opening: "If you want to see how you or your children can hope to travel among the planets someday, catch 2001: A Space Odyssey." *(May 28, 1969)*

•

The Bureau of Standards atomic clock, the paragon of accuracy, mysteriously slows down every sunrise.

•

Arthur Clarke once wrote for a magazine, "The first version of the novel [of *2001*] was handed to Stanley on the 24th of December, 1964, and he promptly fired me. True, I began work next day under a new contract, but I like to claim that I was sacked on Christmas eve." Kubrick had a chance to edit Clarke's article, adding such notations: ". . . the implication here is that you wrote novel alone. 'Fired me' is confusing. No one will know what you mean. It sounds like it was no good."

•

"I took Charlie and Oona to the ABC Fulham Road Cinema to see 2001. Both were overwhelmed, and Charlie wept at the sheer beauty of the accomplishment."

Jerry Epstein, producer of The Countess of Hong Kong

•

Abbie Hoffman, in *Revolution for the Hell of It*: "*2001* has things to feel in it and it's fascinating how all the human emotions, joy, sadness, love, anxiety, jealousy, hatred, on and on, come through so clearly in a film that on its surface seems to deal so much with machines and the mastery of them. I mean, where the fuck are the tits and ass that we have been conditioned to see as dealing with the emotional side of man?"

•

ADVENTURE ON MARS
By Chris Cerf

In the year of darkness 2001 A.D., two people from Earth rocketed off to Mars! The cargo they quickly loaded into the Lezairo, the bigest FLYING Saucer on Earth!

J. Dope said, "How's your wife, David." "That's rather irrelevant J."

Finnaly they arrived on Mars, the first people to visit another planet besides Earth!

Christopher Bennett Cerf wrote this story, set it with rubber type, and published it on a toy press when he was in the sixth grade in Friends' Seminary in New York City. He is now 29 years old, a science-fiction anthologizer, an author, and an editor at Random House.

•

Clarke: *"We had our first freakout in Los Angeles. A kid went up to the screen and screamed, 'It's God, it's God.' The movie seems to be alive. People are telling Stanley and me things we didn't realize were in the movie. A theological student said he saw the Sign of the Cross — and he may have, which would have been interesting, since Stanley is a Jew and I'm an atheist."*

•

College papers are being written on *2001*. Brooks Riley, in New York University's Graduate Cinema Program, whose instructor was Andrew Sarris: "When one can sit in front of a television screen for two hours waiting for Robert Kennedy's funeral train to pass, just sit before a view of a railroad track, then one can easily give up the laws of drama which demand a beginning, middle and end, which demand concentrated conflict and action within a two-hour span, which demand that every minute be as exciting as the next. Pace, which is part of

any art which involves the passage of time (performance), has
only been fully defined by music. Therefore, in discussing the
pace of a film, one is tempted to use musical definitions. For
pace implies rhythm or tempo. These are primarily musical
qualities. How can one define the pace of *2001* or any other
film? To say that it is slow does nothing more than conjure up
the prejudice that the film is a bore. . . ." Sarris gave Miss Riley
a B+.

•

*On the eve of the Washington premiere, Richard L. Coe
of the* Washington Post *interviewed the president of
M-G-M, Robert H. O'Brien:*

"Of course computers are human." The speaker was M-G-M
president Robert H. O'Brien, a man not noted for whimsical
sayings. Having weathered one of the great proxy battles of the
century, O'Brien next put a sizable slice of Metro's millions
into *2001: A Space Odyssey*. It is in that film that a major confrontation concerns a sneaky computer's plot against two human astronauts.

"We installed a giant computer in our Culver City studios about
ten years ago, using it for all sorts of things such as feeding
the staff and maintaining the locations of all our records and
personnel details. Things worked splendidly and the investment
was worth the fortune it cost.

"After a year or so we decided one Monday to give it the pay-
roll job, and that's when old Charley cut loose. To people earn-
ing a couple of thousand a week he assigned checks of $8.57,
and to people getting $50-odd his checks read $125,000. I can
tell you there was hell breaking all over, and before Friday,
payday, we had to hire every accountant in Los Angeles County
to straighten out the mess.

"So don't tell me computers aren't human. That's why I had no
trouble understanding Stanley Kubrick's story about H.A.L.
9000 and his plot against Keir Dullea and Gary Lockwood."
Considering the august position of O'Brien, a Montana mining
student who took law and high finance, his grasp on the computer mind seemed worth passing along.

•

More from Kubrick aides:

"Stanley's fascination for communication was intense; he was concerned that anyone asking him a question should supply sufficient information for him to make a decision. Once you realized it, it was incredible how many people go through life not knowing how to present a problem. . . . Stanley preferred either his blue suit or a duck-hunting jacket that had enough pockets for his innumerable items of camera gear. He usually carried two or three cameras, two or three watches, and half a dozen pens. His pain about clothing is best expressed by the time his wife, Christiane, convinced him to get away from the studio long enough to buy a new suit. She arranged an appointment for Saturday morning at Harrods in Knightsbridge, and his driver managed to get him all the way down there. While the entire tailoring staff stood at the ready, Stanley chanced to make his approach through the ready-to-wear department, paused by Medium, fingered a sleeve of blue, tried on the coat, said fine, I'll take four, and hurried back to the car. 2001 rolled on."

Gordon Moore, art director, TV Times, *London, who selected stills for publicity purposes:*

"I was immensely impressed with the absolute perfection Stanley was trying to obtain. There has never been a film, surely, where the dominance and single-minded character of the director was so obvious in every frame. His attention to detail was legend. He even involved himself in the making of the cardboard frames that went around the stills I chose. I saw him working seven days a week in the gloom of his cutting room with music sounding incessantly, but he was very approachable. He was looking very haggard toward the end of the production, racing against time as he was editing the film. There were lots of visitors to the studios, as Stanley is a magnet to talent, but he was very cautious with his film. I was not allowed to see several takes, and his colleagues were pretty tight-lipped."

Jeremy Bernstein, who was almost in *2001* (see pages 27, 40), wrote thrice in *The New Yorker* about *2001* — a Talk of the Town article (page 24), a Profile of Kubrick (page 58), and a review of Clarke's novel, based on the screenplay, in which the following appears:

". . . the final version of the film was almost a total surprise to me, even though Kubrick had allowed me to watch the shooting of several scenes, though we had discussed extensively the theme of the film . . . I am sure that he was the only person involved with the picture who could actually visualize what the final product would look like."

•

Freeman Dyson, of the Institute for Advanced Study, Princeton, one of the experts interviewed for the proposed prologue (see page 42):

"When I saw Kubrick at work on *Space Odyssey* in London, I was immediately struck by the fact that he was interested in the gadgetry rather than in the people. Watching the finished movie, I found the lack of human characterization even more remarkable. It seemed that Kubrick was forcing himself with iron self-discipline to avoid the brilliant character-sketching and fast dialogue that made *Strangelove* great. The result was for me unsatisfactory. As a scientist, I took the gadgetry for granted, and I wished we had had a chance to see Keir Dullea act.

"I was pleasantly surprised to find that the reaction of my teen-age children and their friends to the movie was quite different. They found it exciting and moving. I conclude from this that Kubrick knew what he was doing. He was pitching his message to the young people, not to middle-aged professors, and the message got through. I ought not to have found this surprising, for I am myself of the generation that was bowled over by Disney's *Fantasia* thirty years ago, while our sophisticated elders complained in vain of our shocking bad taste.

"After seeing *Space Odyssey*, I read Arthur Clarke's book. I found the book gripping and intellectually satisfying, full of the tension and clarity which the movie lacks. All the parts of the movie that are vague and unintelligible, especially the beginning and the end, become clear and convincing in the book. So I recommend to my middle-aged friends who find the movie bewildering that they should read the book; their teen-age kids don't need to."

•

ARTHUR CLARKE WENT ON A WHIRLWIND TOUR PROMOTING *2001*:

Nature has a lot of surprises up her sleeve.

It isn't possible to predict the political future, but it is possible to map technological trends.

Pericles never had to go to a daily job. Neither did Socrates. No freeman of ancient Athens had to labor to live. Man's purpose in the universe should be to enjoy himself—and it is about time that he did. Future man will have millions of superior machines to do the world's work.

If man lives to be 125, he may attend some form of school until he is at least 120. By abolishing sleep, man may be able to enjoy life 24 hours a day, instead of 16.

I have two main regrets—that I never learned to play the piano and that I never learned to speak at least one foreign language. It would be a good thing if all high school students could live for a year in a foreign country—one with an entirely different culture, like India for U.S. students.

There's an awful lot of symbolism in my fiction, some of it intentional, some unconscious.

Best political comment I've seen was in a men's washroom in Cleveland. On one of those hot-air machines that dry your hands, someone had written, "Press for 5-minute speech by L.B.J."

The television interviewer implied that the space program was a waste of money. I hit back—hard.

As a child, I read all the science-fiction magazines I could get my hands on. Science fiction is an education in itself.

I fully expect to go to the Moon. Probably in 1977 or 1978—that's when they'll start commercial service.

Nothing would surprise me less than learning that intelligent things have been here before.

There are only civilized men and uncivilized men. Civilized men can do whatever they set their minds to.

I don't know what to think about UFOs. They're being seen by reliable people. There may be something odd going on.

I want to work as little as possible for as long as possible. Maybe a few short stories. I'll be able to mine the debris from *2001* for years.

In the future, sex, obviously, will have to be separated from reproduction. No family will be allowed to have more than 2.1 children.

An educated person can never be bored. My ambition: to become a beachcomber.

Many people thought I was some kind of nut when I predicted the enormous and revolutionary impact of communications satellites.

All the problems of the universe — pollution, population, weather, and so on — can only be solved by going into space. With the help of communications and educational satellites, we will be able to make this planet livable for future generations.

I became interested in science fiction when I read the March 30, 1930, issue of *Astounding* magazine. Don't ask me why, but it did the trick.

If man can live in Manhattan, he can live anywhere. I regard space as a great emotional experience.

I've really got no use for young people who drop out completely. Why don't they just commit suicide rather than cluttering up the streets?

The goal of the future is full unemployment, so we can play. That's why we have to destroy the present politico-economic system.

Nature does not give up her secrets easily. She always turns out to be richer, more complex, fuller of surprises than we could possibly have dreamed.

It is highly probable that Earth has been visited many times in the past and will be visited many times in the future, although what we think are flying saucers aren't from outer space, but are probably atmospheric phenomena. When there are really flying saucers from outer space, we'll know it.

One of the prominent changes of the future will be the disinvention of work.

The sheep and the cow today are less than ten percent efficient as a mobile food producer and will go out about the end of the century.

One hundred thousand people is the optimum population for a world in which the work will be done by robots.

Some of us have a chance of seeing the end of the Dark Ages.

Any sufficiently advanced technology is indistinguishable from magic.

The only way to define the limits of the possible is by going beyond them into the impossible.

When a distinguished but elderly scientist states that something is possible, he is almost certainly right. When he states that something is impossible, he is very probably wrong.

•

From *Childhood's End:* "I DON'T KNOW YET, BUT WE'LL THINK OF SOMETHING."

Page 34, *2001: A Space Odyssey:* "For a few seconds Moon-Watcher stood uncertainly above his new victim, trying to grasp the strange and wonderful fact that the dead leopard could kill again. Now he was master of the world, and he was not quite sure what to do next. But he would think of something."

Page 221, *2001: A Space Odyssey:* "Then he [the star-child] waited, marshaling his thoughts and brooding over his still untested powers. For though he was master of the world, he was not quite sure what to do next. But he would think of something."

•

KEIR DULLEA WENT ON A WHIRLWIND TOUR PROMOTING *2001:*

HAL is more human than I am in the picture.

Explaining 2001 *is a little like trying to describe* Romeo and Juliet *to someone who has never heard of Shakespeare.*

Except for *2001, The Fox* is the only artistically honorable film I've made since *David and Lisa.* It has scenes with a girl, and that's helpful for someone with my image.

I knew Kubrick's reputation and would have worked for him for nothing. The picture took two years to make, and while I did all right financially during my seven months of working, it was more of an enriching experience, artistically speaking.

I'm frankly in awe to be in 2001. *I'm only an important plastic material of the film, but it will open a new genre of filmmaking. There is no similarity between the script and the final picture, because it is all visual, and even the director couldn't know from reading it how it would evolve in terms of modern technology.*

I was disturbed by its ambiguity when I first saw the film. But I think it will turn out to be the *Citizen Kane* of our era.

Kubrick left a lot of it ambiguous, since he obviously believes that art is subliminal, that each person can bring his own experience and interpretation to it. You have to approach it with an open mind, because it's a very different concept of what a movie should be.

HAL is more personable than I am. To play a 21st-Century astronaut, I tried to show him as a man without emotional highs and lows — an intelligent, highly trained man, lonely and alienated, not too imaginative.

2001 *is really like an odyssey into infinity. It suggests death and life as an eternal circle, as in the Eastern philosophies.*

Kubrick hired me without an audition. He screened everything I'd ever done, including *Hoodlum Priest,* and gave me the chance to do something different than an introverted, neuter young boy with parent problems, usually my mother. That image was driving me up the wall, and I stopped doing dramatic shows on television because of type casting. I never met Kubrick until the first day of work. He gave me a breath of fresh air.

I feel like Mona Lisa must have felt after seeing herself in the painting. As years go on, our appreciation of it will increase, and kids will be studying it in a ramshackle building on 53d Street in New York in 2001.

Any similarity between the script I first read and the movie is purely coincidental. All I saw was a science-fiction story with a very visual approach.

I had no idea the film would be so stunning when we were making it. I was disturbed by it the first time and uplifted the second time.

•

GARY LOCKWOOD WENT ON A WHIRLWIND TOUR PROMOTING *2001:*

I first worked for Kubrick in 1959 as an extra in *Spartacus*. I got $50 a day and a hot meal.

Keir has the big scene with HAL. I hated him for having it, but he is the star.

Working with Kubrick is like working with a great military commander. He had this huge labor force working for him and he was always in control of every detail. What was really impressive was that he knew when to make a change even though it could change the set plans and cost a great deal of money.

It should change a lot of people's minds about a lot of notions.

I want to see *2001* about three times when it's finished. Then I'll go back and catch it occasionally. You'll understand what I mean when you see it, too.

I created the role of Frank Poole pretty much myself, although Stanley certainly told me when to change things. But the conception had to be worked out personally. Of course, we had long bull sessions with NASA advisers to understand human reactions in space.

I got used to the centrifuge, after a while, but there'd be days in London when I'd be walking down a street and all of a sudden start aiming off in a 45-degree angle, you know, UP.

You know, I would like to go to the Moon.

While we were filming *2001*, I also directed a film, an 18-minute short, a black comedy. I might as well tell you we copped M-G-M equipment to do it.

•

College and "underground" publications equaled the attention given *2001* in the consumer press: three *Harvard Crimson* critics wrote the longest film review to appear in that paper (see page 215); the University of Wisconsin's *Daily Cardinal* published a special eight-page supplement; *Berkeley Barb* repeatedly talked about the film after running a full-page review.

The most prestigious, however, came from the faculty side. *Hartford Studies in Literature* (University of Hartford, West Hartford, Connecticut 06117; Leonard F. Manheim, general editor) published in its first issue a symposium on *2001*. The journal is intended to develop literary insights that stem from any art, science, or scholarly discipline. *2001* was the subject of four essays, with allusions to Hawthorne, Sophocles, Descartes, Hemingway, Henry James, William Styron, Goethe, Schopenhauer, Dostoevsky, Melville, Thomas Mann, Karel Capek, Walt Disney, and Mary W. Shelley.

> Alan Brody, assistant professor of English, University of Hartford: "*2001* is a film in the tradition of the American literary romance."
> Norman N. Holland, professor of English, State University of New York at Buffalo: "The film centers on the theme of 'life support systems.'"
> Robert Plank, a psychiatric social worker: "Men in *2001* are not the masters of their fate." Robert Rogers, Department of English, Buffalo, and author in the field of psychoanalytic criticism: "When the cosmonaut sees a series of his doubles at the climax, one infers that the dimensions of ordinary time and space have been transcended."

Trumpet (published three or four times a year at Box 523, Richardson, Texas 75080) published in its issue number nine three articles on *2001:* Harlan Ellison's very personal guide to understanding *2001: A Space Odyssey* "so you don't look like a schmuck when you come out of the theater and try explaining it to your husband or wife, blues." "Notes on *2001*" by Richard Hodgens: "*2001* is a great work." "*2001:* A Parable Detailed, and a Devilish Advocacy," by Alex Eisenstein: "Though I enjoyed the film greatly, I still have more than minor misgivings about the plot in the third segment. Much of it is sheer technical stupidity."

•

Early ads for 2001 *contained some misinformation that no doubt threw off viewers, who expected to see what they had read about:*

"As soon as your ship lands inside the 150-mile-wide crater Clavius, you are met by scientists from the newly-built research station. It is a small underground city, almost entirely self-supporting. Oxygen and water are obtained by chemical processing from the lunar rocks; plants growing in pressurized conservatories provide food, and help to purify the air. Already, children have been born here who know no other home."

•

Douglas Trumbull: *"The tremendous potential in my future is due entirely to my association with Stanley and* 2001." (Trumbull has made many television films since *2001*.)

•

Con Pederson: "Working with Kubrick is great. I never have enjoyed working more. He is remarkable, with characteristics that do tend to make many people defensive, but I couldn't imagine any director tolerating everything. He really is stupendous."

•

Trumbull: *"I didn't realize until just before production got underway that Stanley intended to keep the star-child in the movie.* 2001 *could have been the funniest movie ever made. Stanley's alternative scenes were hilarious. At an early stage, all the astronauts were to make it to the room in the penultimate scene. I told Stanley to kill all except Bowman, and he told me I was ridiculously stupid."*

•

Barron's, April, 1969: "The electronic brain will largely take care of its own scheduling, rendering daily or weekly reports on its progress. It even will keep track of its human attendants, assigning them to specific chores and eventually filling out their time sheets. When you have a new task you want the robot to take on, it will check and give you a rundown on whether it has time, what the cost will be, and what personnel will be required."

•

JOURNEY BEYOND THE STARS

The original screenplay, when it was still known as Journey Beyond the Stars, *included extraterrestrials. This is a synopsis of the ending of that screenplay:*

Astronauts Dave Bowman and Peter Whitehead take their separate pods and descend into the slot-tunnel that is in the center of the flat side of the satellite Jupiter-V. Their crew had already tested the depth of the slot-tunnel to a depth in excess of 9050 miles, though the entire satellite only possessed a depth of 100 miles. As Dave descends, he notices that time comes to a halt. He compares the sensations of the slot-tunnel trip to those he had in training on Earth when he was given a hallucinogenic drug. When the slot-tunnel ends, time starts again. He sees a globular cluster, the first Earthling to do so. He is passing over the surface of a planet that is covered with similar slot-tunnel openings. He passes over a spaceship wreckage on the surface and goes by a large (1000 feet long and 300 feet wide) golden spindle that moves through the skies with no visible means of propulsion. He descends to the surface and enters another slot-tunnel, and once more time stops. He has the insight that he is going through an enormous cosmic switching device. He emerges to a world of binary suns and approaches a Saturn-like world with silvery rings. He sinks into one of its oceans and encounters a variety of lifelike things, "trees," etc. He is attracted to a light that seems to roar, and he enters a city.

The inhabitants are visible to him as he sails over their heads in his pod. They have two arms and two legs and stand upright. They move with a smooth, flowing motion that makes Earthlings seem jumpy and awkward by comparison. He sees the vehicles of the city move only in one area—about 50 feet thick and some 100 feet above the ground. The ETs are eight feet tall. Dave sees through his rear-view mirror that one ET is taking his picture. The city is complete; there are no signs anywhere of demolition or construction. He passes over a playground, where children five feet tall are playing. One appears to shoot at Dave's pod with a toy ray-gun. Momentarily, Dave is worried, but only a silver vortex ring hits the pod, doing no harm. Dave notes, again in his rear-view mirror, that an elder takes the child's gun away after the incident. Dave notices, as he flies along, that he attracts very little notice for an alien, though some of the ETs do consider him with interest.

He flies over a spaceport and enters a tunnel. As he emerges, he sees some nonhuman intelligences: Squat cones with tube-like legs, and a variety of other species. The pod lands in the exact center of a circle — in a Washington hotel room.

The room is "a set" made to resemble TV information received by the Moon monolith two years before the Discovery voyage. Dave realizes this. His mind is read, but the feeling is not unpleasant: "If the situation demanded that his privacy be sacrificed on the altar of truth, so be it." Dave goes to sleep, only to be awakened by — a telephone ringing in the distance. He answers it:

"Good evening, Mr. Bowman [says a voice]. You have adapted yourself well, both mentally and physically. You are correct in having no fear. You will not be harmed, nor will you suffer any discomfort. You will be returned to your world without any ill effects within a reasonable period of time."

He is requested to go through a door when he is ready. "He was as ready now as he would ever be." He has the feeling that he is "standing on the threshold of the universe." He goes through the door and sits in a chair. He is in a total void. A light glimmers and Dave sees the outlines of a transparent cube.

.

.

HOW THE BOOK ENDS

In the final book version, as in the film, Bowman is the lone surviving astronaut. He passes through a star-gate but does not encounter extraterrestrials. He too ends up, however, in "a Washington hotel room," where for the last time he sleeps. "There being no further use for it, the furniture of the suite dissolved back into the mind of its creator. Only the bed remained — and the walls, shielding this fragile organism from the energies it could not yet control." Bowman is reborn a star-child:

Here he was, adrift in this great river of suns, halfway between the banked fires of the galactic core and the lonely, scattered sentinel stars of the rim. And *here* he wished to be, on the far side of this chasm in the sky, this serpentine band of darkness, empty of all stars. He knew that this formless chaos, visible only by the glow that limned its edges from fire-mists far beyond, was the still unused stuff of creation, the raw material of evolution yet to be. Here, Time had not begun; not until the suns that now burned were long since dead would light and life reshape this void.

Unwittingly, he had crossed it once; now he must cross it again—this time, of his own volition. The thought filled him with a sudden, freezing terror, so that for a moment he was wholly disorientated, and his new vision of the universe trembled and threatened to shatter into a thousand fragments.

It was not fear of the galactic gulfs that chilled his soul, but a more profound disquiet, stemming from the unborn future. For he had left behind the time scales of his human origin; now, as he contemplated that band of starless night, he knew his first intimations of the Eternity that yawned before him.

Then he remembered that he would never be alone, and his panic slowly ebbed. The crystal-clear perception of the universe was restored to him—not, he knew, wholly by his own efforts. When he needed guidance in his first faltering steps, it would be there.

Confident once more, like a high diver who had regained his nerve, he launched himself across the light-years. The galaxy burst forth from the mental frame in which he had enclosed it; stars and nebulae poured past him in an illusion of infinite speed. Phantom suns exploded and fell behind as he slipped like a shadow through their cores; the cold, dark waste of cosmic dust which he had once feared seemed no more than the beat of a raven's wing across the face of the Sun.

The stars were thinning out; the glare of the Milky Way was dimming into a pale ghost of the glory he had known—and, when he was ready, would know again.

He was back, precisely where he wished to be, in the space that men called real.

There before him, a glittering toy no Star-Child could resist, floated the planet Earth with all its peoples.

He had returned in time. Down there on that crowded globe the alarms would be flashing across the radar screens, the great tracking telescopes would be searching the skies—and history as men knew it would be drawing to a close.

A thousand miles below, he became aware that a slumbering cargo of death had awoken, and was stirring sluggishly in its orbit. The feeble energies it contained were no possible menace to him; but he preferred a cleaner sky. He put forth his will, and the circling megatons flowered in a silent detonation that brought a brief, false dawn to half the sleeping globe.

Then he waited, marshaling his thoughts and brooding over his still untested powers. For though he was master of the world, he was not quite sure what to do next.

But he would think of something.

"I'm sure it beefed up morale a helluva lot."

Technical information and ideas were donated to the production by the following:

Aerojet-General Corporation
Covina, California
Instrumentation design and rationale, particularly for vehicle monitoring and display.

Aeronautical Chart and Information Center
St. Louis, Missouri, and Washington branch: Arlington, Virginia
Charts of vast areas of the lunar surface, detailed data on Pic de Midi lunar photography, and support in obtaining such photography. Also, charts of the surface of Mars. In Washington: photographs of Earth taken from high-altitude rockets and from satellites.

Aerospace Medical Division
Wright-Patterson Air Force Base, Ohio
Full pressure spacesuit design, operating instructions, use and accessories.

USAF School of Aerospace Medicine
San Antonio, Texas
Photography of the Earth seen from extreme altitude manned balloons (Manhigh). Obtention of medical data in support of space medical aspects of film.

Department of the Air Force
The Pentagon, Washington, D. C.
Nuclear rocket propulsion.

Air Force Cambridge Research Laboratories
Bedford, Massachusetts
Extreme altitude photography.

Analytical Laboratories, Ltd.
Corsham, Wiltshire, England
Biological and medical instrumentation for centrifuge and for research panels for planetary and planetary moon probing.

Army Map Service
Washington, D. C.
Maps of the Moon.

U. S. Army Natick Laboratories
Natick, Massachusetts
Data and photographs of space foods and associated equipment.

Barnes Engineering Co.
Stamford, Connecticut
Design concepts of telescopes and antennas, and their console instrumentation.

Bell Telephone Laboratories, Inc.
Murray Hill, New Jersey
1. Space Station V's picture- or vision-phone design, including rationale of routines to be followed in conducting orbit-Earth communications on a regular commercial basis. Assistance included typical jargon to be employed.
2. Communications console for Discovery's centrifuge, including design and means of routine and nonroutine transmitting and receiving. Typical jargon was suggested.

Bendix Field Engineering Corp.
Owings Mills, Maryland
Control centers, consoles, and readout devices of manned space flight network.

Boeing Company, Aero-Space Division
Seattle, Washington
Space simulation facilities information and photographs.

Chrysler Corp.
New Orleans, Louisiana
Interplanetary missions of scientific nature, particularly use of spaceship-mounted telescopes.

Computer Control Co.
Framingham, Massachusetts
Computer operations, terminology, console jargon.

Department of Defense
Washington, D. C.
Color photography of Earth and general support in obtaining information of DoD space activities.

Douglas Aircraft Co.
Santa Monica, California
Instrumentation; vehicle design; console layouts; space vehicle films.

Elliott Automation, Ltd.
Borham Wood, Hertfordshire, England
Close support in supplying information on computer functions, readout materials, computer module design, computer terminology, and component miniaturization.

Individual (Don Flickinger, M.D., Gen. USAF, ret.)
Washington, D. C.
Appearance of the Earth from extreme altitudes.

Institute for Advanced Study, School of Mathematics
Princeton, New Jersey
Nuclear propulsion for Discovery.

Flight Research Center, National Aeronautics and Space Administration
Edwards, California
Lunar landing research vehicle design and operation. Design and utilization of Gemini spacesuits.

General Atomic-Division General Dynamics Corp.
San Diego, California
Propulsion system concepts for Discovery and capabilities of interplanetary spaceship.

General Dynamics-Convair
San Diego, California
Films on Mars manned exploration missions; trajectory studies on manned interplanetary missions; mission mode concepts; advanced spacesuit design.

General Electric Co., Missile and Space Division
Philadelphia, Pennsylvania
Design, instrumentation and rationale applicable to Space Station V lunar roving vehicles, lunar bus design, instrumentation applicable to lunar base design, rationale, console instrumentation and operation of Discovery's propulsion; this is the system actually used. Detailed description of system and instrumentation.

Goddard Space Flight Center
Greenbelt, Maryland
General support (1) surveying Goddard facility by photography; (2) photo and information files on spacecraft, tracking systems, computers, instrumentation consoles.

Grumman Aircraft Engineering Corp.
Bethpage, New York
Apollo LEM mockup, detailed guided review, including instrumentation panels. Apollo mission planning; flight profile; activities of crew during entire mission; communications, etc., all applicable to Aries IB and Orion.

Harbor General Hospital (A. T. K. Crockett, M.D., Chief of Urology)
Torrance, California
Consultation in the hibernation sequences, monitoring devices. Note: Crockett is co-author of the paper "Total Body Hypothermia for Prolonged Space Travel." Ideas incorporated to extend, as modified by Ormand Mitchell.

Hawker Siddeley Dynamics, Ltd.
Stevenage, Hertfordshire, England
Hawker Siddeley provided us the basic design of the interior of the space pods, including details of all the panels. They sent several experts to us on three or four occasions and a number of meetings were held at Stevenage with Clarke, Ordway, and Lange. They also aided us in antenna design and console instrumentation for antenna operation.

Honeywell, Inc.
Minneapolis, Minnesota
Assistance in instrumentation ranging from panels in Discovery and Pod Bay to the monitoring devices on the moon and the cockpit of Orion. Ideas were generated for the various docking sequences, leak detection aboard the Discovery, extravehicular activities, etc., etc. Honeywell prepared for us a special report entitled "A Prospectus for 2001 Interplanetary Flight." As for hardware, Honeywell provided us with many buttons and switches.

Illinois Institute of Technology, Research Institute
Chicago, Illinois

International Business Machines
Armonk, New York
S.K. received very broad and valuable support from IBM through the making of the film, ranging from the design and construction by IBM subcontractors of computer panels and consoles to the establishment of futuristic computer jargon and astronaut-computer interface. Also supplied valuable information on how computer-generated information would be displayed in future. Hardware contributions: panels for the Aries IB and the Orion cockpits plus buttons for many other sets, including Discovery's Command Module and centrifuge. IBM assigned Eliot Noyes & Associates, industrial designers (q.v.), as their consultants to work with us. Their personnel made several visits to the M-G-M studios in London during the course of making the film.

International Business Machines, Ltd.
London, England
IBM U.K. Ltd. provided the direct technical input to the IBM-built panels; see IBM entry and that of Eliot Noyes & Associates. IBM U.K. personnel visited the studios on a number of occasions, and many meetings were held in their offices.

Detailed documentation on experiments that could be made from Discovery of the asteroids and the planet Jupiter, and its twelve moons.

Jet Propulsion Laboratory, California Institute of Technology
Pasadena, California
Spacecraft information, photography of lunar surface mission, analysis of the asteroid belt and Jupiter fly-by probes.

Langley Research Center
Hampton, Virginia
Detailed photographic tour of the center; gathering of large quantities of technical information relevant to *2001*, including photographs of laboratories, research vehicles, simulated docking and lunar landing devices, and film depicting appearance of man walking on the moon (simulator device). Considerable time spent in space station laboratory, viewing models and reports of space stations, and receiving briefings on rationale of space station technology.

Lear Siegler, Inc.
Grand Rapids, Michigan
Design concepts of advanced space vehicle instrumentation and display devices.

Food Technology Research Center, Libby, McNeil and Libby
Chicago, Illinois
Food selection and menus for long space voyages; basis of menu selection for the centrifuge.

Lick Observatory
Mt. Hamilton, California
Photography of the moon.

Ling-Temco-Vought, Inc.
Dallas, Texas
Reports on means and methods of displaying flight and other information to a crew undertaking an interplanetary space mission.

Lowell Observatory
Flagstaff, Arizona
Photography of the moon and planets.

Lunar and Planetary Laboratory, University of Arizona
Tucson, Arizona
Photography and charts of the moon.

Manned Spacecraft Center, National Aeronautics and Space Administration
Houston, Texas
Detailed photographic survey of the center; reports and miscellaneous technical documentation on many aspects of manned space flight, with particular emphasis on Apollo lunar spaceship and space station technology. Very valuable cooperation

in securing dozens of color photographs of the Earth taken from Mercury and Gemini spacecraft. Computer design and functioning; instrumentation; training techniques, astronaut routines, and conference room design and rationale utilized on lunar base sequence. MSC supplied six reels of Gemini tape in which mission control and pilot cross-talk was recorded. Maintenance and repair of space vehicles; Apollo mission rationale, time sequential analysis of crew activities and probable conversation with mission control, and advanced post-Apollo spacesuit design.

George C. Marshall Space Flight Center
National Aeronautics and Space Administration
Huntsville, Alabama
Detailed photographic survey of the Marshall Center, including manufacturing and test areas; design and utilization of display and recording instrumentations; design of advanced space vehicles; dozens of technical documents and photographs required during the film preparation.

Martin Co.
Baltimore, Maryland
Technical instrumentation.

Minnesota Mining & Manufacturing Co.
St. Paul, Minnesota
A broad program of cooperation was outlined at original meetings in St. Paul.

Mt. Wilson & Palomar Observatories
California Institute of Technology
Pasadena, California
Photography of the moon.

National Aeronautics and Space Administration Headquarters
Washington, D. C.
Space station philosophy, effects of rotation on man; speed of rotation. Photography made by Ranger lunar probes; photography of space vehicles and NASA facilities; photography of planet Mars, general and overall support from NASA; capabilities of man as scientific observers during deep space voyage; continuing documentation of myriad subjects throughout progress of film.

National Aeronautics and Space Council
Washington, D. C.
Feasibility of scene wherein a non-helmeted astronaut is very briefly exposed to space conditions.

National Institute of Medical Research
London, England
Hibernational techniques and instrumentation.

U. S. Naval Observatory
Flagstaff, Arizona

Photography of the asteroids.

Office of Naval Research, Brand Office,
Embassy of U. S. A.
London, England
Obtention of U.S. Navy full-pressure flight
suit, including pressurization attachments,
shoes, helmet; plus, technical documentation—all used in developing our own suits.

N. Y. U. College of Medicine
New York City
Development of techniques of placing man
into hibernation and monitoring him when
he is in the state. Very complete discussion of displays needed, design of the
hibernaculums, a term devised by Dr.
Ormand G. Mitchell, Assistant Professor
of Anatomy, from whose many sketches
were derived our final designs.

North American Aviation, Inc., Space and
Information Systems Division
Downey, California
Photographs and documentation of the
Apollo lunar spaceship. Simulated lunar
base experimentations; nature of the lunar
surface.

Eliot Noyes & Associates
New Canaan, Connecticut
Cooperation in design and rationale as
appointed agents of IBM in all computer
sequences for Aries IB and Orion, as well
as spacesuit arm controls.

State of Oregon, Department of Geology &
Mineral Information
Portland, Oregon
Extraction of useful resources from lunar
surface materials, utilizing SNAP nuclear
reactors as heat sources.

Paris Match
Paris, France
Supplied special futuristic cover for the
magazine featured in Space Station V.

Philco Corp.
Philadelphia, Pennsylvania
NASA-Manned Spacecraft Center Mission
Control Center documentation, photog-
raphy, and description of use of computer
complex.

Royal Greenwich Observatory
Herstmonceux, Surrey, England
Design and rationale of the astronomical
observatory and console in the centrifuge.

Societé de Prospection Electrique Schlumberger
Paris, France
Geophysical instrumentation for the centrifuge. Cooperation included a meeting
in Paris, two trips by Schlumberger per-

sonnel to London, submission of design
concepts and rationale for use.

Smithsonian Astrophysical Observatory
Cambridge, Massachusetts
Micrometeoroid danger to space flight;
means of detection; nature of space in
terms of Discovery's flight through the
asteroids.

Soviet Embassy
London, England
Films of Soviet space programs. Stills of
Luna 9 lunar photography.

United Kingdom Atomic Energy Authority,
Dorchester, England
Instrumentation of nuclear reactor con-
trol consoles in the centrifuge and in the
Command Module. Meetings at Dragon
reactor site and in studios.

University of London
Mill Hill, Hertfordshire, England
Advice on models of lunar surface; visit to
studios and tour of laboratories at Mill Hill,
including inspection of simulated lunar surface materials.

University of Manchester, Department of
Astronomy
Manchester, England
Photography of the moon from Pic de Midi
sources; large scale photos of Tycho and
Clavius craters; charts and maps of many
areas of the moon; consultation on surface
characteristics of moon, nature of soil materials. Consultation on nature of celestial sphere as viewed from the Moon, i.e.,
the appearance of the heavens. Two meetings held in Manchester and one at the
studios with members of Professor Kopal's
staff.

University of Minnesota, School of Physics
Minneapolis, Minnesota
Extreme altitude conditions, appearance of
Earth from high altitude balloons.

Vickers, Ltd., Medical Division
London, England
Advice on hibernation and health-monitor-
ing equipment and techniques for the centrifuge.

U. S. Weather Bureau
Washington, D. C.
Detailed photographic coverage of the
center; selection of documentation and
photographs of appearance of Earth from
satellite altitudes.

Whirlpool Corp., Systems Division
St. Joseph, Michigan
Development of the Aries IB kitchen and
planning of eating programs and routines.

"Just a moment. Just a moment."

Ted Mahar, *Portland Oregonian*
Academy Awards are gross travesties. They are blatantly commercial awards given to con yokels into believing that some kind of final word has been delivered on the relative quality of a movie. . . . They defy artistic expression and reflect the waning dinosaur groans of a movie generation sinking into senility and richly deserved oblivion. . . . *2001* was obviously too new and too advanced for the rank and file.

•

John Hinterberger, *Seattle Times*
2001 is probably the only film since the experimental days of Eisenstein that seriously attempted to expand the horizons of film as a medium. In that respect it was the ONLY film this year that was important and significant.

•

1968 Oscar Award Winner:
Special visual effects: *2001: A Space Odyssey*, Stanley Kubrick.

•

British Film Academy Awards:
Geoffrey Unsworth was cited for Best Cinematography. Tony Masters, Harry Lange, and Ernie Archer were cited for Best Art Direction. Winston Ryder was cited for Best Soundtrack.

•

The Italian motion picture industry conferred its annual David Di Donatello Golden Statue on *2001: A Space Odyssey* as the year's best film from the West.

•

The Second International Film Festival, in Rio, in the Spring of 1969 honored *2001: A Space Odyssey*. It presented a Black Monolith to Arthur C. Clarke.

•

2001: A SPACE ODYSSEY
The Best Film of 1968

The David Di Donatello Award (the Italian Oscar)
The Film Critics Circle of Spain
The Antwerp Film Critics Circle
The Kansas City Film Critics Circle
"The Critics," BBC Radio, Alex Walker and Dilys Powell
Newsday, Joseph Gelmis
"Critical People," WBAI-FM, Al Lees, New York
Film Bulletin, Jack Ano
The San Francisco Examiner, Stanley Eichelbaum
Films and Filming, London
The Post-Intelligencer, Seattle, John Voorhees
The Oregonian, Portland, Ted Mahar
The Star, Washington, D.C., Harry McArthur
The Cincinnati Enquirer, E. B. Racliffe
WBZ-TV, Boston, Pat Collins
The Fort Worth Star, Perry Stuart
The Catholic Sentinel, James W. Arnold
The Houston Post, Nathan Fain
Winston-Salem Journal & Sentinel, Jim Shertzer
The States-Item, New Orleans, James A. Perry
The Houston Chronicle, Jeff Millar
The Denver Register, Tom Officer
The Bulletin, Sydney, Australia, Beverly Tivey
The Toronto Star, Martin Knelman
Seattle Times, John Hinterberger & John Hartl
Los Angeles Free Press Readers' Poll
The Beau Prix
The Record News, Kingsville Bishop, Texas, Jack Trussell
The Stanford Daily, Stanford, California, Todd McCarthy

THE NATIONAL CATHOLIC OFFICE
FOR MOTION PICTURES
PRESENTS
ITS 1968 AWARD
BEST FILM OF EDUCATIONAL VALUE
TO

2001: A SPACE ODYSSEY

which, by the scope of its imaginative vision of man—his origins, his creative encounter with the universe, and his unfathomed potential for the future—immerses the eye, the ear, and the intuitive responses of the viewer in a uniquely stimulating human experience.

•

The *Saturday Review*, in December, 1969, declared that *2001: A Space Odyssey* was "the motion picture of the decade . . . an extraordinary masterpiece that gathered into one dynamic image a major challenge to some of the assumptions that dominated serious writing for at least a hundred years."

"I really think I'm entitled to an answer to that question."

PLAYBOY INTERVIEW: STANLEY KUBRICK*

Playboy: Much of the controversy surrounding *2001* deals with the meaning of the metaphysical symbols that abound in the film—the polished black monoliths, the orbital conjunction of Earth, Moon and sun at each stage of the monoliths' intervention in human destiny, the stunning final kaleidoscopic maelstrom of time and space that engulfs the surviving astronaut and sets the stage for his rebirth as a "star-child" drifting toward Earth in a translucent placenta. One critic even called *2001* "the first Nietzschean film," contending that its essential theme is Nietzsche's concept of man's evolution from ape to human to superman. What *was* the metaphysical message of *2001*?

Kubrick: It's not a message that I ever intend to convey in words. *2001* is a nonverbal experience; out of two hours and 19 minutes of film, there are only a little less than 40 minutes of dialog. I tried to create a *visual* experience, one that bypasses verbalized pigeonholing and directly penetrates the subconscious with an emotional and philosophic content. To convolute McLuhan, in *2001* the message is the medium. I intended the film to be an intensely subjective experience that reaches the viewer at an inner level of consciousness, just as music does; to "explain" a Beethoven symphony would be to emasculate it by erecting an artificial barrier between conception and appreciation. You're free to speculate as you wish about the philosophical and allegorical meaning of the film—and such speculation is one indication that it has succeeded in gripping the audience at a deep level—but I don't want to spell out a verbal road map for *2001* that every viewer will feel obligated to pursue or else fear he's missed the point. I think that if *2001* succeeds at all, it is in reaching a wide spectrum of people who would not often give a thought to man's destiny, his role in the cosmos and his relationship to higher forms of life. But even in the case of someone who is highly intelligent, certain ideas found in *2001* would, if presented as abstractions, fall rather lifelessly and be automatically assigned to pat intellectual categories; experienced in a moving visual and emotional context, however, they can resonate within the deepest fibers of one's being.

Playboy: Without laying out a philosophical road map for the viewer, can you tell us your own interpretation of the meaning of the film?

Kubrick: No, for the reasons I've already given. How much would we appreciate *La Gioconda* today if Leonardo had written at the bottom of the canvas: "This lady is smiling slightly because she has rotten teeth" — or "because she's hiding a secret from her lover"? It would shut off the viewer's appreciation and shackle him to a "reality" other than his own. I don't want that to happen to *2001*.

Playboy: Arthur Clarke has said of the film, "If anyone understands it on the first viewing, we've failed in our intention." Why should the viewer have to see a film twice to get its message?

Kubrick: I don't agree with that statement of Arthur's, and I believe he made it facetiously. The very nature of the visual experience in *2001* is to give the viewer an instantaneous, visceral reaction that does not — and should not — require further amplification. Just speaking generally, however, I would say that there are elements in any good film that would increase the viewer's interest and appreciation on a second viewing; the momentum of a movie often prevents every stimulating detail or nuance from having a full impact the first time it's seen. The whole idea that a movie should be seen only once is an extension of our traditional conception of the film as an ephemeral entertainment rather than as a visual work of art. We don't believe that we should hear a great piece of music only once, or see a great painting once, or even read a great book just once. But the film has until recent years been exempted from the category of art — a situation I'm glad is finally changing.

Playboy: Some prominent critics — including Renata Adler of *The New York Times*, John Simon of *The New Leader*, Judith Crist of *New York* magazine and Andrew Sarris of the *Village Voice* — apparently felt that *2001* should be among those films still exempted from the category of art; all four castigated it as dull, pretentious and overlong. How do you account for their hostility?

Kubrick: The four critics you mention all work for New York publications. The reviews across America and around the world have been 95 percent enthusiastic. Some were more perceptive than others, of course, but even those who praised the film on relatively superficial grounds were able to get something of its message. New York was the only really hostile city. Perhaps there is a certain element of the lumpen literati that is so dogmatically atheist and materialist and Earth-bound that it finds the grandeur of space and the myriad mysteries of cosmic intelligence anathema. But film critics, fortunately, rarely have any effect on the general public; houses everywhere are packed and the film is well on its way to becoming the greatest moneymaker in M-G-M's history. Perhaps this sounds like a crass way to evaluate one's work, but I think that, especially with a film that is so obviously *different*, record audience attendance means people are saying the right things to one another after they see it — and isn't this really what it's all about?

Playboy: Speaking of what it's all about — if you'll allow us to return to the philosophical interpretation of *2001* — would you agree with those critics who call it a profoundly religious film?

Kubrick: I will say that the God concept is at the heart of *2001* — but not any traditional, anthropomorphic image of God. I don't believe in any of Earth's monotheistic religions, but I do believe that one can construct an intriguing *scientific* definition of God, once you accept the fact that there are approximately 100 billion stars in our galaxy alone, that each star is a life-giving sun and that there are approximately 100 billion galaxies in just the *visible* universe. Given a planet in a stable orbit, not too hot and not too cold, and given a few billion years of chance chemical reactions created by the interaction of a sun's energy on the planet's chemicals, it's fairly certain that life in one form or another will eventually emerge. It's reasonable to assume that there must be, in fact, countless *billions* of such planets where biological life has arisen, and the odds of some proportion of such life developing intelligence are high. Now, the sun is by no means an old star, and its planets are mere children in cosmic age, so it seems likely that there are billions of planets in the universe not only where intelligent life is on a lower scale than man but other billions where it is approximately equal and others still where it is hundreds of thousands of millions of years in advance of us. When you think of the giant technological strides that man has made in a few millennia — less than a microsecond in the chronology of the universe — can you imagine the evolutionary development that much older life forms have taken?

They may have progressed from biological species, which are fragile shells for the mind at best, into immortal machine entities—and then, over innumerable eons, they could emerge from the chrysalis of matter transformed into beings of pure energy and spirit. Their potentialities would be limitless and their intelligence ungraspable by humans.

Playboy: Even assuming the cosmic evolutionary path you suggest, what has this to do with the nature of God?

Kubrick: Everything—because these beings would *be* gods to the billions of less advanced races in the universe, just as man would appear a god to an ant that somehow comprehended man's existence. They would possess the twin attributes of all deities—omniscience and omnipotence. These entities might be in telepathic communication throughout the cosmos and thus be aware of everything that occurs, tapping every intelligent mind as effortlessly as we switch on the radio; they might not be limited by the speed of light and their presence could penetrate to the farthest corners of the universe; they might possess complete mastery over matter and energy; and in their final evolutionary stage, they might develop into an integrated collective immortal consciousness. They would be incomprehensible to us except as gods; and if the tendrils of their consciousness ever brushed men's minds, it is only the hand of God we could grasp as an explanation.

Playboy: If such creatures do exist, why should they be interested in man?

Kubrick: They may not be. But why should man be interested in microbes? The motives of such beings would be as alien to us as their intelligence.

Playboy: In *2001*, such incorporeal creatures seem to manipulate our destinies and control our evolution, though whether for good or evil—or both, or neither—remains unclear. Do you really believe it's possible that man is a cosmic plaything of such entities?

Kubrick: I don't really *believe* anything about them; how can I? Mere speculation on the possibility of their existence is sufficiently overwhelming, without attempting to decipher their motives. The important point is that all the standard attributes assigned to God in our history could equally well be the characteristics of biological entities who billions of years ago were at a stage of development similar to man's own and evolved into something as remote from man as man is remote from the primordial ooze from which he first emerged.

Playboy: In this cosmic phylogeny you've described, isn't it possible that there might be forms of intelligent life on an even higher scale than these entities of pure energy — perhaps as far removed from them as they are from us?

Kubrick: Of course there could be; in an infinite, eternal universe, the point is that *anything* is possible, and it's unlikely that we can even begin to scratch the surface of the full range of possibilities. But at a time [1968] when man is preparing to set foot on the Moon, I think it's necessary to open up our Earthbound minds to such speculation. No one knows what's waiting for us in the universe. I think it was a prominent astronomer who wrote recently, "Sometimes I think we are alone, and sometimes I think we're not. In either case, the idea is quite staggering."

Playboy: You said there must be billions of planets sustaining life that is considerably more advanced than man but has not yet evolved into non- or suprabiological forms. What do you believe would be the effect on humanity if the Earth were contacted by a race of such ungodlike but technologically superior beings?

Kubrick: There's a considerable difference of opinion on this subject among scientists and philosophers. Some contend that encountering a highly advanced civilization — even one whose technology is essentially comprehensible to us — would produce a traumatic cultural shock effect on man by divesting him of his smug ethnocentrism and shattering the delusion that he is the center of the universe. Carl Jung summed up this position when he wrote of contact with advanced extraterrestrial life that the "reins would be torn from our hands and we would, as a tearful old medicine man once said to me, find ourselves 'without dreams' . . . we would find our intellectual and spiritual aspirations so outmoded as to leave us completely paralyzed." I personally don't accept this position, but it's one that's widely held and can't be summarily dismissed.

In 1960, for example, the Committee for Long Range Studies of the Brookings Institution prepared a report for the National Aeronautics and Space Administration warning that even indirect contact — i.e., alien artifacts that might possibly be discovered through our space activities on the Moon, Mars or Venus or via radio contact with an interstellar civilization — could cause severe psychological dislocations. The study cautioned that "Anthropological files contain many examples of societies, sure of their place in the universe, which have disintegrated when they have had to associate with previously unfamiliar societies espousing different ideas and different life ways; others that survived such an experience usually did so by paying the price of changes in values and attitudes and behavior." It concluded that since intelligent life might be discovered at any time, and that since the consequences of such a discovery are "presently unpredictable," it was advisable that the Government initiate continuing studies on the psychological and intellectual impact of confrontation with extraterrestrial life. What action was taken on this report I don't know, but I assume that such studies are now under way. However, while not discounting the possible adverse emotional impact on some people, I would personally tend to view such contact with a tremendous amount of excitement and enthusiasm. Rather than shattering our society, I think it could immeasurably enrich it.

Another positive point is that it's a virtual certainty that all intelligent life at one stage in its technological development must have discovered nuclear energy. This is obviously the watershed of any civilization; does it find a way to use nuclear power without destruction and harness it for peaceful purposes, or does it annihilate itself? I would guess that any civilization that has existed for 1000 years after its discovery of atomic energy has devised a means of accommodating itself to the bomb, and this could prove tremendously reassuring to us — as well as give us specific guidelines for our own survival. In any case, as far as cultural shock is concerned, my impression is that the attention span of most people is quite brief; after a week or two of great excitement and oversaturation in newspapers and on television, the public's interest would drop off and the United Nations, or whatever world body we then had, would settle down to discussions with the aliens.

Playboy: You're assuming that extraterrestrials would be benevolent. Why?

Kubrick: Why should a vastly superior race *bother* to harm or destroy us? If an intelligent ant suddenly traced a message in the sand at my feet reading, "I am sentient; let's talk things over," I doubt very much that I would rush to grind him under my heel. Even if they weren't superintelligent, though, but merely more advanced than mankind, I would tend to lean more toward the benevolence, or at least indifference, theory. Since it's most unlikely that we would be visited from within our own solar system, any society capable of traversing light-years of space would have to have an extremely high degree of control over matter and energy. Therefore, what possible motivation for hostility would they have? To steal our gold or oil or coal? It's hard to think of any nasty intention that would justify the long and arduous journey from another star.

Playboy: You'll admit, though, that extraterrestrials are commonly portrayed in comic strips and cheap science-fiction films as bug-eyed monsters scuttling hungrily after curvaceous Earth maidens.

Kubrick: This probably dates back to the pulp science-fiction magazines of the Twenties and Thirties and perhaps even to the Orson Welles Martian-invasion broadcast in 1938 and the resultant mass hysteria, which is always advanced in support of the hypothesis that contact would cause severe cultural shock. In a sense, the lines with which Welles opened that broadcast set the tone for public consideration of extraterrestrial life for years to come. I've memorized them: "Across an immense ethereal gulf, minds that are to our minds as ours are to the beasts in the jungle—intellects vast, cool and unsympathetic— regarded this Earth with envious eyes and slowly and surely drew their plans against us. . . ." Anything we can imagine about such other life forms is possible, of course. You could have psychotic civilizations, or decadent civilizations that have elevated pain to an aesthetic and might covet humans as gladiators or torture objects, or civilizations that might want us for zoos, or scientific experimentation, or slaves or even for food. While I am appreciably more optimistic, we just can't be sure *what* their motivations will be.

I'm interested in the argument of Professor Freeman Dyson of Princeton's Institute for Advanced Study, who contends that it would be a mistake to expect that all potential space visitors will be altruistic, or to believe that they would have *any* ethical or moral concepts comparable to mankind's. Dyson writes, if I remember him correctly, that "Intelligence may indeed be a benign influence creating isolated groups of philosopher kings far apart in the heavens," but it's just as likely that "Intelligence may be a cancer of purposeless technological exploitation, sweeping across a galaxy as irresistibly as it has swept across our own planet." Dyson concludes that it's "just as unscientific to impute to remote intelligence wisdom and serenity as it is to impute to them irrational and murderous impulses. We must be prepared for either possibility and conduct our searches accordingly."

This is why some scientists caution, now that we're attempting to intercept radio signals from other solar systems, that if we do receive a message we should wait awhile before answering it. But we've been transmitting radio and television signals for so many years that any advanced civilization could have received the emissions long ago. So in the final analysis, we really don't have much choice in this matter; they're either going to contact us or they're not, and if they do we'll have nothing to say about their benevolence or malevolence.

Even if they prove to be malevolent, their arrival would have at least one useful by-product in that the nations of the Earth would stop squabbling among themselves and forge a common front to defend the planet. I think it was André Maurois who suggested many years ago that the best way to realize world peace would be to stage a false threat from outer space; it's not a bad idea. But I certainly don't believe we should view contact with extraterrestrial life forms with foreboding, or hesitate to visit other planets for fear of what we may find there. If others don't contact us, we must contact them; it's our destiny.

Playboy: You indicated earlier that intelligent life is extremely unlikely elsewhere within our solar system. Why?

Kubrick: From what we know of the other planets in this system, it appears improbable that intelligence exists, because of surface temperatures and atmospheres that are inhospitable to higher life forms. Improbable, but not impossible. I will admit that there are certain tantalizing clues pointing in the other direction. For example, while the consensus of scientific opinion dismisses the possibility of intelligent life on Mars—as opposed to plant or low orders of organic life—there are some eminently respectable dissenters. Dr. Frank B. Salisbury, professor of plant physiology at Utah State University, has contended in a study in *Science* magazine that if vegetation exists on a planet, then it is logical that there will be higher orders of life to feed on it. "From there," he writes, "it is but one more step—granted, a big one—to intelligent beings."

Salisbury also points out that a number of astronomers have observed strange flashes of light, possibly explosions of great magnitude, on Mars' surface, some of which emit clouds; and he suggests that these could actually be nuclear explosions. Another intriguing facet of Mars is the peculiar orbits of its twin satellites, Phobos and Deimos, first discovered in 1877—the same year, incidentally, that Schiaparelli discovered his famous but still elusive Martian "canals." One eminent astronomer, Dr. Josif Shklovsky, chairman of the department of radio astronomy at the Shternberg Astronomical Institute in Moscow, has propounded the theory that both moons are artificial space satellites launched by the Martians thousands of years ago in an effort to escape the dying surface of their planet. He bases this theory on the unique orbits of the two moons, which, unlike the 31 other satellites in our solar system, orbit *faster* than the revolution of their host planet. The orbit of Phobos is also deteriorating in an inexplicable manner and dragging the satellite progressively closer to Mars' surface. Both of these circumstances, Shklovsky contends, make sense only if the two moons are *hollow.*

Shklovsky believes that the satellites are the last remnants of an extinct ancient Martian civilization; but Professor Salisbury goes a step further and suggests that they were launched within the past hundred years. Noting that the moons were discovered by a relatively small-power telescope in 1877 and not detected by a much more powerful telescope observing Mars in 1862 — when the planet was appreciably nearer Earth — he asks: "Should we attribute the failure of 1862 to imperfections in the existing telescope, or may we imagine that the satellites were launched into orbit between 1862 and 1877?" There are no answers here, of course, only questions, but it is fascinating speculation. On balance, however, I would have to say that the weight of available evidence dictates against intelligent life on Mars.

Playboy: How about possibilities, if not the probabilities, of intelligent life on the other planets?

Kubrick: Most scientists and astronomers rule out life on the outer planets since their surface temperatures are thousands of degrees either above or below zero and their atmospheres would be poisonous. I suppose it's possible that life could evolve on such planets with, say, a liquid ammonia or methane base, but it doesn't appear too likely. As far as Venus goes, the Mariner probes indicate that the surface temperature of the planet is approximately 800 degrees Fahrenheit, which would deny the chemical basis for molecular development of life. And there could be no indigenous intelligent life on the Moon, because of the total lack of atmosphere — no life as we know it, in any case; though I suppose that intelligent rocks or crystals, or statues, with a silicone life base are not really impossible, or even conscious gaseous matter or swarms of sentient electric particles. You'd get no technology from such creatures, but if their intelligence could control matter, why would they need it? There could be nothing about them, however, even remotely humanoid — a form that would appear to be an eminently practicable universal life prototype.

Playboy: What do you think we'll find on the Moon?

Kubrick: I think the most exciting prospect about the Moon is that if alien races have ever visited Earth in the remote past and left artifacts for man to discover in the future, they probably chose the arid, airless lunar vacuum, where no deterioration would take place and an object could exist for millennia. It would be inevitable that as man evolved technologically, he would reach his nearest satellite and the aliens would then expect him to find their calling card—perhaps a message of greeting, a cache of knowledge or simply a cosmic burglar alarm signaling that another race had mastered space flight. This, of course, was the central situation of *2001*.

But an equally fascinating question is whether there could be another race of intelligent life on Earth. Dr. John Lilly, whose research into dolphins has been funded by the National Aeronautics and Space Administration, has amassed considerable evidence pointing to the possibility that the bottle-nosed dolphin may be as intelligent as or more intelligent than man. [See *Deep Thinkers* in PLAYBOY, August 1968—*Ed.*] He bases this not only on its brain size—which is larger than man's and with a more complex cortex—but on the fact that dolphins have evolved an extensive language. Lilly is currently attempting, with some initial success, to decipher this language and establish communication with the dolphins. NASA's interest in this is obvious, because learning to communicate with dolphins would be a highly instructive precedent for learning to communicate with alien races on other planets. Of course, if the dolphins are really intelligent, theirs is obviously a nontechnological culture, since without an opposable thumb, they could never create artifacts. Their intelligence might also be on a totally different order than man's, which could make communication additionally difficult. Dr. Lilly has written that, "It is probable that their intelligence is comparable to ours, though in a very strange fashion . . . they may have a new class of large brain so dissimilar to ours that we cannot within our lifetime possibly understand its mental processes." Their culture may be totally devoted to creating works of poetry or devising abstract mathematical concepts, and they could conceivably share a telepathic communication to supplement their high-frequency underwater language.

What is particularly interesting is that dolphins appear to have developed a concept of altruism; the stories of shipwrecked sailors rescued by dolphins and carried to shore, or protected by them against sharks, are by no means all old wives' tales. But I'm rather disturbed by some recent developments that indicate not only how we may treat dolphins but also how we may treat intelligent races on other planets. The Navy, impressed by the dolphin's apparent intelligence, is reported to have been engaging in underwater-demolition experiments in which a live torpedo is strapped to a dolphin and detonated by radio when it nears a prototype enemy submarine. These experiments have been officially denied; but if they're true, I'm afraid we may learn more about man through dolphins than the other way around. The Russians, paradoxically, seem to be one step ahead of us in this area; they recently banned all catching of dolphins in Russian waters on the grounds that "Comrade Dolphin" is a fellow sentient being and killing him would be morally equivalent to murder.

Playboy: Although flying saucers are frequently an object of public derision, there has been a good deal of serious discussion in the scientific community about the possibility that UFOs could be alien spacecraft. What's your opinion?

Kubrick: The most significant analysis of UFOs I've seen recently was written by L. M. Chassin, a French Air Force general who had been a high-ranking NATO officer. He argues that by any legal rules of evidence, there is now sufficient sighting data amassed from reputable sources—astronomers, pilots, radar operators and the like—to initiate a serious and thorough worldwide investigation of UFO phenomena. Actually, if you examine even a fraction of the extant testimony you will find that people have been sent to the gas chamber on far less substantial evidence. Of course, it's possible that all the governments in the world really *do* take UFOs seriously and perhaps are already engaging in secret study projects to determine their origin, nature and intentions. If so, they may not be disclosing their findings for fear that the public would be alarmed—the danger of cultural shock deriving from confrontation with the unknown which we discussed earlier, and which is an element of *2001*, when news of the monolith's discovery on the Moon is suppressed. But I think even the two percent of sightings that the Air Force's Project Blue Book admits is unexplainable by conventional means should dictate a serious, searching probe. From all indications, the current Government-authorized investigation at the University of Colorado is neither serious nor searching.

One hopeful sign that this subject may at last be accorded the serious discussion it deserves, however, is the belated but exemplary conversion of Dr. J. Allen Hynek, since 1948 the Air Force's consultant on UFOs and currently chairman of the astronomy department at Northwestern University. Hynek, who in his official capacity pooh-poohed UFO sightings, now believes that UFOs deserve top-priority attention—as he wrote in PLAYBOY [December 1967]—and even concedes that the existing evidence may indicate a possible connection with extra-

errestrial life. He predicts: "I will be surprised if an intensive
study yields nothing. To the contrary, I think that mankind may
be in for the greatest adventure since dawning human intelligence turned outward to contemplate the universe." I agree
with him.

Playboy: If flying saucers are real, who or what do you think
they might be?

Kubrick: I don't know. The evidence proves they're up there,
but it gives us very little clue as to what they are. Some science-
fiction writers theorize half-seriously that they could be time
shuttles flicking back and forth between eons to a future age
when man has mastered temporal travel; and I understand that
biologist Ivan Sanderson has even advanced a theory that they
may be some kind of living space animal inhabiting the upper
stratosphere—though I can't give much credence to that suggestion. It's also possible that they are perfectly natural phenomena, perhaps chain lightning, as one American science
writer has suggested; although this, again, does not explain
some of the photographs taken by reputable sources, such as
the Argentine navy, which clearly show spherical metallic objects hovering in the sky. As you've probably deduced, I'm
really fascinated by UFOs and I only regret that this field of investigation has to a considerable extent been pre-empted by a
crackpot fringe that claims to have soared to Mars on flying
saucers piloted by three-foot-tall green humanoids with pointy
heads. That kind of kook approach makes it very easy to dismiss the whole phenomenon which we do at our own risk.

I think another problem here—and one of the reasons that,
despite the overwhelming evidence, there has been remarkably
little public interest—is that most people don't really *want* to
think about extraterrestrial beings patrolling our skies and perhaps observing us like bugs on a slide. The thought is too
disturbing; it upsets our tidy, soothing, sanitized suburban
Weltanschauung; the cosmos is more than light-years away
from Scarsdale. This could be a survival mechanism, but it
could also blind us to what may be the most dramatic and important moment in man's history—contact with another civilization.

Playboy: Among the reasons adduced by those who doubt the
interstellar origin of UFOs is Einstein's special theory of relativity, which states that the speed of light is absolute and that
nothing can exceed it. A journey from even the nearest star to
Earth would consequently take thousands of years. They claim
this virtually rules out interstellar travel—at least for sentient

beings with life spans as short as the longest known to man. Do you find this argument valid?

Kubrick: I find it difficult to believe that we have penetrated to the ultimate depths of knowledge about the physical laws of the universe. It seems rather presumptuous to believe that in the space of a few hundred years, we've figured out most of what there is to know. So I don't think it's right to declaim with unshakable certitude that light is the absolute speed limit of the universe. I'm suspicious of dogmatic scientific rules; they tend to have a rather short life span. The most eminent European scientists of the early 19th Century scoffed at meteorites, on the grounds that "stones can't fall from the sky"; and just a year before Sputnik, one of the world's leading astrophysicists stated flatly that "space flight is bunk." Actually, there are already some extremely interesting theoretical studies underway—one by Dr. Gerald Feinberg at Columbia University—which indicate that short cuts could be found that would enable some things under certain conditions to exceed the speed of light.

In addition, there's always the possibility that the speed-of-light limitation, even if it's rigid, could be circumvented via a space-time warp, as Arthur Clarke has proposed. But let's take another, slightly more conservative, means of evading the speed of light's restrictions: If radio contact is developed between ourselves and another civilization, within 200 years we will have reached a stage in genetic engineering where the other race could transmit its genetic code to us by radio and we could then re-create their DNA pattern and artificially duplicate one of their species in our laboratories—and vice versa. This sounds fantastic only to those who haven't followed the tremendous breakthroughs being made in genetic engineering.

But actual interstellar travel wouldn't be impossible even if light speed *can't* be achieved. Whenever we dismiss space flight beyond our solar system on the grounds that it would take thousands of years, we are thinking of beings with life spans similar to ours. Fruit flies, I understand, live out their entire existence—birth, reproduction and death—within 24 hours; well, man may be to other creatures in the universe as the fruit fly is to man. There may be countless races in the universe with life spans of hundreds of thousands or even millions of years, to whom a 10,000-year journey to Earth would be about as intimidating as an afternoon outing in the park. But even in terms of our own time scale, within a few years it should be possible to freeze astronauts or induce a hibernatory suspension of life functions for the duration of an interstellar journey. They could spend 300 or 1000 years in space and be awakened automatically, feelng no different than if they had had a hearty eight hours' sleep. The speed-of-light theory, too, could work in favor of long ourneys; the peculiar "time dilation" factor in Einstein's relativity theory means that as an object accelerates toward the speed of light, time slows down. Everything would appear normal to those on board; but if they had been away from Earth for, say, 56 years, upon their return they would be merely 20 years older than when they departed. So, taking all these factors into consideration, I'm not unduly impressed by the claims of some scientists that the speed-of-light limitation renders interstellar travel impossible.

Playboy: You mentioned freezing astronauts for lengthy space ourneys, as in the "hibernacula" of *2001*. As you know, phys- cist Robert Ettinger and others have proposed freezing *dead* bodies in liquid nitrogen until a future time when they can be revived. What do you think of this proposal?

Kubrick: I've been interested in it for many years, and I con- sider it eminently feasible. Within ten years, in fact, I believe that freezing of the dead will be a major industry in the United States and throughout the world; I would recommend it as a field of investment for imaginative speculators. Dr. Ettinger's thesis is quite simple: If a body is frozen cryogenically in liquid nitrogen at a temperature near absolute zero—minus 459.6 degrees Fahrenheit—and stored in adequate facilities, it may very well be possible at some as-yet-indeterminate date in the future to thaw and revive the corpse and then cure the dis- ease or repair the physical damage that was the original cause of death. This would, of course, entail a considerable gamble; we have no way of knowing that future science will be sufficiently advanced to cure, say, terminal cancer, or even successfully revive a frozen body. In addition, the dead body undergoes damage in the course of the freezing process itself; ice crystal- izes within the blood stream. And unless a body is frozen at the precise moment of death, progressive brain-cell deterioration also occurs. But what do we have to lose? Nothing—and we have immortality to gain. Let me read you what Dr. Ettinger has written: "It used to be thought that the distinction between life and death was simple and obvious. A living man breathes, sweats and makes stupid remarks; a dead one just lies there, pays no attention, and after a while gets putrid. But nowadays nothing is that simple."

Actually, when you really examine the concept of freezing the dead, it's nowhere nearly as fantastic—though every bit as revolutionary—as it appears at first. After all, countless thou- sands of patients "die" on the operating table and are revived by artificial stimulation of the heart after a few seconds or even a few minutes—and there is really little substantive difference between bringing a patient back to life after three minutes of clinical death or after an "intermezzo" stage of 300 years. Fortunately, the freezing concept is now gaining an increasing amount of attention within the scientific community. France's Dr. Jean Rostand, an internationally respected biologist, has proposed that every nation begin a freezer program immediately, funded by government money and utilizing the top scientific minds in each country. "For every day that we delay," he says, "untold thousands are going to an unnecessary grave."

Playboy: Are you interested in being frozen yourself?

Kubrick: I would be if there were adequate facilities available at the present time—which, unfortunately, there are not. A number of organizations are attempting to disseminate information and raise funds to implement an effective freezing program—the Life Extension Society of Washington, the Cryonics Society of New York, etc.—but we are still in the infancy of cryobiology. Right now, all existing freezer facilities—and there are only a handful—aren't sufficiently sophisticated to offer any realistic hope. But that could and probably will change far more rapidly than we imagine.

A key point to remember, particularly by those ready to dismiss this whole concept as preposterous, is that science has made fantastic strides in just the past 40 years; within this brief period of time, a wide range of killer diseases that once were the scourge of mankind, from smallpox to diphtheria, have been virtually eliminated through vaccines and antibiotics; while others, such as diabetes, have been brought under control—though not yet completely eliminated—by drugs such as insulin. Already, heart transplants are almost a viable proposition, and organ banks are being prepared to stock supplies of spleens, kidneys, lungs and hearts for future transplant surgery.

Dr. Ettinger predicts that a "freezee" who died after a severe accident or massive internal damage would emerge resuscitated from a hospital of the future a "crazy quilt of patchwork." His internal organs—heart, lungs, liver, kidneys, stomach and the rest—may be grafts, implanted after being grown in the laboratory from someone's donor cells. His arms and legs may be "bloodless artifacts of fabric, metal and plastic, directed by tiny motors." His brain cells, writes Ettinger, "may be mostly new, regenerated from the few which would be saved, and some of his memories and personality traits may have had to be imprinted onto the new cells by micro-techniques of chemistry and physics." The main challenge to the scientist of the future will not be revival but eliminating the original cause of death; and in this area, we have every reason for optimism as a result of recent experience. So before anyone dismisses the idea of freezing, he should take a searching look at what we have accomplished in a few decades — and ponder what we're capable of accomplishing over the next few centuries.

Playboy: If such a program does succeed, the person who is frozen will have no way of knowing, of course, if he will ever be successfully revived. Do you think future scientists will be willing, even if they're able, to bring their ancestors back to life?

Kubrick: Well, 20th-Century man may not be quite the cup of tea for a more advanced civilization of even 100 years in the future; but unless the future culture has achieved immortality — which is scientifically quite possible — they themselves would be frozen at death, and every generation would have a vested interest in the preservation of the preceding frozen generation in order to be, in turn, preserved by its own descendants. Of course, it would be something of a letdown if, 300 years from now, somebody just pulled the plug on us all, wouldn't it?

Another problem here, quite obviously, is the population explosion; what will be the demographic effect on the Earth of billions of frozen bodies suddenly revived and taking their places in society? But by the time future scientists have mastered the techniques to revive their frozen ancestors, space flight will doubtless be a reality and other planets will be open for colonization. In addition, vast freezer facilities could possibly be constructed on the dark side of the Moon to store millions of bodies. The problems are legion, of course, but so are the potentialities.

Playboy: Opponents of cryogenic freezing argue that death is the natural and inevitable culmination of life and that we shouldn't tamper with it — even if we're able to do so. How would you answer them?

Kubrick: Death is no more natural or inevitable than smallpox or diphtheria. Death is a disease and as susceptible to cure as any other disease. Over the eons, man's powerlessness to prevent death has led him to force it from the forefront of his mind, for his own psychological health, and to accept it unquestioningly as the unavoidable termination. But with the advance of science, this is no longer necessary — or desirable. Freezing is only one possible means of conquering death, and it certainly would not be binding on everyone; those who desire a "natural" death can go ahead and die, just as those in the 19th Century who desired "God-ordained" suffering resisted anesthesia. As Dr. Ettinger has written, "To each his own, and to those who choose not to be frozen, all I can say is—rot in good health."

Playboy: Freezing and resuscitation of the dead is just one revolutionary scientific technique that could transform our society. Looking ahead to the year of your film, 2001, what major social and scientific changes do you foresee?

Kubrick: Perhaps the greatest breakthrough we may have made by 2001 is the possibility that man may be able to eliminate old age. We've just discussed the steady scientific conquest of disease; even when this is accomplished, however, the scourge of old age will remain. But too many people view senile decay, like death itself, as inevitable. It's nothing of the sort. The highly respected Russian scientist V. F. Kuprevich has written, "I am sure we can find means for switching off the mechanisms which make cells age." Dr. Bernard Strehler, an eminent gerontology expert, contends that there is no inherent contradiction, no inherent property of cells or of Metazoa that precludes their organization into perpetually functioning and self-replenishing individuals.

One encouraging indication that we may already be on this road is the work of Dr. Hans Selye, who in his book *Calciphylaxis* presents an intriguing and well-buttressed argument that old age is caused by the transfer of calcium within the body —a transfer that can be arrested by circulating throughout the system specific iron compounds that flush out the calcium, absorb it and prevent it from permeating the tissue. Dr. Selye predicts that we may soon be able to prevent the man of 60 from progressing to the condition of the man of 90. This is something of an understatement; Selye could have added that the man of 60 could *stay* 60 for hundreds or even thousands of years if all other diseases have been eradicated. Even accidents would not necessarily impair his relative immortality; even if a man is run over by a steam-roller, his mind and body will be completely re-creatable from the tiniest fragment of his tissue, if genetic engineering continues its rapid progress.

Playboy: What impact do you think such dramatic scientific breakthroughs will have on the life style of society at the turn of the century?

Kubrick: That's almost impossible to say. Who could have predicted in 1900 what life in 1968 would be like? Technology is, in many ways, more predictable than human behavior. Politics and world affairs change so quickly that it's difficult to predict the future of social institutions for even ten years with a modicum of accuracy. By 2001, we could be living in a Gandhiesque paradise where all men are brothers, or in a neofascist dictatorship, or just be muddling along about the way we are today. As technology evolves, however, there's little doubt that the whole concept of leisure will be both quantitatively and qualitatively improved.

Playboy: What about the field of entertainment?

Kubrick: I'm sure we'll have sophisticated 3-D holographic television and films, and it's possible that completely new forms of entertainment and education will be devised. You might have a machine that taps the brain and ushers you into a vivid dream experience in which you are the protagonist in a romance or an adventure. On a more serious level, a similar machine could directly program you with knowledge; in this way, you might, for example, easily be able to learn fluent German in 20 minutes. Currently, the learning processes are so laborious and time-consuming that a breakthrough is really needed.

On the other hand, there are some risks in this kind of thing; I understand that at Yale they've been engaging in experiments in which the pleasure center of a mouse's brain has been localized and stimulated by electrodes; the result is that the mouse undergoes an eight-hour orgasm. If pleasure that intense were readily available to all of us, we might well become a race of sensually stultified zombies plugged into pleasure stimulators while machines do our work and our bodies and minds atrophy. We could also have this same problem with psychedelic drugs; they offer great promise of unleashing perceptions, but they also hold commensurate dangers of causing withdrawal and disengagement from life into a totally inner-directed kind of Soma world. At the present time, there are no ideal drugs; but I believe by 2001 we will have devised chemicals with no adverse physical, mental or genetic results that can give wings to the mind and enlarge perception beyond its present evolutionary capacities.

Actually, up to now, perception on the deepest level has really, from an evolutionary point of view, been detrimental to survival; if primitive man had been content to sit on a ledge by his cave absorbed in a beautiful sunset or a complex cloud configuration, he might never have exterminated his rival species — but neither would he have achieved mastery of the planet. Now, however, man is faced with the unprecedented situation of potentially unlimited material and technological resources at his disposal and a tremendous amount of leisure time. At last, he has the opportunity to look both within and beyond himself with a new perspective — without endangering or impeding the progress of the species. Drugs, intelligently used, can be a valuable guide to this new expansion of our consciousness. But if employed just for kicks, or to dull rather than to expand perception, they can be a highly negative influence. There should be fascinating drugs available by 2001; what *use* we make of them will be the crucial question.

Playboy: Have you ever used LSD or other so-called consciousness-expanding drugs?

Kubrick: No. I believe that drugs are basically of more use to the audience than to the artist. I think that the illusion of oneness with the universe, and absorption with the significance of every object in your environment, and the pervasive aura of peace and contentment is not the ideal state for an artist. It tranquilizes the creative personality, which thrives on conflict and on the clash and ferment of ideas. The artist's transcendence must be within his own work; he should not impose any artificial barriers between himself and the mainspring of his subconscious. One of the things that's turned me against LSD is that all the people I know who use it have a peculiar inability to distinguish between things that are really interesting and stimulating and things that *appear* so in the state of universal bliss the drug induces on a "good" trip. They seem to completely lose their critical faculties and disengage themselves from some of the most stimulating areas of life. Perhaps when *everything* is beautiful, nothing is beautiful.

Playboy: What stage do you believe today's sexual revolution will have reached by 2001?

Kubrick: Here again, it's pure speculation. Perhaps there will have been a reaction against present trends, and the pendulum will swing back to a kind of neo-puritanism. But it's more likely that the so-called sexual revolution, midwifed by the pill, will be extended. Through drugs, or perhaps via the sharpening or even mechanical amplification of latent ESP functions, it may be possible for each partner to simultaneously experience the sensations of the other; or we may eventually emerge into polymorphous sexual beings, with the male and female components blurring, merging and interchanging. The potentialities for exploring new areas of sexual experience are virtually boundless.

Playboy: In view of these trends, do you think romantic love may have become unfashionable by 2001?

Kubrick: Obviously, people are finding it increasingly easy to have intimate and fulfilling relationships outside the concept of romantic love—which, in its present form, is a relatively recent acquisition, developed at the court of Eleanor of Aquitaine in the 12th Century—but the basic love relationship, even at its most obsessional, is too deeply ingrained in man's psyche not to endure in one form or another. It's not going to be easy to circumvent our primitive emotional programming. Man still has essentially the same set of pair-bonding instincts—love, jealousy, possessiveness—imprinted for individual and tribal survival millions of years ago, and these still lie quite close to the surface, even in these allegedly enlightened and liberated times.

Playboy: Do you think that by 2001 the institution of the family, which some social scientists have characterized as moribund, may have evolved into something quite different from what it is today?

Kubrick: One can offer all kinds of impressive intellectual arguments against the family as an institution—its inherent authoritarianism, etc.; but when you get right down to it, the family is the most primitive and visceral and vital unit in society. You may stand outside your wife's hospital room during childbirth muttering, "My God, what a responsibility! Is it right to take on this terrible obligation? What am I really doing here?"; and then you go in and look down at the face of your child and—zap!—that ancient programming takes over and your response is one of wonder and joy and pride. It's a classic case of genetically imprinted social patterns. There are very few things in this world that have an unquestionable importance in and of themselves and are not susceptible to debate or rational argument, but the family is one of them. Perhaps man has been too "liberated" by science and evolutionary social trends. He has been turned loose from religion and has hailed the death of his gods; the imperative loyalties of the old nation-state are dissolving and all the old social and ethical values, however reactionary and narrow they often were, are disappearing. Man in the 20th Century has been cut adrift in a rudderless boat on an uncharted sea; if he is going to stay sane throughout the voyage, he must have someone to care about, something that is more important than himself.

Playboy: Some critics have detected not only a deep pessimism but also a kind of misanthropy in much of your work. In *Dr. Strangelove*, for example, one reviewer commented that your directorial attitude, despite the film's antiwar message, seemed curiously aloof and detached and unmoved by the annihilation of mankind, almost as if the Earth were being cleansed of an infection. Is there any truth to that?

Kubrick: Good God, no. You don't stop being concerned with man because you recognize his essential absurdities and frailties and pretensions. To me, the only real immorality is that which endangers the species; and the only absolute evil, that which threatens its annihilation. In the deepest sense, I believe in man's potential and in his capacity for progress. In *Strangelove*, I was dealing with the inherent irrationality in man that threatens to destroy him; that irrationality is with us as strongly today, and must be conquered. But a recognition of insanity doesn't imply a celebration of it — nor a sense of despair and futility about the possibility of curing it.

Playboy: In the five years since *Dr. Strangelove* was released, the two major nuclear powers, the U.S. and the U.S.S.R., have reached substantial accommodation with each other. Do you think this has reduced the danger of nuclear war?

Kubrick: No. If anything, the overconfident Soviet-American *détente increases* the threat of accidental war through carelessness; this has always been the greatest menace and the one most difficult to cope with. The danger that nuclear weapons may be used — perhaps by a secondary power — is as great if not greater than it has ever been, and it is really quite amazing that the world has been able to adjust to it psychologically with so little apparent dislocation.

Particularly acute is the possibility of war breaking out as the result of a sudden unanticipated flare-up in some part of the world, triggering a panic reaction and catapulting confused and frightened men into decisions they are incapable of making rationally. In addition, the serious threat remains that a psychotic figure somewhere in the modern command structure could start a war, or at the very least a limited exchange of nuclear weapons that could devastate wide areas and cause innumerable casualties. This, of course, was the theme of *Dr. Strangelove*; and I'm not entirely assured that somewhere in the Pentagon or the Red army upper echelons there does not exist the real-life prototype of General Jack D. Ripper.

Playboy: Fail-safe strategists have suggested that one way to obviate the danger that a screwball might spark a war would be to administer psychological-fitness tests to all key personnel in the nuclear command structure. Would that be an effective safeguard?

Kubrick: No, because any seriously disturbed individual who rose high within the system would have to possess considerable self-discipline and be able to effectively mask his fixations. Such tests already do exist to a limited degree, but you'd really have to be pretty far gone to betray yourself in them, and the type of individual we're discussing would have to be a highly controlled psychopathic personality not to have given himself away long ago. But beyond those tests, how are you going to objectively assess the sanity of the President, in whom, as Commander-in-Chief, the ultimate responsibility for the use of nuclear weapons resides? It's improbable but not impossible that we could someday have a psychopathic President, or a President who suffers a nervous breakdown, or an alcoholic President who, in the course of some stupefying binge, starts a war. You could say that such a man would be detected and restrained by his aides—but with the powers of the Presidency what they are today, who really knows? Less farfetched and even more terrifying is the possibility that a psychopathic individual could work his way into the lower echelons of the White House staff. Can you imagine what might have happened at the height of the Cuban Missile Crisis if some deranged waiter had slipped LSD into Kennedy's coffee—or, on the other side of the fence, into Khrushchev's vodka? The possibilities are chilling.

Playboy: Do you share the belief of some psychiatrists that our continued reliance on the balance of nuclear power, with all its attendant risks of global catastrophe, could reflect a kind of collective death wish?

Kubrick: No, but I think the *fear* of death helps explain why people accept this Damoclean sword over their heads with such bland equanimity. Man is the only creature aware of his own mortality and is at the same time generally incapable of coming to grips with this awareness and all its implications. Millions of people thus, to a greater or lesser degree, experience emotional anxieties, tensions and unresolved conflicts that frequently express themselves in the form of neuroses and a general joylessness that permeates their lives with frustration and bitterness and increases as they grow older and see the grave yawning before them. As fewer and fewer people find solace in religion as a buffer between themselves and the terminal moment, I actually believe that they unconsciously derive a kind of perverse solace from the idea that in the event of nuclear war, the world dies with them. God is dead, but the bomb endures; thus, they are no longer alone in the terrible vulnerability of their mortality. Sartre once wrote that if there was one thing you could tell a man about to be executed that would make him happy, it was that a comet would strike the earth the next day and destroy every living human being. This is not so much a collective death wish or self-destructive urge as a reflection of the awesome and agonizing loneliness of death. This is extremely pernicious, of course, because it aborts the kind of fury and indignation that should galvanize the world into defusing a situation where a few political leaders on both sides are seriously prepared to incinerate millions of people out of some misguided sense of national interest.

Playboy: Are you a pacifist?

Kubrick: I'm not sure what pacifism really means. Would it have been an act of superior morality to have submitted to Hitler in order to avoid war? I don't think so. But there have also been tragically senseless wars such as World War One and the current mess in Vietnam and the plethora of religious wars that pockmark history. What makes today's situation so radically different from anything that has gone before, however, is that, for the first time in history, man has the means to destroy the entire species—and possibly the planet as well. The problem of dramatizing this to the public is that it all seems so abstract and unreal; it's rather like saying, "The sun is going to die in a billion years." What is required as a minimal first corrective step is a concrete alternative to the present balance of terror—one that people can understand and support.

Playboy: Do you believe that some form of all-powerful world government, or some radically new social, political and economic system, could deal intelligently and farsightedly with such problems as nuclear war?

Kubrick: Well, none of the present systems has worked very well, but I don't know what we'd replace them with. The idea of a group of philosopher kings running everything with benign and omniscient paternalism is always attractive, but where do we find the philosopher kings? And if we do find them, how do we provide for their successors? No, it has to be conceded that democratic society, with all its inherent strains and contradictions, is unquestionably the best system anyone ever worked out. I believe it was Churchill who once remarked that democracy is the worst social system in the world, except for all the others.

Playboy: You've been accused of revealing, in your films, a strong hostility to the modern industrialized society of the democratic West, and a particular antagonism—ambivalently laced with a kind of morbid fascination—toward automation. Your critics claim this was especially evident in *2001*, where the archvillain of the film, the computer HAL 9000, was in a sense the only human being. Do you believe that machines are becoming more like men and men more like machines—and do you detect an eventual struggle for dominance between the two?

Kubrick: First of all, I'm not hostile toward machines at all; just the opposite, in fact. There's no doubt that we're entering a mechanarchy, however, and that our already complex relationship with our machinery will become even more complex as the machines become more and more intelligent. Eventually, we will have to share this planet with machines whose intelligence and abilities far surpass our own. But the interrelationship—if intelligently managed by man—could have an immeasurably enriching effect on society.

Looking into the distant future, I suppose it's not inconceivable that a semisentient robot-computer subculture could evolve that might one day decide it no longer needed man. You've probably heard the story about the ultimate computer of the future: For months scientists think of the first question to pose to it, and finally they hit on the right one: "Is there a God?" After a moment of whirring and flashing lights, a card comes out, punched with the words: THERE IS NOW. But this problem is a distant one and I'm not staying up nights worrying about it; I'm convinced that our toasters and TVs are fully domesticated, though I'm not so sure about integrated telephone circuits, which sometimes strike me as possessing a malevolent life all their own.

Playboy: Speaking of futuristic electronics and mechanics, *2001*'s incredibly elaborate gadgetry and scenes of space flight have been hailed—even by hostile critics—as a major cinematic breakthrough. How were you able to achieve such remarkable special effects?

Kubrick: I can't answer that question technically in the time we have available, but I can say that it was necessary to conceive, design and engineer completely new techniques in order to produce the special effects. This took 18 months and $6,500,000 out of a $10,500,000 budget. I think an extraordinary amount of credit must go to Robert H. O'Brien, the president of M-G-M, who had sufficient faith to allow me to persevere at what must have at times appeared to be a task without end. But I felt it was necessary to make this film in such a way that every special-effects shot in it would be completely convincing—something that had never before been accomplished in a motion picture.

Playboy: Thanks to those special effects, *2001* is undoubtedly the most graphic depiction of space flight in the history of films —and yet you have admitted that you yourself refuse to fly, even in a commercial jet liner. Why?

Kubrick: I suppose it comes down to a rather awesome awareness of mortality. Our ability, unlike the other animals, to conceptualize our own end creates tremendous psychic strains within us; whether we like to admit it or not, in each man's chest a tiny ferret of fear at this ultimate knowledge gnaws away at his ego and his sense of purpose. We're fortunate, in a way, that our body, and the fulfillment of its needs and functions, plays such an imperative role in our lives; this physical shell creates a buffer between us and the mind-paralyzing realization that only a few years of existence separate birth from death. If man really sat back and thought about his impending termination, and his terrifying insignificance and aloneness in the cosmos, he would surely go mad, or succumb to a numbing sense of futility. Why, he might ask himself, should he bother to write a great symphony, or strive to make a living, or even to love another, when he is no more than a momentary microbe on a dust mote whirling through the unimaginable immensity of space?

Those of us who are forced by their own sensibilities to view their lives in this perspective—who recognize that there is no purpose they can comprehend and that amidst a countless myriad of stars their existence goes unknown and unchronicled —can fall prey all too easily to the ultimate *anomie*. I can well understand how life became for Matthew Arnold "a darkling plain . . . where ignorant armies clash by night . . . and there is neither love nor hope nor certitude nor faith nor surcease from pain." But even for those who lack the sensitivity to more than vaguely comprehend their transience and their triviality, this inchoate awareness robs life of meaning and purpose; it's why "the mass of men lead lives of quiet desperation," why so many of us find our lives as absent of meaning as our deaths.

The world's religions, for all their parochialism, did supply a kind of consolation for this great ache; but as clergymen now pronounce the death of God and, to quote Arnold again, "the sea of faith" recedes around the world with a "melancholy, long, withdrawing roar," man has no crutch left on which to lean—and no hope, however irrational, to give purpose to his existence. This shattering recognition of our mortality is at the root of far more mental illness than I suspect even psychiatrists are aware.

Playboy: If life is so purposeless, do you feel that it's worth living?

Kubrick: Yes, for those of us who manage somehow to cope with our mortality. The very meaninglessness of life forces man to create his own meaning. Children, of course, begin life with an untarnished sense of wonder, a capacity to experience total joy at something as simple as the greenness of a leaf; but as they grow older, the awareness of death and decay begins to impinge on their consciousness and subtly erode their *joie de vivre*, their idealism—and their assumption of immortality. As a child matures, he sees death and pain everywhere about him, and begins to lose faith in faith and in the ultimate goodness of man. But if he's reasonably strong—and lucky—he can emerge from this twilight of the soul into a rebirth of life's *élan*. Both because of and in spite of his awareness of the meaninglessness of life, he can forge a fresh sense of purpose and affirmation. He may not recapture the same pure sense of wonder he was born with, but he can shape something far more enduring and sustaining. The most terrifying fact about the universe is not that it is hostile but that it is indifferent; but if we can come to terms with this indifference and accept the challenges of life within the boundaries of death—however mutable man may be able to make them—our existence as a species can have genuine meaning and fulfillment. However vast the darkness, we must supply our own light.

Playboy: Will we be able to find any deep meaning or fulfillment, either as individuals or as a species, as long as we continue to live with the knowledge that all human life could be snuffed out at any moment in a nuclear catastrophe?

Kubrick: We *must*, for in the final analysis, there may be no sound way to eliminate the threat of self-extinction without changing human nature; even if you managed to get every country disarmed down to the bow and arrow, you would still be unable to lobotomize either the knowledge of how to build nuclear warheads or the perversity that allows us to rationalize their use. Given these two categorical imperatives in a disarmed world, the first country to amass even a few weapons would have a great incentive to use them quickly. So an argument might be made that there is a greater chance for *some* use of nuclear weapons in a totally disarmed world, though less chance of global extinction; while in a world armed to the teeth, you have less chance for *some* use—but a great chance of extinction if they're used.

If you try to remove yourself from an Earthly perspective and look at this tragic paradox with the detachment of an extraterrestrial, the whole thing is totally irrational. Man now has the power in one mad, incandescent moment, as you point out, to exterminate the entire species; our own generation could be the last on Earth. One miscalculation and all the achievements of history could vanish in a mushroom cloud; one misstep and all of man's aspirations and strivings over the millennia could be terminated. One short circuit in a computer, one lunatic in a command structure and we could negate the heritage of the billions who have died since the dawn of man and abort the promise of the billions yet unborn—the ultimate genocide. What an irony that the discovery of nuclear power, with its potential for annihilation, also constitutes the first tottering step into the universe that must be taken by all intelligent worlds. Unhappily, the infant-mortality rate among emerging civilizations in the cosmos may be very high. Not that it will matter except to us; the destruction of this planet would have no significance on a cosmic scale; to an observer in the Andromeda nebulae, the sign of our extinction would be no more than a match flaring for a second in the heavens; and if that match does blaze in the darkness, there will be none to mourn a race that used a power that could have lit a beacon in the stars to light its funeral pyre. The choice is ours.

"The Unhinged Doors of Gaza," painted in 1962 by Austrian fantastic-realist Ernst Fuchs. Fuchs says that "the floating, monolithic angelic matter signifies the cosmic power of the angels."

Stonehenge. Is it possible . . . ?

Space columns by Peter Kolisnyk, of Toronto.

In a letter to a fan on June 19, 1968, Stanley Kubrick wrote that he expected *2001* would run for two years on Broadway. Six months later, however, *2001* ended its engagement at the Cinerama Theatre, thus becoming the first roadshow film to close during a profitable New York run, said M-G-M.

The closing caused much trade speculation, some insisting that M-G-M sacrificed the engagement to open its long-completed *Ice Station Zebra* in time for Christmas business. (New York was then in the uncomfortable position of having only one theater equipped to show a Cinerama film. Loew's Capitol, the theater where *Space Odyssey* had premiered in New York, was torn down in September, 1968.)

Although agreeing that the film was still showing a clear profit after an eight-month booking, M-G-M felt that the margin was too small to warrant a continued reserved-seat playoff. A New York opening is always prohibitively expensive, with almost all films winding up in the red. This can be attributed to high advertising costs, the huge overhead of all Broadway theaters, and, in the case of reserved-seat films, the additional expense of employing a treasurer and mail-order personnel. In Los Angeles and San Francisco, *2001* played for over a year and a half at a consistent, highly profitable pace. Apart from the early days of reserved-seat films (*Around the World in Eighty Days*, *West Side Story*), few hard-ticket attractions stay for over a year in any one location.

Receiving British Film Academy Award for *2001* "best art direction" from Lord Mountbatten, left to right: Tony Masters, Harry Lange, Ernest Archer, production designers.

SHOWCASE photos of SHEILA FORD by BRUCE REED

The Repeaters: They see the same

Many people see *2001* over and over and over and over and over again. Jack Cottingham, manager of a Toronto theater, told Clyde Gilmour, of the Toronto *Telegram*: "Some of the repeaters here can fairly be described as hippies, but [*sic*] they are well-behaved. So far as I am aware, they are not smoking pot in the theater, although such occurrences have been reported sporadically in the U.S. If we detected anything like that here, of course, we'd put a stop to it in a hurry."

Ed Seeman, a New York filmmaker, said he was inspired by *2001* to make "Space Oddity," an eleven-minute short. He zoomed his camera around eight nude women on black velvet blackdrops, achieving a nonbackground in which the models appeared to float.

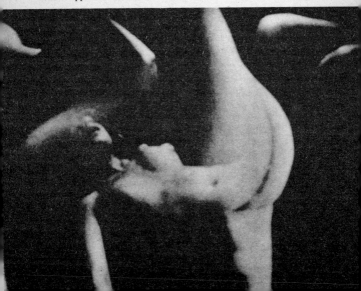

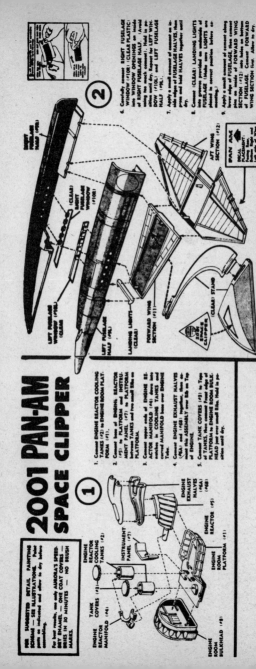

2001 PAN-AM SPACE CLIPPER

FOR SUGGESTED DETAIL PAINTING DETAIL — SEE ILLUSTRATIONS. Paint where indicated and allow to dry before assembling.

For best results, use only AURORA'S SPEED-DRY ENAMEL. ONE COAT COVERS — DRIES IN 30 MINUTES — NO BRUSH MARKS.

①

1. Cement ENGINE REACTOR COOLING TANKS (#2) to ENGINE ROOM PLATFORM (#1).

2. Cement base of ENGINE REACTOR (#5) to PLATFORM and INSTRUMENT PANEL (#7) to PLATFORM between TANKS and two small libs on PLATFORM.

3. Cement upper section of ENGINE REACTOR MANIFOLD (#4) into notches in COOLING TANKS and cement MANIFOLD base over ENGINE Tube.

4. Cement ENGINE EXHAUST HALVES (#6A) and (#6B) together, then cement this ASSEMBLY over Tab on Top of ENGINE.

5. Cement TANK COVERS (#3) to Top of TANKS, then cement Front edge of PLATFORM to ENGINE ROOM BULKHEAD just over small libs. Hold in position until dry.

TANK COVERS (#3)
ENGINE REACTOR COOLING TANKS (#2)
ENGINE REACTOR MANIFOLD (#4)
INSTRUMENT PANEL (#7)
ENGINE EXHAUST HALVES (#6A) (#6B)
ENGINE REACTOR (#5)
ENGINE ROOM PLATFORM (#1)
ENGINE ROOM BULKHEAD (#8)

②

6. Carefully cement RIGHT FUSLAGE WINDOW (#10R) (CLEAR PLASTIC) into WINDOW OPENINGS on inside of RIGHT FUSELAGE HALF. (Avoid using too much cement). Used in the same way cement LEFT FUSELAGE WINDOW (#10L) and LEFT FUSELAGE HALF (#9L).

7. Carefully cement along inside edges of FUSELAGE HALVES, then press and hold HALVES together until dry.

8. Cement (CLEAR) LANDING LIGHTS into opening on bottom of FUSELAGE (Make sure LIGHTS are placed in correct position, before cementing.)

9. Apply a small amount of cement along upper edge of FUSELAGE, then cement upper edge of FORWARD WING SECTION (#12) into FORWARD WING SECTION (#12) into FORWARD WING SECTION. Cement FORWARD WING SECTION first. Allow to dry.

RIGHT FUSELAGE HALF (#9R)
RIGHT FUSELAGE WINDOW (#10R) (CLEAR)
LEFT FUSELAGE WINDOW (#10L) (CLEAR)
LEFT FUSELAGE HALF (#9L)
LANDING LIGHTS (CLEAR)
FORWARD WING SECTION (#11)
AFT WING SECTION (#12)
PAN AM DECAL PAN AM (CLEAR) STAND

Make your own *2001* space clipper, a model kit produced by Aurora Plastics Corp., West Hempstead, N.Y.

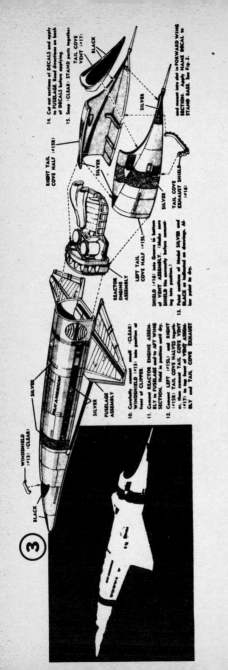

③

WINDSHIELD
(#13) (CLEAR)

BLACK

SILVER

Plus-A Attachment

SILVER

FUSELAGE
ASSEMBLY

REACTOR ENGINE
ASSEMBLY

LEFT TAIL
COVE HALF (#15L)

RIGHT TAIL
COVE HALF (#15R)

SILVER

SILVER

BLACK

TAIL COVE VENT
(#17)

TAIL COVE
STAND

SILVER

TAIL COVE
EXHAUST SHIELD (#16)

10. Carefully cement small (CLEAR) WINDSHIELD (#13) into position at front of CLIPPER.

11. Cement REACTOR ENGINE ASSEMBLY to FUSELAGE and to AFT WING SECTION. Hold in position until dry.

12. Cement LEFT (#15L) and RIGHT (#15R) TAIL COVE HALVES together, then cement TAIL COVE VENT (#17) to top. Cement TAIL COVE ASSEMBLY and TAIL COVE EXHAUST

13. Paint sections of Model SILVER and BLACK as indicated on drawings. Allow to dry.

SHIELD (#16) into Groove (at bottom of VENT ASSEMBLY. (Make sure SHIELD fits securely before cementing into position.)

14. Cut out sections of DECALS and apply to FUSLAGE. Read directions on back of DECALS before applying.

15. Snap (CLEAR) STAND parts together.

and cement into slot in FORWARD WING SECTION. Apply NAME DECAL to STAND BASE. See Fig. 2.

"Did you have a good flight?"

2001 Timetable

- PRODUCTION BEGINS IN LONDON — December 29, 1965
- KUBRICK ARRIVES IN THE UNITED STATES, CUTTING FILM EN ROUTE TO M-G-M FACILITIES IN CALIFORNIA — March 13, 1968
- SCREENING FOR *LIFE* MAGAZINE — March 29, 1968
- WASHINGTON PRESS PREVIEWS — March 31, April 1, 1968
- WASHINGTON WORLD PREMIERE — April 2, 1968
- NEW YORK PRESS PREVIEWS — April 1-2, 1968
- NEW YORK PREMIERE — April 3, 1968
- LOS ANGELES PREMIERE — April 4, 1968
- KUBRICK CUTS 19 MINUTES FROM FILM — April 4-5, 1968
- FINAL CUT SHOWN IN NEW YORK — April 6, 1968

Comments From *Time* Magazine

August 2, 1968

2001: A Space Odyssey has as its key character a shining oblong object symbolizing a great extraterrestrial intelligence that has overseen mankind since the Pliocene age. Though it fails as drama, Stanley Kubrick's venture succeeds as dazzling visual art.

August 30, 1968

2001: A Space Odyssey. Director Stanley Kubrick attempts to create a new language to describe the future on the screen. His grammar is faultless, his pronunciation beautiful, his message obscure.

October 10, 1968

2001: A Space Odyssey. Stanley Kubrick's cosmic parable of the history and future of man contains some of the most stunning and visual pyrotechnics in the history of the motion picture.

October 18, 1968

2001: A Space Odyssey. Stanley Kubrick's cosmic parable of the history and future of man contains the most stunning technical effects and visual pyrotechnics in motion-picture history.

December 27, 1968

2001: A Space Odyssey. An epic film about the history and future of man, brilliantly directed by Stanley Kubrick. The special effects are mind-blowing.

September 12, 1969

2001: A Space Odyssey. Man's first step on the Moon lends new immediacy to Stanley Kubrick's epic film about a voyage to Jupiter that assumes awesome metaphysical consequences. Kubrick is one of the best American filmmakers, and *2001* may be his masterpiece.

ILLUSTRATION CREDITS

Cover, M-G-M; 3, Douglas Trumbull; 6, M-G-M;
7, M-G-M; 14, M-G-M; 73, M-G-M; 74, Douglas Trumbull;
75t, M-G-M; 75b, Douglas Trumbull; 76, M-G-M;
77, M-G-M; 78t, Douglas Trumbull; 78b, M-G-M;
79, M-G-M; 80, M-G-M; 81, M-G-M;
82t, Douglas Trumbull; 82b, M-G-M;
83, Douglas Trumbull; 84, M-G-M; 85, M-G-M;
86, M-G-M; 87, M-G-M; 88, M-G-M; 89, M-G-M;
90t, Douglas Trumbull; 90bl, M-G-M;
90br, Douglas Trumbull; 91, M-G-M; 92, M-G-M;
93, M-G-M; 94-95, M-G-M; 96, M-G-M;
97t, Douglas Trumbull; 97b, M-G-M; 98t, M-G-M;
98bl, M-G-M; 98br, UPI Photo; 99t, Douglas Trumbull;
99m, M-G-M; 99b, M-G-M; 100, M-G-M; 101t, M-G-M;
101m, M-G-M; 101b, Douglas Trumbull; 102t, M-G-M;
102ml, Douglas Trumbull; 102mr, Douglas Trumbull;
102bl, M-G-M; 102br, M-G-M;
103, Frederick I. Ordway III;
104t (inset), Douglas Trumbull; 104, M-G-M;
104m (inset), M-G-M; 105, M-G-M; 106, M-G-M;
107t, M-G-M; 107m, M-G-M; 107b, Douglas Trumbull;
108t, M-G-M; 108m, M-G-M; 108b, Douglas Trumbull;
109, M-G-M; 110, M-G-M; 111, M-G-M; 112-113, M-G-M;
114tl, Douglas Trumbull; 114tr, Douglas Trumbull;
114b, M-G-M; 115t, Douglas Trumbull; 115bl, M-G-M;
115br, M-G-M; 116, M-G-M; 117, M-G-M; 118, Stratford;
119, M-G-M; 120tl, Douglas Trumbull;
120tr, Douglas Trumbull; 120b, M-G-M; 121, M-G-M;
122t, Douglas Trumbull; 122m, M-G-M; 122b, M-G-M;
123, M-G-M; 124, M-G-M; 125, M-G-M;
126tl, Douglas Trumbull; 126tr, M-G-M; 126b, M-G-M;
127, M-G-M; 128t, Douglas Trumbull;
128ml, Douglas Trumbull; 128mr, Douglas Trumbull;
128b, M-G-M; 129, Stanley Kubrick;
130, Douglas Trumbull; 131, Douglas Trumbull;
132, Douglas Trumbull; 133, M-G-M; 134, M-G-M;
135, M-G-M; 136, M-G-M; 137, M-G-M;
138, Douglas Trumbull; 139, Douglas Trumbull;
140tl, Douglas Trumbull; 140tr, Douglas Trumbull;
140b, M-G-M; 141, M-G-M; 142, M-G-M;
143, Douglas Trumbull; 144, M-G-M; 145, M-G-M;
146, M-G-M; 147, M-G-M; 148, M-G-M;
149t, Stanley Kubrick; 149bl, M-G-M;
149br, Douglas Trumbull; 150, M-G-M;

151, Douglas Trumbull; 152, Douglas Trumbull;
153, Douglas Trumbull; 154, M-G-M;
155, Douglas Trumbull; 156, M-G-M; 157, M-G-M;
158, M-G-M; 159, M-G-M; 160, M-G-M; 161, M-G-M;
162t, M-G-M; 162b (inset drawing), Douglas Trumbull;
163, M-G-M; 164, M-G-M;
174, Randy Clower & Stephen Dilling;
194, Frederick I. Ordway III;
201, Margaret Stackhouse; 206, Foto Schikola;
355, By permission of the Artist, Ernst Fuchs;
356, UPI Photo; 357, Kolisnyk; 358, J. Paul Kirouac;
359, P.I.C. Photos Ltd.; 360t, Toronto Telegram
Showcase Photos of Sheila Ford by Bruce Reed;
360b, By permission of the Filmmaker, Ed Seeman;
361, Aurora Plastics Corp; 362, Aurora Plastics Corp.

"Of course I saw *2001: A Space Odyssey* — but now I'm not so sure I did."

> — *Proofreader of this book.*

"Apollo officials learned from Apollo 8, which orbited the Moon ten times Christmas eve, that there are more problems navigating around the lunar sphere than originally supposed. These problems are caused by unexplained buried lumps or heavy spots below the Moon's surface, like raisins in a piece of bread, which scientists call mass concentrations or 'mascons.' The mascons cause the force of lunar gravity to vary, making a spacecraft speed up and slow down unpredictably."

> — *The New York Times*, March 25, 1969

"If you understood *2001* completely, we failed. We wanted to raise far more questions than we answered."

> — Arthur C. Clarke.

"This week, several hundred books on Napoleon were shipped from Paris to the London office of Stanley Kubrick."

> — *L'Express*, September 23, 1968

"Its origin and purpose still a total mystery."